WORLD CUP '98

For Juliet, family and friends
Tim Oldham

For Pip, Edward and April
Glen Phillips

A COMPLETE
CHAMPIONSHIP GUIDE

WORLD
CUP '98

GLEN PHILLIPS & TIM OLDHAM

B▥XTREE

First published in Great Britain 1998 by Boxtree
an imprint of Macmillan Publishers Ltd
25 Eccleston Place London SW1W 9NF
and Basingstoke

Associated companies throughout the world

ISBN 0 7522 1136 6

1 3 5 7 9 8 6 4 2

A CIP catalogue record for this book is available from
the British Library.

Typeset by Blackjacks, London

Printed and bound by Mackays of Chatham Plc, Chatham, Kent.

CONTENTS

INTRODUCTION

For football fans everywhere, the World Cup is the chance to see the finest concentration of international stars in action in one competition. It is the stage on which every player is prepared to give his all in an uncompromising effort to achieve the ultimate accolade.

Every tournament has witnessed a great player come to the fore and dominate the finals. Pelé, Eusebio, Cruyff, Platini and most sensationally, Maradona, have all left their mark on the competition, but whose turn will it be this year? With most of the finest players in the world on display in France this summer, including Ronaldo, Shearer, Zidane, Batistuta, Raul, Bergkamp, Schmeichel, Kanu, Suker and Maldini (to name but a few), there are plenty of candidates. France '98 is their big opportunity.

The eventual winners will have to play seven tough games in just four weeks against tough opposition. These days, there are few easy matches; the footballing minnow is now something of a rarity as even the debutants will be well drilled and prepared.

It is widely believed that Africa will produce a World Cup winning team in the near future. The semi-finals could possibly be in sight for Nigeria this time round as they will include many of the players who won the Olympic gold medal in 1994. For the likes of South Africa, Japan and Jamaica, just reaching the finals has been a great achievement, but for Brazil, Italy, Germany and, dare we say it, England, failure to reach the semi-finals will be considered a disaster.

The pressures on each team will be immense but none will be greater, one suspects, than those on France. Playing at home in front of your own supporters can be a big advantage but the pressure of expectation can weigh too heavily and the record of host nations in recent tournaments has not been good.

Whatever the outcome, it is going to be a memorable World Cup and we hope this book will enhance your enjoyment of the event. It contains a comprehensive history of the tournament from the inaugural competition in 1930 to the present day. There are profiles of each of the 32 teams, looking at how they qualified, who the key players are, and how each country has fared in previous finals. There is also a complete schedule of matches, venues, and a fill-in guide so that you can create your own record of what promises to be a wonderful competition.

Brazil are the deserved favourites but there are five or six other teams who seem evenly matched. We'll go for Brazil, Argentina, Italy and England to reach the semi-finals with the sheer brilliance of Ronaldo and Denilson lifting Brazil to a fifth World Cup victory.

THE TEAMS

Group A

Brazil, Scotland, Morocco, Norway

With three teams competing for the runners-up spot behind Brazil, the game between Scotland and Norway in Bordeaux on 16 June looks critical and should decide who progresses to the second round. It should be a close call as both managers are renowned for their immaculate preparation. Egil Olsen already has a victory over Brazil under his belt but it's unlikely that Norway will repeat that feat in the finals. However, the Norwegians have a far better squad than the one which was so unadventurous four years ago and should narrowly pip the Scots for second place.

FIXTURES

Brazil v Scotland	10 June, 15.30, Stade de France	**BBC**
Morocco v Norway	10 June, 19.00, Montpellier	**ITV**
Scotland v Norway	16 June, 15.30, Bordeaux	**ITV**
Brazil v Morocco	16 June, 19.00, Nantes	**ITV**
Scotland v Morocco	23 June, 19.00, Saint Etienne	**BBC**
Brazil v Norway	23 June, 19.00, Marseille	**BBC**

Brazil

Federation
Confederacao Brasileira de Futbol

Founded
1914

Strip
Yellow shirts with green trim, blue shorts, white socks
with green trim

Coach
Mario Zagalo

Qualification
Qualified as holders

Pelé once described football as the beautiful game and it's a phrase
that sums up samba soccer. The Brazilians are the best exponents
of it, both on and off the pitch. It seems that every supporter gets
caught up with the craze of decorating themselves in the vibrant
gold and green.

Winning the World Cup is an obsession for everyone involved in
Brazilian football. They have entered and qualified for every tour-
nament – the only country to do so – and for many people, a World
Cup would be unthinkable without the brilliant Brazilians.

Once again, there will be no team to touch the Brazilians going
forward. Romario and Bebeto were the star strikeforce in the team
which won a record fourth World Cup in 1994 and with coach
Mario Zagalo seemingly settled on a 4–4–2 system, Brazil's
attacking riches will be battling to partner the precocious and
prolific Ronaldo.

The 21-year-old Inter Milan striker is a goalscorer of great pace,
power and control and was the overwhelming choice for the 1997
FIFA Player of the Year award. His place in the side is virtually
assured – barring injury – but his striking partner is up for grabs.

Despite a spell in the wilderness at Valencia in Spain, Romario has once again found his scoring edge back in Brazil with Flamengo. He scored a great goal in the 2–1 win over South Africa and two more against Saudi Arabia in the Confederations Cup. However, there is certainly a question mark against his temperament and Zagalo was not pleased when, after limping off against Peru in the Copa America, Romario proceeded to spend the night on the town.

Romario's partner in 1994, Bebeto, has moved from club to club recently and needs to establish himself quickly to be considered while Dodo's meteoric rise at Sao Paulo has earned him a place in the national team as back-up to Ronaldo.

There is even one player who, on recent form, can claim to be better than Ronaldo. Edmundo's goalscoring exploits in the Brazilian championship have been sensational. He scored a record 29 goals for Vasco da Gama including six in one game and a hat-trick against arch rivals Flamengo.

There is no doubt that he is one of the most dangerous strikers in more than one sense. Along with his record-breaking goalscoring he has also set new heights in cautions and sendings off and on his last appearance for Brazil against Bolivia he elbowed an opponent in the face. The referee missed the incident but Zagalo didn't and substituted him immediately.

It will be a hard decision for Zagalo to pick him. Now with Fiorentina, Edmundo is certainly a match-winner but a hot-blooded moment and Brazil could be down to ten men. 'Whatever I do, I'm going to be criticised,' said Zagalo. 'Everybody wants him in the team now but what happens if I pick him and then he gets sent off during a match in the World Cup? Then they'll be saying I shouldn't have selected him.' It's tough being a manager.

Two enormously talented midfielders have come through in the past year. Djalminha looked the likely choice but he in turn was overshadowed by the dazzling Denilson. He was a revelation at Le Tournoi in France and looks set to become the world's most expensive player next season. He was picked out for special praise by Zagalo, who compared him to some of the great Brazilian wingers of the past.

Juninho is almost certainly out of the World Cup after suffering a serious injury while playing for Atletico Madrid. The former

Middlesbrough forward was stretchered off after being fouled and he was later diagnosed as having a fractured fibula and torn ankle ligaments, keeping him out for five months.

With the range of talent on display it is tempting to suggest that other teams are simply playing for second prize. Yet the Brazilian defence is far less convincing. Roberto Carlos is an exciting attacking left-back who can produce stunning free-kicks, but less gifted as a full-back.

In goal, Taffarel remains Zagalo's favourite, somewhat controversially given some of his recent blunders for both his country and his club side, Atletico Mineiro. Flavio Conceicao has ousted original choice Mauro Silva as Dunga's partner in front of the defence while Leonardo emerged as favourite for the role of playmaker during the Copa America.

Despite being spared the marathon South American World Cup qualifying competition, Brazil have been packing the fixtures in and their form has been awesome.

In 1997, Zagalo's team played in the Copa America, the Tournoi de France and a further nine friendlies. Critics argued that some friendlies, such as those at home to below-strength Chile and injury-weakened Wales, were a waste of time. Zagalo argued that they gave him a chance to test players and see how they reacted to wearing the famous yellow shirt.

There have been no arguments, however, about Brazil's form. The run of wins began in the Tournoi de France with a 1–0 win over England. They then won six games in a row, scoring 22 goals, on their way to winning the Copa America in Bolivia, even overcoming the difficulties of playing at altitude to beat the hosts in the final. This was followed by wins away to South Korea and Japan and at home to Ecuador, Morocco and Wales.

Since the last World Cup, Brazil have only lost three times, going down 2–0 to Mexico in the final of the 1996 Gold Cup, 4–2 against Norway in a friendly in May 1997 and, most recently, an embarrassing 1–0 defeat to the USA in the semi-final of this year's Gold Cup. However, it is the result against Norway which bears the closest scrutiny.

Norway caught the Brazilian defence cold to take a 2–0 lead after just 20 minutes and added weight to the suggestion that Zagalo had not done his homework on the Norwegians. Their manager Olsen believes the Brazilians do have weaknesses and often underestimate the opposition.

Having said that, the events are unlikely to be repeated when the sides meet in Marseille on 23 June. The four-time winners may make it five on 12 July.

WORLD CUP HISTORY

Brazil were knocked out in the first round of both the 1930 and 1934 tournaments but reached the semi-finals four years later. Here, they committed the error of resting their star striker, Leonidas, against Italy, believing that they would reach the final without him. This self-assurance proved costly as Italy scored twice to win the match.

In 1950, Brazil, the hosts, were overwhelming favourites to win but, requiring only a draw, they continued to play attacking football when they could have defended a lead and allowed Uruguay to score twice and snatch the title.

The 1954 quarter-final defeat against Hungary is perhaps best forgotten. It was sad that a game between the two most attacking teams should prove to be one of the most violent games in the history of the competition.

In 1958 Brazil, inspired by Didi, Garrincha and a 17-year-old prodigy called Pelé, finally won the World Cup. In Chile in 1962, it belonged to them again but not to Pelé who was injured in the second game and missed the rest of the tournament. Amarildo proved a marvellous replacement but the show belonged to Garrincha.

Pelé again did not have a happy time in 1966 when Brazil lost their crown to England. He threatened never to play in the World Cup again but thankfully he was to join the likes of Tostao, Gerson, Rivelino and Jairzinho for the 1970 finals. The team that won the World Cup in Mexico was one of the best ever to take the field in a World Cup. Apart from England, no-one came close to matching the sublime skills of the Brazilians.

Since 1970, the national team has reverted to a more defensive style and it was only in 1982 that Brazil produced a team which promised the same supreme footballing skills of old. Falcao,

Socrates and Zico played in a style reminiscent of the golden era but lost to Italy, the eventual champions, in a classic encounter. Requiring only a draw, Brazil again paid the penalty of pressing forward to win the game.

History was made twice at the 1994 World Cup finals. Brazil secured a fourth title to add to their triumphs in 1958, 1962, and 1970. But to do so they needed to win the first-ever penalty shoot-out after a goalless final against Italy.

The game itself was one of few chances and even though they were the best team at USA '94, the Brazilians had lost their zip after a tough schedule of seven games in 28 days. Italy had also run out of legs so after a hugely entertaining month the final was a bit of a damp squib.

Finals appearances: 15 (1930–1994)
Biggest win: 7–1 v Sweden (1950)
Biggest defeat: 2–4 v Hungary (1954)

1930 Eliminated first round
    Group Two: 1–2 v Yugoslavia, 4–0 v Bolivia
1934 Eliminated first round
    First round: 1–3 v Spain
1938 Third
    First round: 6–5 v Poland; second round: 1–1 v Czechoslovakia,
    2–1 v Czechoslovakia (replay); semi-final: 1–2 v Italy;
    third-place play-off: 4–2 v Sweden
1950 Runners-up
    Group One: 4–0 v Mexico, 2–2 v Switzerland,
    2–0 v Yugoslavia; final pool: 7–1 v Sweden, 6–1 v Spain,
    1–2 v Uruguay
1954 Quarter-finalists
    Group One: 5–0 v Mexico, 1–1 v Yugoslavia;
    quarter-final: 2–4 v Hungary
1958 Winners
    Group Four: 3–0 v Austria, 0–0 v England, 2–0 v Soviet Union;
    quarter-final: 1–0 v Wales; semi-final: 5–2 v France;
    final: 5–2 v Sweden

1962 Winners
Group Three: 2–0 v Mexico, 0–0 v Czechoslovakia,
2–1 v Spain; quarter-final: 3–1 v England;
semi-final: 4–2 v Chile; final: 3–1 v Czechoslovakia

1966 Eliminated first round
Group Three: 2–0 v Bulgaria, 1–3 v Hungary, 1–3 v Portugal

1970 Winners
Group Three: 4–1 v Czechoslovakia, 1–0 v England,
3–2 v Romania; quarter-final: 4–2 v Peru;
semi-final: 3–1 v Uruguay; final: 4–1 v Italy

1974 Fourth
Group Two: 0–0 v Yugoslavia, 0–0 v Scotland, 3–0 v Zaire;
Group A: 1–0 v East Germany, 2–1 v Argentina,
0–2 v Holland; third-place play-off: 0–1 v Poland

1978 Third
Group Three: 1–1 v Sweden, 0–0 v Spain, 1–0 v Austria;
Group B: 3–0 v Peru, 0–0 v Argentina, 3–1 v Poland;
third-place play-off: 2–1 v Italy

1982 Eliminated second round
Group Six: 2–1 v Soviet Union, 4–1 v Scotland,
4–0 v New Zealand; Group C: 3–1 v Argentina; 2–3 v Italy

1986 Quarter-finalists
Group D: 1–0 v Spain, 1–0 v Algeria, 3–0 v Northern Ireland;
second round: 4–0 v Poland; quarter-final: 1–1 v France
(3–4 on penalties)

1990 Eliminated second round
Group C: 2–1 v Sweden, 1–0 v Costa Rica, 1–0 v Scotland;
second round: 0–1 v Argentina

1994 Winners
Group B: 2–0 v Russia, 3–0 v Cameroon, 1–1 v Sweden;
second round: 1–0 v USA; quarter-final: 3–2 v Holland;
semi-final: 1–0 v Sweden; final: 0–0 v Italy (3–2 on penalties)

Scotland

Federation
Scottish Football Association

Founded
1873

Strip
Dark blue shirts, white shorts, blue socks

Coach
Craig Brown

Qualification
Best second-placed team in European Zone after finishing
second in Group Four

Twenty years on, it is safe to assume that Scotland's coach Craig
Brown will not repeat the folly of his predecessor Ally McLeod. In
1978, McLeod took a Scotland squad to the World Cup finals in
Argentina buoyed by his ambitious and ridiculous claims that they
were good enough to win the World Cup. As before, and since,
they were eliminated in the first round.

Brown has seen enough in his five years as national coach to
know what Scotland can achieve in France. And to become the first
coach to see Scotland successfully past the first round would represent a feat of which he could be justly proud.

Brown played for Scotland at schoolboy, youth and junior
level and spent his career at Rangers and Dundee – where he
won a league championship medal in 1962. A knee injury cut
short his playing career and he pursued a career in education
before returning to football in 1974 as Motherwell's assistant
manager.

He took over as Scotland coach from Andy Roxburgh in 1993
and has made the most of the limited resources available to him.
As with Euro '96, Brown can look back over a tough but pleasing
qualification.

The team may not be sparkling but they are efficient and particularly mean in defence. Brown prefers to have a squad he can rely on, so Scotland will travel to France next June without Everton striker Ferguson who has retired from international football at the age of 25. Brown insisted that if Ferguson's heart was in it, he would still consider him but the big striker has effectively closed the door on his chances.

Ferguson's contribution to Scotland's qualification was limited by a long-running injury problem and he played only two games. In the meantime, it has been the goalscoring heroics of Blackburn striker Gallacher that have been the most pleasing aspect of Scotland's progress.

Scotland's World Cup campaign got underway in Vienna in August 1996, with the Scots squandering chances in a goalless draw against Austria, one of the their chief rivals, but the point was a good start.

Two months later, on 5 October, the Scots defeated Latvia 2–0 in Riga, thanks to a wonderful free-kick from Collins and Jackson's first goal for his country.

Three days after the win in Riga, Scotland travelled to the neighbouring Baltic state to play Estonia only to discover that the Estonian team had refused to show. In a farcical incident, the Estonians refused to comply to FIFA's request for an earlier kick-off because of fears over the adequacy of the floodlighting.

The Scots believed, quite reasonably, they would be awarded all three points but FIFA surprisingly ordered a replay on a neutral ground.

Before the replay, Scotland scored a crucial home win over favourites Sweden to go top of the group. They then contrived to make things difficult for themselves with an awful 0–0 draw in the re-run fixture against Estonia in Monaco. It was their poorest performance and could have proved costly.

They gained some revenge in March when a first international goal from Celtic defender Boyd ensured a 2–0 win over Estonia at Kilmarnock.

Four days later came the crunch game of the group. In front of 50,000 passionate fans, a superb double by Gallacher gave Scotland a vital win over group rivals Austria. It was the highlight of the qualifiers and a memorable night for Gallacher whose second goal was a corker.

The Blackburn striker was on the scoresheet again four weeks later but this time Scotland succumbed to their only defeat of the campaign against Sweden.

A McAllister penalty sealed a narrow win over Belarus but three months later at home, the Scots produced a more dominant performance to run out 4–1 winners in the return leg with Gallacher adding another two. It was only fitting that Gallacher should score the first in Scotland's 2–0 win over Latvia to clinch qualification in the final match.

Scotland's success is built on its defence. Only two goals were conceded en route to France, which compared with the three lost in qualifying for Euro '96, makes Brown's side one of the most miserly around.

Even at 39, veteran keeper Leighton is still in inspired form. His performance at Ibrox against Sweden was a particularly fine one and was as important as Scotland's winning goal.

Hendry may not be the most skilled of central defenders in the competition but no-one will match him for do or die commitment. He will once again have to put up with the Braveheart references.

In midfield, Lambert has recently joined Celtic to perform the anchor and man-marking role that earned him a Champions' League medal with Borussia Dortmund, while Collins' experience at Monaco may prove invaluable.

Brown was delighted when FIFA declared an amnesty for players who had picked up one or two yellow cards during qualification for France. It meant that Collins will be available for the first match against Brazil. He has become a key player and his local knowledge could prove important.

Collins' energetic running combined with McAllister's leadership, drive and great distribution were crucial to Scotland. They provide the creativity, inspiration and aggression to carry Scotland through.

So it came as a big disappointment for Craig Brown when McAllister was forced to accept that a knee injury would keep him out of the World Cup.

While Gallacher's form has taken some of the pressure off the strikers, the goal drought that Scotland suffered in the European Championship is still an area that needs attention. The Scots' shortage in attack is such that McCoist, at 35 and not playing regularly for Rangers, remains a candidate for his country.

Scotland have a tough, competent side but they just lack the touch and vision of a truly world-class player. But if Brown can harness greater attacking threat to what is a strong midfield and at the same time maintain the new found defensive solidity, ambition need not be seen as fanciful. Brown is painstaking in his preparation, identifying the key man in the opposition and devising ways to neutralise the threat.

This might well reap reward against Morocco and Norway but Brazil possess too many individual talents for the Scots to cover. Their main hope is that, in the opening game, they can catch the Brazilians a bit cold.

RECORD AGAINST WORLD CUP OPPONENTS

Games against Brazil (Scotland's score listed first)
25 June 1966 (Glasgow) 1–1; 5 July 1972 (Rio de Janeiro) 0–1; 30 June 1973 (Glasgow) 0–1; 18 June 1974 (Frankfurt) 0–0 (WC); 23 June 1977 (Rio de Janeiro) 0–2; 18 June 1982 (Seville) 1–4 (WC); 26 May 1987 (Glasgow) 0–2; 20 June 1990 (Turin) 0–1 (WC)

Games against Norway
28 May 1929 (Oslo) 7–3; 5 May 1954 (Glasgow) 1–0; 19 May 1954 (Oslo) 1–1; 4 June 1963 (Bergen) 3–4; 7 Nov 1963 (Glasgow) 6–1; 6 June 1974 (Oslo) 2–1; 25 Oct 1978 (Glasgow) 3–2 (EC); 7 June 1979 (Oslo) 4–0 (EC); 14 Sept 1988 (Oslo) 2–1 (WC); 15 Nov 1989 (Glasgow) 1–1 (WC); 3 June 1992 (Oslo) 0–0

No fixtures against Morocco

HOW THEY QUALIFIED

Results: Austria 0 **Scotland 0**; Latvia 0 **Scotland 2**; **Scotland 1** Sweden 0; Estonia 0 **Scotland 0**; **Scotland 2** Estonia 0; **Scotland 2** Austria 0; Sweden 2 **Scotland 1**; Belarus 0 **Scotland 1**; **Scotland 4** Belarus 1; **Scotland 2** Latvia 0

	P	W	D	L	F	A	Pts
Austria	10	8	1	1	17	4	25
Scotland	**10**	**7**	**2**	**1**	**15**	**3**	**23**
Sweden	10	7	0	3	16	9	21
Latvia	10	3	1	6	10	14	10
Estonia	10	1	1	8	4	16	4
Belarus	10	1	1	8	5	21	4

Top goalscorers: 6, Gallacher; 2, Hopkin.

WORLD CUP HISTORY

Scotland did not enter the World Cup until 1950 and then decided that as they had not finished top of their qualifying group they wouldn't compete after all.

The same argument did not deter them from travelling to Switzerland four years later – again having finished second to England in the Home Championship, which then served as a qualifying group. However, a 7–0 drubbing by Uruguay ensured a short stay.

The national side made steady progress through the 1960s – during which time Celtic became the first British club to win the European Cup – and qualified for five consecutive World Cup finals from 1974. The Scots have never progressed beyond the first round despite getting close on occasion. In 1974, they remained unbeaten but failed to score enough goals against lowly Zaire.

After a desperate start in 1978, Scotland needed to beat Holland by three clear goals in their final game and nearly caused an upset when Gemmill's super goal put them 3–1 ahead. In 1982, it was again a matter of goals scored as Scotland conceded the qualifying spot to the Soviet Union on goal difference.

In 1986, a win over ten-man Uruguay would have seen them qualify in third spot but even that was beyond them. Drawn in Brazil's group in 1990 it was a 'lowly' central American side which threw the spanner in the works. A win over Sweden and a battling game against Brazil, in which they so nearly held out for the necessary point, all came to nought after their opening defeat by Costa Rica.

Finals appearances: 7 (1954–58, 1974–90)
Biggest win: 5–2 v New Zealand (1982)
Biggest defeat: 0–7 v Uruguay (1954)

1950 Withdrew
1954 Eliminated first round
  Group Three: 0–1 v Austria, 0–7 v Uruguay
1974 Eliminated first round
  Group Two: 2–0 v Zaire, 0–0 v Brazil, 1–1 v Yugoslavia
1978 Eliminated first round
  Group Four: 1–3 v Peru, 1–1 v Iran, 3–2 v Holland
1982 Eliminated first round
  Group Six: 5–2 v New Zealand, 1–4 v Brazil,
  2–2 v Soviet Union
1986 Eliminated first round
  Group Five: 0–1 v Denmark, 1–2 v West Germany,
  0–0 v Uruguay
1990 Eliminated first round
  Group C: 0–1 v Costa Rica, 2–1 v Sweden, 0–1 v Brazil

Morocco

Federation
Royal Moroccan Football Federation

Founded
1955

Strip
Red shirts, green shorts, red socks

Coach
Henri Michel

Qualification
First in African Zone Group Five

Morocco became the first African side to qualify for the finals in 1970, and have made steady progress since, even applying to host the finals in 1984 and 1998. Their presence in their third World Cup in 1994 was confirmation that, along with Cameroon, they are one of the leading countries of the African continent.

However, following three disappointing straight defeats in 1994 the structure of the domestic game was revolutionised with the express intention of preparing Moroccan football for a real comeback.

It seemed to do the trick as the Lions of the Atlas won their group and held off the challenge of Ghana, one of Africa's strongest sides, in the process.

But probably the most important factor in Morocco's success was the arrival in October 1995 of new French coach, Michel. Capped 58 times for his country, he played in the 1978 World Cup in Argentina alongside Platini. He took his native France to Mexico in 1986 and Cameroon to the United States last time around. France '98 will be his fourth World Cup and his third as a coach.

Michel came to Morocco on the recommendation of another former French national team coach, Hidalgo, who works for the Moroccan federation as a consultant.

Quite simply, Michel's team knows exactly what international football is all about. He took time to choose his original squad – watching them play some 20 friendly games. He evidently made the right choices as they romped through qualification and also pulled off a string of impressive friendly results, among them a 2–0 defeat of Nigeria and a 2–2 draw with Croatia. The Moroccans are now Africa's top-ranked team.

The squad is built around a blend of youth and experience. Naybet is a trusty pillar in defence, his defensive qualities making him one of Africa's leading exports to Europe. He currently plays for Deportivo La Coruna alongside his national team-mate, the sublimely talented Hadji.

Hadji will be one of Morocco's most influential players in France where he began his career with Nantes. In 1993, he was forced to choose between an international career with France or Morocco and he finally decided on the place of his birth. He made his debut against Zambia but like the rest of the Moroccan team, made little impact at USA '94. Since then he has matured as a creative midfielder with a delightful array of skills.

Prolific striker Bassir is a big crowd favourite, as is Raghib whose header gave Morocco victory over Ghana and a World Cup spot. They will be no walkover in France.

HOW THEY QUALIFIED

Results: Morocco 4 Sierra Leone 0; Ghana 2 **Morocco 2**; Gabon 0 **Morocco 4**; Sierra Leone 0 **Morocco 1**; **Morocco 1** Ghana 0; **Morocco 2** Gabon 0

	P	W	D	L	F	A	Pts
Morocco	6	5	1	0	14	2	16
Sierra Leone	6	2	1	2	4	6	7
Ghana	6	1	3	2	7	7	6
Gabon	5	0	1	4	1	11	1

Top goalscorers: 4, Bassir; 3, Raghib.

WORLD CUP HISTORY

Ever since they put the wind up Germany in 1970 no-one has underestimated the Moroccans. In 1986 they held England and Poland to a draw and only lost 1–0 to West Germany in the second round.

The three defeats in the United States in 1994 were a big disappointment and led to a restructuring of the domestic game.

Finals appearances: 3 (1970, 1986, 1994)
Biggest win: 3–1 v Portugal (1986)
Biggest defeat: 0–3 v Peru (1970)

1970 Eliminated first round
      Group Four: 1–2 v West Germany, 0–3 v Peru, 1–1 v Bulgaria
1986 Eliminated second round
      Group F: 0–0 v Poland, 0–0 v England, 3–1 v Portugal;
      second round: 0–1 v West Germany
1994 Eliminated first round
      Group F: 0–1 v Belgium, 1–2 v Saudi Arabia, 1–2 v Holland

Norway

Federation
Norges Fotballforbund

Founded
1902

Strip
Red shirts, white shorts, blue socks

Coach
Egil Olsen

Qualification
First in European Zone Group Three

Norway reached the World Cup finals without losing a game, qualifying for the second time in succession and enhancing coach Egil Olsen's reputation in Norway as a football genius.

Repeating what many thought was a one-off feat in 1994, Olsen led his team to six wins and two draws to top European Group Three, well clear of Hungary, Finland, the disappointing Switzerland and Azerbaijan. They were rarely troubled in what was, in truth, a rather weak group.

Norway led right from the start, beating Azerbaijan 5–0 in Oslo in June 1996. Solskjaer stole the show scoring twice including a spectacular drive and giving Alex Ferguson every reason to sign him from Molde for a bargain basement fee of £1.5 million. Solbakken, who has since moved to Wimbledon, also scored twice and Strandli got the fifth.

Against Hungary, Rekdal wrapped up one of the quickest hat-tricks in international history and gave the scoreline a more emphatic appearance than it possibly deserved. With seven minutes to play and a goalless draw on the horizon, Rekdal stepped up to score from a free-kick. He added a second with a stunning volley from 20 yards in the 89th minute and completed the hat-trick with a penalty seconds before the final whistle.

Switzerland were expected to dominate the group alongside Norway but blotted their copybook with a disastrous 1–0 defeat by, of all teams, Azerbaijan. This gave the game against Norway added significance but despite going close through Chapuisat the Swiss were faced with a mountain to climb when Leonhardsen set Norway on the way to victory with the only goal.

Three wins from three games, nine goals scored and none conceded, was the perfect start for 'Professor' Olsen and despite faltering slightly against Finland and Hungary they romped home.

Norway trimmed Nordic rivals Finland with a 4–0 win in Helsinki. Solbakken opened the scoring, Sheffield Wednesday's Rudi scored four minutes later and brothers Jostein and Tore-Andre Flo scored in the second half. Switzerland and Hungary drew 1–1 on the same night, making Norway's place in France all but certain. The Swiss, who had reached the second round of USA '94, were hugely disappointing.

Norway finally secured their place in France on 6 September with a 1–0 victory over Azerbaijan, thanks to a long-range special from Tore-Andre Flo.

Although they were through, the Norwegians applied a healthy sprinkling of salt onto the hapless Swiss and destroyed any hopes they had of qualifying as runners-up in the group by knocking in five goals without reply in Oslo.

While the impact of Olsen, and the exposure of Norwegian players to high levels of competitive football around Europe, has helped improve the team, they still have to prove themselves at the highest level.

Norway disappointed in USA '94 and were eliminated in the first round. They had got to the finals ahead of Holland and eliminated England with a vibrant style but after three cautious, defensive displays no-one was sorry to see them out.

Egil Olsen has helped transform Norway from a bunch of part-timers to World Cup finalists. He is nothing if not meticulous in his match preparations and it was this, as much as Brazil's jet lag, that contributed to their amazing 4–2 victory in a friendly over the world champions in Oslo last year.

Olsen says he could well quit the international team after the World Cup and has been linked with a move to Wimbledon, now part-owned by two Norwegian businessmen.

He has brought a professional approach to the game in Norway. This is reflected in the quality of players who are now much in demand, particularly in the Premiership. Such is the concentration of players in England that Olsen has found it easier to organise training sessions with his team in Blackburn.

Manchester United alone have three on their books in Solskjaer, Berg and Johnsen. With Liverpool's Bjornebye, Haaland of Leeds and Lundekvam of Southampton, the entire defence plays in England's top division.

The game with Scotland in Bordeaux on 16 June should decide who joins Brazil in the second round, and it's probably one both sides will have to win. That won't frighten Craig Brown, himself a great planner, who already knows much about Professor Olsen's team.

HOW THEY QUALIFIED

Results: Norway 5 Azerbaijan 0; **Norway 3** Hungary 0; Switzerland 0 **Norway 1**; **Norway 1** Finland 1; Hungary 1 **Norway 1**; Finland 0 **Norway 4**; Azerbaijan 0 **Norway 1**; **Norway 5** Switzerland 0

	P	W	D	L	F	A	Pts
Norway	8	6	2	0	21	2	20
Hungary	8	3	3	2	10	8	12
Finland	8	3	2	3	11	12	11
Switzerland	8	3	1	4	11	12	10
Azerbaijan	8	1	0	7	3	22	3

Top goalscorers: 4, Solbakken; 3, Solskjaer, Rekdal, T-A Flo.

WORLD CUP HISTORY

In 1994, billed as no-hopers, they topped their World Cup qualifying group finishing above Holland and qualifying ahead of England and Poland. They were, however, the most negative side in the USA and went out in the first round.

Finals appearances: 2 (1938, 1994)
Biggest win: 1–0 v Mexico (1994)
Biggest defeat: 1–2 v Italy (1938)

1938 Eliminated first round
First round: 1–2 v Italy
1994 Eliminated first round
Group E: 1–0 v Mexico, 0–1 v Italy, 0–0 v Republic of Ireland

Group B

Italy, Chile, Cameroon, Austria

Having squeaked through the qualifying round Italy are now in familiar territory. World Cup history is on their side and having made it to the finals, they should put up a bold show. Don't expect them to make it look easy in the first round but they should qualify unbeaten. Cameroon are no longer the force of eight years ago and have a young squad whilst the Austrians are likely to be exposed by their lack of firepower. This leaves Chile. With Salas and Zamorano in attack, goals are not likely to be a problem. And if the defence shows the same frugality as they did against England earlier in the year, they should qualify alongside Italy.

FIXTURES

Italy v Chile	11 June, 15.30, Bordeaux	**BBC**
Cameroon v Austria	11 June, 19.00, Toulouse	**ITV**
Chile v Austria	17 June 15.30, Saint Etienne	**ITV**
Italy v Cameroon	17 June, 19.00, Montpellier	**ITV**
Italy v Austria	23 June, 14.00, Stade de France	**BBC**
Chile v Cameroon	23 June, 14.00, Nantes	**BBC**

Italy

Federation
Federazione Italiana Gioco Clacio

Founded
1898

Strip
Blue shirts, white shorts, blue socks

Coach
Cesare Maldini

Qualification
Second in European Group Two. Beat Russia in play-off

Italy will be one of the favourites in France on the grounds of tradition rather than form. England beat them to the automatic qualification spot in Group Two with that gutsy 0–0 draw in the final match in Rome but Italy were the only team to remain unbeaten in the group – an ability they have used to great effect in previous finals.

It all started so positively for the Italians. With two wins under their belt, Italy arrived at Wembley full of confidence and with a new man in charge, Cesare Maldini. The former AC Milan sweeper is an extremely experienced coach having joined the national team coaching staff in 1980. He worked alongside the great Enzo Bearzot during Italy's victorious 1982 World Cup run and took the national Under-21 side to three European titles.

Maldini could hardly have got off to a better start as Zola stunned the Wembley crowd with the only goal of the game. But having done the hard work, Italy dropped points away to Poland and then disastrously to Georgia. This was the game that did for Italy as Georgia put in a much improved performance. Zola hit the bar early on but Georgia held their own.

Meanwhile, England were scooping up maximum points to lead the group by one point and set up a decider in Rome which Italy needed to win. Vieri nearly won the game for Italy in the dying seconds but it would not have been a fair reflection of the game.

Facing a play-off against Russia, Italy battled to a 1–1 away draw before ensuring qualification with a 1–0 win in the return leg in Naples.

Now they have reached the finals, Maldini knows he must inject greater flair and invention into the squad and it came as no surprise to see him use a January friendly against Slovakia to give new players a run. The most intriguing change was the introduction of midfielders Di Biagio, Moriero and Cois. All performed well enough and could challenge the established midfield order of Dino Baggio, Albertini and Di Matteo. All three are tough, competitive and capable of scoring goals but it is vital that Maldini has cover for them.

Moriero's pace and willingness to take on defenders added a fresh dimension to the Italians' game and could be rewarded in the summer. Maldini certainly needs somebody to unlock opposing defences. On paper he has a glut of top strikers but needs one of them to succeed in the role of goalscorer just as Rossi did so effectively in 1982 when Italy last won the World Cup.

Considering Maldini has the choice of Casiraghi, Chiesa, Vieri, Zola, Ravanelli and Del Peiro to choose from it is amazing that Italy found goals so hard to come by in qualification. Real Madrid's Vieri and Lazio's Casiraghi will compete for the target-man role favoured by Maldini while the other three will battle for the striking partner position.

Chiesa has pace and the ability to shoot with either foot while Zola is still one of the most talented forwards in Europe. Essentially, he plays just in front of the midfield and uses his excellent vision and awareness to release team-mates with perfectly weighted passes. He is a deceptively strong runner on the ball, a tenacious tackler and strikes the ball so well with both feet that he is probably the best free-kick specialist in Europe. But perhaps Del Piero will be the star of France '98. He has flair and skill in abundance and could carry Italy all the way.

Italy still maintain their traditional frugality in defence despite the retirement of the great Baresi. There is little more to be said about Maldini junior – one of the world's greatest attacking defenders and an inspirational leader. The experienced Costacurta has made a decent fist of filling Baresi's shoes although Maldini now faces the prospect of replacing the irreplaceable – Juventus defender

Ferrara broke his leg in January and looks certain to miss the finals.

If Maldini can find the key to unlocking the undoubted talent in attack, Italy have the experience and tradition to reach the final stages in July. He has a squad of players that can see him through the exhausting number of games and, more importantly, players who can handle the big occasion. The first round is tight but shouldn't trouble the *Azzurri*. Expect to see them competing to the death.

HOW THEY QUALIFIED

Results: Moldova 1 **Italy 3**; **Italy 1** Georgia 0; England 0 **Italy 1**; **Italy 3** Moldova 0; Poland 0 **Italy 0**; **Italy 3** Poland 0; Georgia 0 **Italy 0**; **Italy 0** England 0. Play-off: Russia 1 **Italy 1**; **Italy 1** Russia 0

	P	W	D	L	F	A	Pts
England	8	6	1	1	15	2	19
Italy	**8**	**5**	**3**	**0**	**11**	**1**	**18**
Poland	8	3	1	4	10	12	10
Georgia	8	3	1	4	7	9	10
Moldova	8	0	0	8	2	21	0

Top goalscorer: 3, Ravanelli.

WORLD CUP HISTORY

The 1930s were the golden age of Italian football as the great manager, Vittorio Pozzo, guided the national team to consecutive World Cup victories in 1934 and 1938. There was considerable resentment from Argentina, Brazil and Uruguay when Italy lured their star players away and they seemed to have a point when Pozzo fielded three Argentinians of Italian extraction.

In 1949, Italy was stunned by the news that the aeroplane carrying the brilliant Torino team had crashed into the wall of the Superga Basilica on a hillside near Turin. Every player was killed including eight of the national team.

Italy sent a team to the 1950 World Cup but they lost in the first round. There followed another poor display in 1954 and Italy suffered the ultimate disgrace of failing to qualify four years later.

Although they qualified for both the 1962 and 1966 tournaments, performances were still poor and after defeat by North Korea in 1966 the Italian team were greeted by garbage when they arrived back home.

The decision was taken to limit the import of foreign players in 1964 in the hope that local talent would not be overshadowed. The revival started in 1970 when Italy reached the final but they were unfortunate to come up against probably the finest team ever to play in the World Cup.

But 12 years later the World Cup was Italy's for a third time. After a slow start to the finals, drawing all their opening games, they improved as the tournament progressed with victories over Argentina, Brazil, Poland and West Germany. The star was Rossi but it had taken great teamwork to overcome four good opponents.

In 1994 Italy reached the final of the World Cup through a series of gutsy performances and flourishes of inspiration, chiefly from Roberto Baggio. Having barely survived the opening round the Italians faced a powerful Nigerian side who led 1–0 with only two minutes on the clock. This was the point at which Baggio started his inspirational run, scoring the equaliser and then converting a penalty in extra-time.

It was Baggio again who stole in with a late winner against Spain in the next round and became the match-winner for the third time when scoring twice against Bulgaria in the semi-final.

However, although he played in the final a hamstring injury reduced his effectiveness and with the whole team suffering from the strain of the previous games they hung on for 120 minutes only to lose in the dreaded penalty shoot-out.

Finals appearances: 14 (1934–54, 1962–94)
Biggest win: 7–1 v United States (1934)
Biggest defeat: 1–4 v Switzerland (1954), 1–4 v Brazil (1970)

1934 Winners
First round: 7–1 v United States; second round: 1–1 v Spain, 1–0 v Spain (replay); semi-final: 1–0 v Austria; final: 2–1 v Czechoslovakia

1938 Winners
First round: 2–1 v Norway; second round: 3–1 v France;
semi-final: 2–1 v Brazil; final: 4–2 v Hungary

1950 Eliminated first round
Pool Three: 2–3 v Sweden, 2–0 v Paraguay

1954 Eliminated first round
Pool Four: 1–2 v Switzerland, 4–1 v Belgium, 1–4 v Switzerland

1962 Eliminated first round
Group Two: 0–0 v West Germany, 0–2 v Chile,
3–0 v Switzerland

1966 Eliminated first round
Group Four: 2–0 v Chile, 0–1 v Soviet Union, 0–1 North Korea

1970 Runners-up
Group Two: 1–0 v Sweden, 0–0 v Uruguay, 0–0 v Israel;
quarter-final: 4–1 v Mexico; semi-final: 4–3 v West Germany;
final: 1–4 v Brazil

1974 Eliminated first round
Group Four: 3–1 v Haiti, 1–1 v Argentina, 1–2 v Poland

1978 Fourth
Group One: 2–1 v France, 3–1 v Hungary, 1–0 v Argentina;
Group A: 0–0 v West Germany, 1–0 v Austria, 1–2 v Holland;
third-place play-off: 1–2 v Brazil

1982 Winners
Group One: 0–0 v Poland, 1–1 v Peru, 1–1 v Cameroon;
Group C: 2–1 v Argentina, 3–2 v Brazil;
semi-final: 2–0 v Poland; final: 3–1 v West Germany

1986 Eliminated second round
Group A: 1–1 v Bulgaria, 1–1 v Argentina, 3–2 v South Korea;
second round: 0–2 v France

1990 Third
Group A: 1–0 v Austria, 1–0 v United States,
2–0 v Czechoslovakia; second round: 2–0 v Uruguay;
quarter-final: 1–0 v Republic of Ireland; semi-final:
1–1 v Argentina (3–4 on penalties);
third-place play-off: 2–1 v England

1994 Runners-up
Group E: 0–1 v Rep of Ireland; 1–0 v Norway,
1–1 v Mexico; second round: 2–1 v Nigeria;
quarter-final: 2–1 v Spain; semi-final: 2–1 v Bulgaria;
final: 0–0 v Brazil (2–3 on penalties)

Chile

Federation
Federacion de Futbol de Chile

Founded
1895

Strip
Red shirts, blue shorts, white socks

Coach
Nelson Acosta

Qualification
Fourth in South American Group

When Chile played England at Wembley in February, all eyes were focused on the 18-year-old Liverpool striker Owen – the youngest player this century to play for England. Expectations were high and his debut was a cracking success. Owen was subsequently voted Man of the Match but he would probably be the first to say that Chile's Salas was the more deserving recipient. A goal in each half by Salas – the first a stunning finish, the second a penalty – brought Chile a victory they thoroughly deserved and had many pundits reassessing their views of the South Americans.

Watchers could not have failed to be impressed by the organisation of Chile's defence, the inventiveness of their midfield and, of course, the finishing of Salas. His goals must have made Alex Ferguson, who had chased the £13 million autograph of Salas for many months, rue the fact that the South American decided to join Lazio instead.

The stocky Salas is still only 23 but widely regarded as the best player in South America and although he is an out-and-out-striker, there is more than a passing resemblance to Maradona.

His first goal followed a 40-yard pass from Sierra. The English defence was caught square, Salas outpaced Batty to cushion the dropping ball on his left thigh and then, before the ball dropped further, volleyed it past Martyn. Twelve minutes from time, Sierra again found Salas in space on the left of the penalty area. He tricked Campbell and drew the England defender into a rash challenge. Salas tucked the resulting spot kick inches inside the left-hand post.

It was perhaps a relief for English fans that only one half of the famed Chilean attack was on display. Salas was a handful but who knows what carnage the presence of Zamorano could have caused.

The partnership ran riot in the qualifying games with Zamorano scoring 12 goals and Salas 11 of Chile's 32 – the most, by some margin, of any South American team.

Despite the potent strikeforce, Chile only qualified in fourth place, ahead of Peru on goal difference. And in their first game, against lowly Venezuela, the Chileans came only seconds away from losing. The poor result led to Xavier Azkargorta receiving his marching orders and being replaced by Nelson Acosta – a Uruguayan who has taken out Chilean citizenship.

Victory over Ecuador was followed by defeats by Colombia and Paraguay and their prospects of qualification looked decidedly shaky until a decent run in mid-1997, which included an impressive 4–1 win over Colombia in which Salas scored a hat-trick.

Considering their strike rate, it is surprising that Zamorano and Salas only played together in five of the games – each being sidelined through injury at some stage. Zamorano scored his 12 goals in only 10 matches and Salas scored his 11 in 12 games. And if this duo were not enough, Chile can call on another outstanding goalscorer in the shape of Rozental who joined Rangers last year for £3.5 million. However, he has missed most of the year through injury and surgery.

Goals, then, are not likely to be a problem but their defence conceded 18 goals in 16 qualifiers – a high proportion for a serious challenger. However, their defensive display against England was pretty secure with Owen, Dublin and Shearer getting little joy with chances few and far between.

Their only world-class defender is the tall and skilful Margas at centre-back who also played in the all-star match which preceded the World Cup draw. Reyes, Fuentes and Ponce will most likely form the rest of the defence. Tapia is the best goalkeeper in the Chilean league and pulled off several good saves against England, particularly from Le Saux and Owen. In midfield, Acuna is a promising attack-minded player who played in the last seven of the qualifiers and Sierra of Colo Colo also showed against England that he has great vision and a sweet long-distance delivery. At least Acosta has the opportunity to watch and work with many of his players. Apart from his gifted strikers, most of the national side still play in Chile.

The result against England came as a real bolt from the blue. A few weeks before, Chile had finished bottom of a four-game event with Nigeria, Hong Kong and Iran – none of whom could be considered football's heavyweights. But their performance at Wembley showed that their full-strength side should be taken seriously.

Acosta says he'll be content to reach the second round and this could be well within their reach.

HOW THEY QUALIFIED

Results: Venezuela 1 **Chile 1**; **Chile 4** Ecuador 1; Colombia 4 **Chile 1**; Paraguay 2 **Chile 1**; **Chile 1** Uruguay 0; Argentina 1 **Chile 1**; Peru 2 **Chile 1**; Bolivia 1 **Chile 1**; **Chile 6** Venezuela 0; Ecuador 1 **Chile 1**; **Chile 4** Colombia 1; **Chile 2** Paraguay 1; Uruguay 1 **Chile 0**; **Chile 1** Argentina 2; **Chile 4** Peru 0; **Chile 3** Bolivia 0

	P	W	D	L	F	A	Pts
Argentina	16	8	6	2	23	13	30
Paraguay	16	9	2	5	21	14	29
Colombia	16	8	4	4	23	15	28
Chile	**16**	**7**	**4**	**5**	**32**	**18**	**25**
Peru	16	7	4	5	19	20	25
Ecuador	16	6	3	7	22	21	21
Uruguay	16	6	3	7	18	21	21
Bolivia	16	4	5	7	18	21	17
Venezuela	16	0	3	13	8	41	3

Top goalscorers: 12, Zamorano; 11, Salas; 2, Margas, Reyes.

WORLD CUP HISTORY

Chile made their World Cup debut back in 1930, beating Mexico 3–0 in Uruguay. 32 years later they hosted the finals and produced their best performance in the competition: reaching the semis before going out to Cup winners Brazil. Their tie with Italy in the qualifying stages of that tournament is one of the bloodiest games in football history and has been dubbed 'the battle of Santiago'. One Italian had his nose broken, two were sent off, there was a mass brawl and the match was almost abandoned! Chile eventually won 2–0.

Chile were banned from the 1994 World Cup by FIFA after a bizarre case of cheating during a qualifying match against Brazil in Rio. Brazil were leading 1–0 when a flare, thrown from the crowd, appeared to hit Rojas, Chile's goalkeeper. It was later shown that he had feigned the injury and that other players and officials were in on the attempt to get the result cancelled.

Finals appearances: 6 (1930, 1950, 1962–66, 1974, 1982)
Biggest win: 5–2 v USA (1950)
Biggest defeat: 1–4 v West Germany (1982)

1930 Eliminated first round
   Group One: 3–0 v Mexico, 1–0 v France, 1–3 v Argentina
1950 Eliminated first round
   Group Two: 0–2 v England, 0–2 v Spain, 5–2 v USA
1962 Third
   Group Two: 3–1 v Switzerland, 2–0 v Italy,
   0–2 v West Germany; quarter-final: 2–1 v Soviet Union;
   semi-final: 2–4 v Brazil; third-place play-off: 1–0 v Yugoslavia
1966 Eliminated first round
   Group Four: 0–2 v Italy, 1–1 v North Korea, 1–2 v Soviet Union
1974 Eliminated first round
   Group One: 0–1 v West Germany, 1–1 v East Germany,
   0–0 v Australia
1982 Eliminated first round
   Group Two: 0–1 v Austria, 1–4 v West Germany, 2–3 v Algeria

Cameroon

Federation
Cameroon football federation

Founded
1960

Strip
Green shirt, red shorts, yellow socks

Coach
Jean-Manga Onguene

Qualification
First in African Zone Group Four

Eight years ago, Cameroon heralded the promise of a continent with victory over Argentina in the opening game of Italia '90. The Indomitable Lions reached the quarter-finals before losing narrowly to England but played with such a raw yet swashbuckling style that they earned the respect of the world.

Expected to go from strength to strength, the intervening years have actually witnessed a decline in fortunes and they appear to be in the middle of a transition period and no longer Africa's greatest power.

The performance at USA '94 was a particularly disappointing period culminating, as it did, in the embarrassing 6–1 defeat by Russia – themselves a dispirited, lacklustre team. It seemed a long way from the joyful scenes of 1990 when Milla and his colleagues performed samba dances around the corner flags after scoring.

France '98 represents an opportunity for them to restore their image and coach Onguene has the experience to avoid the disasters of the last World Cup. Onguene is a former international, Africa's player of the year in 1980, and a key figure in helping the Indomitable Lions qualify for the 1982 World Cup finals in Spain – although injury ruled him out of the tournament. As a coach he assisted the national team in the previous two World Cup finals

and since taking over from Henri Depireux last July has set about
creating a youthful squad of overseas and locally based players.

After their 1994 World Cup debacle and poor showing in the
1996 Africa Nations Cup, the Lions surprised critics by emerging
unbeaten at the top of their 1998 World Cup qualifying group.

Money has always been a problem for Cameroon and funds to
buy air tickets for overseas players have to be used carefully. But
the investment paid off with a fairly comfortable qualification.

Having beaten Togo away, Cameroon then drew with group
rivals Angola – who were aiming to qualify for their first finals. But
two home wins in April set them on the way. Against Zimbabwe,
a piece of individual inspiration by Tchoutang, who lobbed goalkeeper Grobbelaar, gave Cameroon a barely deserved win while
late goals by Mboma and Tchoutang saw off Togo.

They finally clinched their ticket for France in August when they
beat Zimbabwe 2–1 in Harare. The hero of that match was again
Mboma whose two long-range strikes proved decisive. He is a
prolific scorer for Japanese J-league side Gambo Osaka and has
been equally successful for the national side. On current form he is
a potential replacement for Omam-Biyik who is desperately trying
to make a comeback.

For the game against Zimbabwe, Onguene managed to call upon
the services of his overseas players and he will need to have the funds
available to repeat that during the Lions' preparation for France.

Fans were not happy when their team came bottom of a four-
nation tournament in Haiti and Onguene had another experi-
mental side on display when Cameroon went down 2–0 to England
at Wembley. The coach's plan to experiment was clearly demonstrated by the introduction of 16-year-old Olembe for that game
and he became the youngest ever international to appear at
Wembley. Another making his debut that night was 19-year-old
striker Job whose impressive performance may see him line up
alongside Mboma in attack.

But what could be a major handicap for Cameroon in France is
the absence of stars of the calibre of Milla. His exploits in Italy put
Cameroon firmly on the world map and it was thanks to
Cameroon's performance – they were the first African nation to
reach the last eight – that FIFA awarded Africa two additional
places at World Cup finals.

Despite the absence of big names, Cameroon can always count on the combative youngsters Tchoutang and Ndjitap in midfield and sharp-shooter Mboma as well as the talented Job.

In addition, Onguene can call on captain and goalkeeper Songo'o, veteran of two World Cup finals and experienced defenders Kalla as well as Song (who made his World Cup debut in 1994 aged just 17).

HOW THEY QUALIFIED

Results: Togo 2 **Cameroon 4**; **Cameroon 0** Angola 0; **Cameroon 1** Zimbabwe 0; **Cameroon 2** Togo 0; Angola 1 **Cameroon 1**; Zimbabwe 1 **Cameroon 2**

	P	W	D	L	F	A	Pts
Cameroon	6	4	2	0	10	4	14
Angola	6	3	1	2	5	5	10
Zimbabwe	6	1	1	4	6	7	4
Togo	6	1	1	4	6	14	4

Top goalscorers: 5, Mboma; 2,Tchami.

WORLD CUP HISTORY

Of all the African nations, Cameroon have made the biggest impact at the World Cup finals. In 1982, they drew all of their games – including with eventual winners Italy – but it was in 1990 that they enthralled the world. The victory over world champions Argentina was one of the biggest upsets in the game but they proved that they were no flash in the pan with exhilarating wins over Romania and Colombia before losing narrowly to England in the quarter-final.

Finals appearances: 3 (1982, 1990, 1994)
Biggest win: 2–1 v Romania (1990), 2–1 v Colombia (1990)
Biggest defeat: 1–6 v Russia (1994)

1982 Eliminated first round
Group One: 0–0 v Peru, 0–0 v Poland, 1–1 v Italy
1990 Quarter-finalists
Group B: 1–0 v Argentina, 2–1 v Romania, 0–4 v Soviet Union;
second round: 2–1 v Colombia; quarter-final: 2–3 v England
1994 Eliminated first round
Group B: 2–2 v Sweden, 0–3 v Brazil, 1–6 v Russia

Austria

Federation
Austrian football federation

Founded
1904

Strip
White shirts, black shorts, white socks

Coach
Herbert Prohaska

Qualification
First in European Zone Group Four

Given their failure to qualify for USA '94 and Euro '96 and with nightmares still of that disastrous defeat by the Faeroe Isles in 1990, Austria's chances of qualifying for France were not rated highly when they were drawn in the same group as Scotland and Sweden.

For coach Herbert Prohaska, who took over the team in 1993, it represented his final chance to re-establish the credibility of Austrian football and restore some much needed pride in the national side.

Bravely, he resisted change and continued to call on the services of players from Rapid, FK Austria and Salzburg along with those playing in the German league.

Failure to beat Scotland at home in their opening game seemed to confirm that Austria were an ageing, toothless team with little creativity, but a few minor changes then brought an unexpected but deserved away win in Sweden. Things were looking up and although they lost to Scotland at Parkhead the Austrians won all their other games to finish top of the table.

Prohaska, who was heavily criticised after Austria failed to make Euro '96, celebrated the biggest success of his coaching career. 'This is a sensation for us,' he said after his team's decisive 4–0 win over Belarus.

How far they will go in France is another question. The fact that they qualified at all is seen as a major success and with Italy, Cameroon and Chile in their group, the Austrians could have hoped for a kinder draw.

At least they should be a tough team to beat. Konsel is a top-class keeper and there is considerable experience in defence. The sweeper Feiersinger is likely to line up with Pfeffer and Schottel – all ultra-reliable and hard-working players.

In midfield, Herzog is Austria's main star and playmaker. Surgery last autumn on a long-standing toe complaint means that he will be out of action for at least five months and Prohaska will be keeping a close eye on his recovery. The two have not always seen eye to eye and the coach once said he would never pick Herzog again after he had preferred to play for Werder Bremen instead of his country.

But the truth is that Prohaska needs a fully fit and committed Herzog in his line-up. He cannot afford to lose his sole world-class player whose creativity and deadly left foot provide the inspiration for an Austrian team high on work rate and low on genuine quality. Herzog made a vital contribution to Austria's qualification, scoring crucial goals at home to Latvia and the winner in both games against Sweden and the 29-year-old could prove to be a leading figure in France.

Herzog should be joined in midfield by Pfeifenberger who was ever-present in the national side during qualification. He's also a handy goalscorer, averaging a goal every three games.

Also in midfield, Prilasnig has been one of the few newcomers to catch the eye. He made his debut against Sweden and did well enough to keep his place for the subsequent qualifiers.

However, Prohaska's main problem lies up front. His main hope is veteran Cologne striker Polster who will be looking to add to an impressive tally of 41 goals in 87 appearances for his country. His seven goals were vital to qualification and confirmed how crucial his presence is to the national side. He is rapidly approaching Hanappi's record of 93 caps but, at 34, is no spring chicken and Prohaska will be praying that the tough German league doesn't take too much out of his star striker as there is no obvious replacement.

The Austrians seemed to surprise even themselves by clinching first place in the qualifying group but the finals are likely to expose their lack of firepower. They will be tough opponents and may not lose games but it's hard to see where the spark to win games is going to come from. Without that, the first round is likely to be their limit.

HOW THEY QUALIFIED

Results: Austria 0 Scotland 0; Sweden 0 **Austria 1**; **Austria 2** Latvia 1; Scotland 2 **Austria 0**; **Austria 2** Estonia 0; Latvia 1 **Austria 3**; Estonia 0 **Austria 3**; **Austria 1** Sweden 0; Belarus 0 **Austria 1**; **Austria 4** Belarus 0

	P	W	D	L	F	A	Pts
Austria	**10**	**8**	**1**	**1**	**17**	**4**	**25**
Scotland	10	7	2	1	15	3	23
Sweden	10	7	0	3	16	9	21
Latvia	10	3	1	6	10	14	10
Estonia	10	1	1	8	4	16	4
Belarus	10	1	1	8	5	21	4

Top goalscorers: 7, Polster; 4, Stoger; 3, Herzog.

WORLD CUP HISTORY

The period between the wars was Austria's most successful era when the 'Wunderteam' swept all before them under the inspired coaching of the legendary Hugo Meisl.

The 1934 World Cup seemed theirs for the taking but defeat by the hosts Italy on a quagmire of a pitch ended their hopes.

Four years later, Austrian chances were destroyed by the German occupation as the Germans also recruited some of Austria's best players into their own team.

A new 'Wunderteam' was developed in the 1950s but, as happens so often, they peaked between finals. Nevertheless, they were still expected to do well in Switzerland in 1958 and after eliminating Scotland and Czechoslovakia they went on to beat the hosts in a memorable quarter-final which ended 7–5. But the Germans again spoiled things, crushing them 6–1 in the semi-final.

A poor showing in Sweden in 1958, admittedly in a nightmare group featuring Brazil, England and the Soviet Union, was followed by a dramatic decline in fortunes.

Their next finals appearance, in South America in 1978, resulted in defeats by Brazil, Holland and Italy but at least they got some satisfaction from a 3–2 win over West Germany.

Qualification in 1982 was soured by a much-criticised 1–0 defeat by West Germany which allowed them both to qualify for the second round at the expense of Algeria.

Italia '90 represented another low point – a narrow victory over the USA following defeats by Italy and Czechoslovakia.

Finals appearances: 6 (1934, 1954, 1958, 1978, 1982, 1990)
Biggest win: 5–0 v Czechoslovakia
Biggest defeat: 6–1 v West Germany

1934 Fourth
First round: 3–2 v France (aet); second round: 2–1 v Hungary; semi-final: 0–1 v Italy; third-place play-off: 2–3 v Germany

1954 Third
Pool Three: 1–0 v Scotland, 5–0 v Czechoslovakia;
quarter-final: 7–5 v Switzerland;
semi-final: 1–6 v West Germany;
third-place play-off: 3–1 v Uruguay

1958 Eliminated first round
Pool Four: 0–3 v Brazil, 0–2 v Soviet Union, 2–2 v England

1978 Eliminated second round
Group Three: 2–1 v Spain, 1–0 v Sweden, 0–1 v Brazil;
Group A: 1–5 v Holland, 0–1 v Italy, 3–2 v West Germany

1982 Eliminated second round
Group Two: 1–0 v Chile, 2–1 v Algeria, 0–1 v West Germany;
Group D: 0–1 v France, 2–2 v Northern Ireland

1990 Eliminated first round
Group A: 0–1 v Italy, 0–1 v Czechoslovakia, 2–1 v USA

Group C

France, South Africa, Saudi Arabia, Denmark

By the time France play Denmark in the final group game they should both be looking ahead to their second-round opponents. Saudi Arabia will be no pushover but the strength and experience of the European squads should prove too strong.

With the likes of Djorkaeff, Zidane, Desailly and Deschamps, France are capable of mounting Europe's strongest challenge. The only problem appears to be the absence of a star striker. But if ever France have the chance of emulating the vintage side from the mid-1980s, now is the time. Certainly coach Aime Jacquet has the quality at his disposal to make a concerted bid for the semi-final stages.

FIXTURES

France v South Africa	12 June, 19.00,	Marseilles	**ITV**
Saudi Arabia v Denmark	12 June, 15.30,	Lens	**BBC**
France v Saudi Arabia	18 June, 19.00,	Stade de France	**BBC**
South Africa v Denmark	18 June, 15.30,	Toulouse	**ITV**
France v Denmark	24 June, 14.00,	Lyon	**BBC**
South Africa v Saudi Arabia	24 June, 14.00,	Bordeaux	**BBC**

France

Federation
Federation Française de Football

Founded
1919

Strip
Blue shirts, white shorts, red socks

Coach
Aime Jacquet

Qualification
As hosts

It's been 12 long years since France last reached the finals of the World Cup and after a disappointing Euro '96 the hosts will be under huge pressure to raise the profile of French football to the level they enjoyed in the early 1980s.

But if ever France have the chance of emulating that vintage side surely now is the time. Certainly coach Aime Jacquet has the quality at his disposal to make a concerted bid for the semi-final stages.

It is the midfield of Zidane, Deschamps, Djorkaeff and Ba which holds so much promise for France and the big question will be whether Jacquet can coax his talented individuals to combine as a team.

There is no doubting Djorkaeff's sublime skills. The former Paris St-Germain favourite came to prominence in 1995 and was snapped up by Inter the following year where he has been instrumental in the Italian giant's resurgence. He can play as an out-and-out striker or operate as a foil to the main striker – such as for Ronaldo at Inter – and has scored stunning goals for club and country.

Djorkaeff has developed a great partnership and understanding with Zidane – another French import who has stamped his authority on Serie A with Juventus. Zidane is an outstandingly inventive player with a lethal left foot and if his partnership with Djorkaeff clicks it could prove the highlight of the finals.

Zidane's Juventus team-mate Deschamps provides the combative edge and steel in midfield while Ba is an electrifying presence on the right wing. His pace alone unnerves defenders and although he may not be an automatic first choice, the Milan winger shone in the Tournoi last summer and could prove an inspired selection.

While Boghossian and Karembeu hope to impress Jacquet for a midfield slot, there is one player whose place is virtually assured – the imposing figure of Desailly. The Ghana-born defender or midfielder possesses skill, vision but above all power and it is his great strength which makes him such an effective player. Desailly is a pillar of impregnability in defence, almost impossible to beat one-on-one through strength or speed. He makes an effective partner for the even more experienced Blanc who is a calming influence at sweeper.

The problem for this French team appears to be the absence of a star striker. Talk of Papin making a return surely smacks of desperation but Jacquet is running out of time to find a partner for Djorkaeff. The 24-year-old PSG striker Maurice has proved at club level that he deserves consideration while the Monaco youngsters of Henry and Trezeguet are also knocking on the coach's door.

Dugarry's form appears to have suffered since the big clubs were attracted to his goalscoring feats at Bordeaux. Unlike Zidane and Djorkaeff, Dugarry spent most of his time on the Milan bench when he moved to Italy and was then sold to Barcelona before a similar experience persuaded him to move back to Marseille. Back on French soil, he may make a late claim for the striker's role.

Jacquet has tried out a lot of players in the forward role and Guivarc'h at least scored on his debut against South Africa. The French won that game 2–1 but were booed off the pitch by fans craving more entertainment.

The clock is ticking for Jacquet. At least there are no unpleasant surprises in the group stages but an in-form striker alongside Zidane and Djorkaeff could make a good French side into one which could challenge for the ultimate prize.

WORLD CUP HISTORY

France's best spell in world football came in the 1980s when the country gloried in one of the most inspired four-man midfields ever to have graced a football pitch. The combined talents of Giresse, Tigana, Fernandez and, of course, Platini were simply outstanding and France's victory, on home soil, in the 1984 European Championship was a fitting tribute to that wonderful side.

That victory went some way towards compensating for the unlucky and controversial defeat by West Germany in the 1982 World Cup semi-final but four years later, in 1986, it was the Germans who again stopped the French in the semi-finals; the defeat coming after Platini had inspired his team-mates to a momentous win over Brazil in the quarter-finals.

Since then, the French have failed to qualify for the World Cup finals and disappointed on both occasions they reached the final stages of the European Championship.

Finals appearances: 9 (1930–38, 1954–58, 1966, 1978–86)
Biggest win: 7–3 v Paraguay (1958)
Biggest defeat: 2–5 v Brazil (1958)

1930 Eliminated first round
     Group One: 4–1 v Mexico, 0–1 v Argentina, 0–1 v Chile
1934 Eliminated first round
     First round: 2–3 v Austria
1938 Quarter-finalists
     First round: 3–1 v Belgium; quarter-final: 1–3 v Italy
1954 Eliminated first round
     Group One: 0–1 v Yugoslavia, 3–2 v Mexico
1958 Third
     Group Two: 7–3 v Paraguay, 2–3 v Yugoslavia, 2–1 v Scotland;
     quarter-final: 4–0 v Northern Ireland; semi-final: 2–5 v Brazil;
     third-place play-off: 6–3 v West Germany
1966 Eliminated first round
     Group One: 1–1 v Mexico, 1–2 v Uruguay, 0–2 v England
1978 Eliminated first round
     Group One: 1–2 v Italy, 1–2 v Argentina, 3–1 v Hungary

1982 Fourth
> Group Four: 1–3 v England, 4–1 v Kuwait,
> 1–1 v Czechoslovakia; second round: 1–0 v Austria,
> 4–1 v Northern Ireland; semi-final: 3–3 v West Germany
> (4–5 on penalties); third-place play-off: 2–3 v Poland

1986 Third
> Group Three: 1–0 v Canada, 1–1 v Soviet Union,
> 3–0 v Hungary; second round: 2–0 v Italy;
> quarter-final: 1–1 v Brazil (4–3 on penalties);
> semi-final: 0–2 v West Germany;
> third-place play-off: 4–2 v Belgium

South Africa

Federation
South African Football Association

Founded
1991

Strip
White, yellow, green and black shirts, green shorts, white socks

Coach
Philippe Troussier

Qualification
First in African Zone Group Three

First rugby World Cup champions, then African Nations Cup champions and now qualification for the World Cup finals. And only five years after the end of South Africa's long sporting isolation.

Success in football has been a major boost to a country where sporting success is seen as an important factor in building a common national identity after the years of apartheid. And more to the point, the mixed race team has done much to break down old racial barriers and unite the country.

South Africa came through a wobbly campaign, starting impressively but then faltering before winning their last two games to finish top of their group. South Africa took all the points against the Democratic Republic of Congo, but were fortunate to have their away match switched by FIFA from the hostilities of Kinshasa to neutral west Africa because of the civil conflict.

South Africa also beat favourites Zambia at home and drew away in Lusaka but Congo proved the biggest obstacle to qualification for 'Bafana Bafana', as the South African team are called – a Zulu term meaning 'the boys'.

Defeat by Congo jolted their campaign and left them needing a result in the return game in Johannesburg – the last match of the qualifiers. However, long-standing favourite Masinga sneaked the vital goal in the 1–0 win – confirming his position as South Africa's key player.

Under the old apartheid regime, football was one of the few racially-integrated activities in South Africa. In 1978 the white National Football League and non-white Professional Soccer League merged to form the National Soccer League. In 1996 South Africa won the African Nations Cup for the first time, beating Tunisia in the final at the Soccer City stadium in Soweto.

The man who took South Africa to this success was coach Clive Barker who was in charge of the national team from early 1994. He won two championships in South Africa and was one of the first white coaches to coach a black club in South Africa's segregated leagues in the 1970s.

However, a run of poor performances late last year, including two defeats at the Confederations Cup in Saudi Arabia, led him to resign as coach. Frenchman Philippe Troussier was appointed to take over in March once he had finished his commitments with Burkina Faso in the Nations Cup.

This left Sono, a club owner in South Africa, to act as caretaker coach for the Nations Cup – not the ideal preparation for a team needing a lift before the World Cup finals.

Troussier will have a range of talent to draw upon. Not that long ago, the whole team would have been based in South Africa but now there are a number dotted around Europe picking up valuable international experience.

Masinga is one of that growing contingent of players competing in the leagues of Europe and he has proved a reliable scorer for the national team. Once with Leeds United and now enjoying success with Bari in Italy, Masinga is a serious test for any defence. His four goals in qualifying proved vital and came after he had threatened to retire from international football because of frequent barracking from home fans.

The captain, Radebe, plies his trade in England with Leeds United and has developed into a defender of international class. Fish, now playing for Bolton after a season with Lazio, is also a key figure in defence.

Others to benefit from action overseas are the Barnsley midfielder, Tinkler, and the midfielder Moshoeu, who plays in

Turkey for Kocaelispor. Mosheou and partner Khumalo are the midfield play-makers in the team with Tinkler the ball-winner. Age will be a problem for Troussier though, with all three of these players plus veteran sweeper Tovey being over 30.

The experience in the squad should mean that 'Bafana Bafana' are no pushovers in their first appearance in the finals but they are unlikely to prevent the European teams from going through.

HOW THEY QUALIFIED

Results: Preliminary round: Malawi 0 **South Africa 1**;
South Africa 3 Malawi 0; Group Three: **South Africa 1**
Republic of Congo 0; Zambia 0 **South Africa 0**; Congo 2
South Africa 0; Republic of Congo 1 **South Africa 2**;
South Africa 3 Zambia 0; **South Africa 1** Congo 0

	P	W	D	L	F	A	Pts
South Africa	6	4	1	1	7	3	13
Congo	6	3	1	2	5	5	10
Zambia	6	2	2	2	7	6	8
Rep of Congo	6	0	2	4	4	9	2

Top goalscorers: 4, Masinga; 2, Bartlett.

WORLD CUP HISTORY

This is South Africa's first appearance in the finals.

Saudi Arabia

Federation
Saudi Arabian Football Federation

Founded
1959

Strip
White shirts, green shorts, white socks

Coach
Carlos Alberto Parreira

Qualification
First in final Asian Zone Group A

There is no doubt about the moment when Saudi Arabia established themselves on the world stage; in the fifth minute of their group match against Belgium at USA '94, Saeed al-Owairan, the 'Desert Pelé', picked up the ball in his own half and ran through the whole Belgian team before scoring the goal that secured their passage to the second round. There they went out to the eventual semi-finalists Sweden, but their free-flowing style had won many admirers and they returned home with the reputation of Saudi football greatly enhanced.

Since then Owairan has served an 18-month ban for 'immoral acts', imposed after he was caught at an illegal drinks party in 1995, flouting the Islamic law against alcohol and illicit sexual relationships. After serving his punishment he has now been welcomed back at the age of 30 in time for France '98.

The national side did not appear to miss their star forward during qualifying. They reached their second successive finals by romping through their first-round Asian group, scoring 18 goals and conceding only one. They then squeezed past Qatar in the final qualifying tie of their second-round group – when four teams still had a chance of taking the automatic qualifying place and the runners-up position. Sami al-Jaber, who came into the reckoning when al-Owairan was banned, won national hero status when he scored the all-important goal in Qatar, and Khaled al-Mulawid finished as the team's top scorer.

The Saudi federation has invested millions in recent years in an attempt to establish professional football in the Desert Kingdom, and their impatience for success has led them to use no fewer than eight national coaches since the start of qualifying. Otto Pfister, the German who actually clinched their place in the finals, has now given way to Carlos Alberto Parreira, who led Brazil to the title in 1994. Parreira's experience – he also managed Kuwait at the 1982 World Cup and the UAE in 1990 – may help the Saudis make things difficult for France, Denmark and South Africa in Group C, but their two heavy defeats by Mexico and Brazil in the Confederations Cup in Riyadh in January do not encourage optimism.

HOW THEY QUALIFIED

Results: First round: Taiwan 0 **Saudi Arabia 2**; Malaysia 0 **Saudi Arabia 0**; Bangladesh 1 **Saudi Arabia 4**; At Djeddah: **Saudi Arabia 3** Bangladesh 0; **Saudi Arabia 3** Malaysia 0; **Saudi Arabia 6** Taiwan 0. Second round: **Saudi Arabia 2** Kuwait 1; Iran 1 **Saudi Arabia 1**; China 1 **Saudi Arabia 0**; **Saudi Arabia 1** Qatar 0; Kuwait 2 **Saudi Arabia 1**; **Saudi Arabia 1** Iran 0; **Saudi Arabia 1** China 1; Qatar 0 **Saudi Arabia 1**

	P	W	D	L	F	A	Pts
Saudi Arabia	8	4	2	2	8	6	14
Iran	8	3	3	2	13	8	12
China	8	3	2	3	11	14	11
Qatar	8	3	1	4	7	10	10
Kuwait	8	2	2	4	7	8	8

Top goalscorers: 8, Khaled Mussaad al-Mulawid; 6, Ahmed Doukhi al-Dossari.

WORLD CUP HISTORY

In 1994 the Saudis surprised fans with their speed on the ball and remarkable control, beating Belgium 1–0 thanks to the famous goal by Owairan.

Their coach, Solari, spoke barely 30 words of Arabic yet under his leadership the Saudis ran Holland close in a 2–1 defeat. When they beat Morocco 2–1 in New York, Saudi Arabia won the first-ever all-Arab clash in the World Cup finals and became only the second Asian side to win a match in the finals, following North Korea's win over Italy in 1966.

Finals appearances: 1 (1994)
Biggest win: 2–1 v Morocco
Biggest defeat: 1–3 v Sweden (1994)

1994 Eliminated second round
Group F: 1–2 v Holland, 2–1 v Morocco, 1–0 v Belgium;
second round: 1–3 v Sweden

Denmark

Federation
Dansk Boldspil Union

Founded
1889

Strip
Red shirts, white shorts, red socks

Coach
Bo Johansson

Qualification
First in European Zone Group One

The most surprising aspect of Denmark's presence at France '98 is that this will be only the second time they have qualified for the finals. But despite their lack of World Cup pedigree, the 1992 European champions will not be intimidated in France and will aim to at least match the achievements of the wonderful Denmark side of 1986.

That team, with players such as Elkjaer, Michael Laudrup, Olsen and Lerby stunned everyone with an awesome display in Mexico. They won all their group matches, including a sensational 6–1 win over Uruguay and a 2–0 victory over eventual finalists Germany before losing in spectacular fashion to Spain.

Denmark won a lot of admirers for their exciting brand of football and this encouraged development in the domestic game from which a new generation of players emerged to win the 1992 European Championship in Sweden.

Coach Bo Johansson took over as Danish national coach in the summer of 1996 after Richard Moeller Nielsen's squad failed to make an impact in Euro '96. He set about revitalising the team with some keen youngsters who have done well in the qualifiers. The Swedish-born coach enjoys great popularity among the Danish public, media and his team, which he is developing into a more aggressive side.

Johansson can also call on several world-class players. First, there is the huge imposing presence of Schmeichel who is surely the world's best goalkeeper. Not only is he decisive, athletic and brave in goal, he is frequently the instigator of swift counter-attacks for both club and country with his intelligent distribution.

In front of Schmeichel is the highly experienced Hogh who has adapted well to Johansson's zonal defence system after so long as the *libero* while Celtic's Rieper and Udinese's Helveg are rock-solid defenders with plenty of caps between them. Helveg in particular has developed into a world-class wing-back and has been an automatic choice for Denmark over the past four years.

In midfield, Nielsen has contributed important goals to his high work rate while Michael Laudrup, the only member of Denmark's squad to have played in the World Cup, is enjoying something of an Indian summer with Ajax and Denmark. As captain, he has had a key role in settling the side and, together with his experienced brother, Brian, has helped the younger players blend and settle.

Denmark got off to a winning start against Slovenia in what was a tough qualifying group that also featured Croatia, Greece and Bosnia. Victory over Greece at home the following month was particularly memorable for a wonderful solo effort by Brian Laudrup – a mazy run took him past four opponents before he hit the back of the net. It was his rather fortunate strike which earned the Danes a draw away to Croatia and after further impressive victories against Slovenia and Bosnia they looked set fair for France.

Against Bosnia in Sarajevo, Johansson's reshaped Danish team suffered its first and only defeat. Although Brian Laudrup was missing, Bosnia totally outplayed Denmark in a 3–0 win which put some unnecessary pressure on them for their last two matches. However, the defeat concentrated their minds and no further mistakes were made – a 3–1 victory over Croatia proving a fitting riposte.

Of the young talents that Johansson has introduced into the team, defenders Colding and Tobiassen have impressed while Newcastle's Tomasson has the ability to force his way into the midfield reckoning.

Denmark will rely heavily on Schmeichel's broad shoulders but the finals are the perfect stage for the Laudrup brothers to demonstrate their dazzling skills. Brian Laudrup has the pace and control to cut swathes through defences and Michael will hope to make up for his disappointing performances at Euro '96.

Denmark certainly don't possess the swashbuckling skills of the 1986 team but it is unlikely that they will fail in such spectacular fashion. Experience in defence will see them past the first round but a shortage of firepower up front makes it difficult to see them going any further.

HOW THEY QUALIFIED

Results: Slovenia 0 **Denmark 2**; **Denmark 2** Greece 1; Croatia 1 **Denmark 1**; **Denmark 4** Slovenia 0; **Denmark 2** Bosnia 0; Bosnia 3 **Denmark 0**; **Denmark 3** Croatia 1; Greece 0 **Denmark 0**

	P	W	D	L	F	A	Pts
Denmark	**8**	**5**	**2**	**1**	**14**	**6**	**17**
Croatia	8	4	3	1	17	12	15
Greece	8	4	2	2	11	4	14
Bosnia	8	3	0	5	9	14	9
Slovenia	8	0	1	7	5	20	1

Top goalscorers: 4, B Laudrup; 3 Nielsen.

WORLD CUP HISTORY

In the heat of Mexico, newcomers Denmark were drawn in the so-called 'group of death' alongside West Germany, Scotland and Uruguay. Denmark made a mockery of the title, winning all three of their games including a 6–1 annihilation of Uruguay in which Elkjaer scored a hat-trick. But having been the revelation of the tournament everything went pear-shaped in the second round when a terrible error by Olsen allowed Spain to equalise just before half-time. From then on it was all Spain who put another four past the bewildered Danes.

Finals appearances: 1 (1986)
Biggest win: 6–1 v Uruguay (1986)
Biggest defeat: 1–5 v Spain (1986)

1986 Eliminated second round

Group Five: 1–0 v Scotland, 6–1 v Uruguay,
2–0 v West Germany; second round: 1–5 v Spain

Group D

Spain, Nigeria, Paraguay, Bulgaria

With Spain, in 1992, and Nigeria, in 1996, this fascinating group boasts the past two winners of the Olympic football gold medal. Spain are a stronger side than the one that lost to Italy four years ago and they enjoyed a good qualifying run. They have the shape and feel of a team that could go far. Nigeria are certainly good enough to get through but so are Bulgaria, who can still call on the sublime skills of Stoichkov.

Nigeria and Bulgaria are unlikely to overcome the strong Spanish team but the Africans should be lifted by the way in which they simply tore through Bulgaria four years ago.

FIXTURES

Paraguay v Bulgaria	12 June, 12.30, Montpellier	**ITV**
Spain v Nigeria	13 June, 12.30, Nantes	**BBC**
Nigeria v Bulgaria	19 June, 15.30, Parc des Princes	**ITV**
Spain v Paraguay	19 June, 19.00, Saint Etienne	**BBC**
Spain v Bulgaria	24 June, 19.00, Lens	**ITV**
Nigeria v Paraguay	24 June, 19.00, Toulouse	**ITV**

Spain

Federation
Real Federacion Espanola de Futbol

Founded
1913

Strip
Red shirts, blue shorts, black socks

Coach
Javier Clemente

Qualification
First in European Zone Group Six

Despite consistently reaching the final stages of both the World Cup and European Championship for the past 20 years, Spain's subsequent performances in the finals themselves have never come up to the high level expected of them and they have frequently been labelled as under-achievers. But there are now signs that they may be on the threshhold of better things and travel to France as one of the favourites.

The root of this optimism can be traced back to the Under-23 side which won gold at the Barcelona Olympics in 1992. Two years later, Spain were unlucky to lose to Italy in the World Cup quarter-final and if Salinas had not missed a golden opportunity when clean through on goal the result could have been very different. As it was, Spain lost a game they deserved to win.

Since then, they have continued to improve. They were unbeaten in qualifying for Euro '96 and the World Cup and have lost only two games since 1994. The first was to England at Euro '96, and that only in the penalty shoot-out, and more recently to France in a friendly to mark the official opening of the Stade de France in January.

One would think that a coach who could boast this sort of record would be considered something of a hero but Clemente has been criticised over his team selection and style of play. Since he took over in 1992, Clemente has both strengthened and breathed new life into the national team, notably by calling on the youngsters, such as Amavisca, Enrique, Abelardo and Kiko, who helped Spain to Olympic gold. Now, with the maturing of those Olympic winners, in particular Alfonso and Kiko, there is a mood of optimism amongst Spain's success-starved supporters.

Although it may not be the most attractive football on display no one will argue that it has not been effective. The veteran goalkeeper Zubizaretta continues to hold his place, and can count on the hugely impressive defensive qualities of Abelardo, Alkorta and Nadal.

Guerrero was thrown in at the deep end when, as a 20-year-old, he was given the job of organising the Spanish midfield in the 1994 competition. Despite injury problems, the Athletic Bilbao player has already played 30 times for his country and he scored a first half hat-trick in the qualifying game at Malta. The 24-year-old alternates between midfield and front-line roles, where his pace, mobility, vision and finishing make him a tremendous all-rounder.

Real Madrid's intelligent midfielder Hierro is the driving force through the centre while his former club team-mate, Enrique (he of the hide-your-head-in-your-shirt style of celebrating a goal), is another attack-minded midfielder who covers plenty of ground. He was ever-present during the World Cup finals in 1994 and his ability to keep on running at defenders in the overwhelming heat was a measure of his fitness and raw energy.

Enrique is enjoying a new lease of life at both international and club level since joining Barcelona from Real Madrid, and has benefited from a shift into midfield from the forward role he filled in the 1994 World Cup.

Spain's real weakness has been in attack. But Clemente may have finally solved this problem by giving Raul, the young Real Madrid forward, his chance. Nevertheless, Clemente took longer than most would have liked to call up the young star, and he has still to pick Barcelona playmaker De la Pena. The coach has often been reluctant to pick 'star' players but Raul's form made it impossible for Clemente to ignore him any longer. He won his first full cap against the Czech Republic aged just 19, and already looks like a seasoned international.

Spain won what beforehand appeared to be a tough group, and did so without losing a game. But they often failed to convert their undoubted superiority into goals. Their lack of goal power could still be a problem in the finals.

They are relying on Raul to change that and, appropriately, it was goals from him and Olympic hero Guardiola, which gave Spain victory over Yugoslavia in the decisive qualifying game of the group.

Spain had begun their campaign with a 6–2 win in the Faeroe Islands, which included a hat-trick by striker Alfonso, and went on to clinch a goalless draw with the Euro '96 runners-up, the Czech Republic, who never looked like posing a threat in Group Six.

It was a Hierro spot kick that made the difference in the 1–0 home win over the Czechs but Clemente's side missed a hatful of chances in that game. They were back on target in both matches against another potentially dangerous team in Slovakia – the second of which clinched their ticket to the finals.

Four years ago, Clemente's side may have been too young and inexperienced. Four years on, they have the shape and feel of a team that could go far.

HOW THEY QUALIFIED

Results: Spain 6 Faeroe Isles 2; Czech Republic 0 **Spain 0; Spain 4** Slovakia 1; **Spain 2** Yugoslavia 0; **Spain 3** Malta 0; **Spain 4** Malta 0; Yugoslavia 1 **Spain 1; Spain 1** Czech Republic 0; **Spain 2** Slovakia 1; **Spain 3** Faeroe Isles 1

	P	W	D	L	F	A	Pts
Spain	10	8	2	0	26	6	26
Yugoslavia	10	7	2	1	29	7	23
Czech Rep	10	5	1	4	16	6	16
Slovakia	10	5	1	4	18	14	16
Faeroe Isles	10	2	0	8	10	31	6
Malta	10	0	0	10	2	37	0

Top goalscorers: 5, Alfonso; 4, Hierro, Enrique; 3, Guerrero.

WORLD CUP HISTORY

Spain's best performance in a World Cup was fourth place in Brazil in 1950, when they beat the United States, Chile and England. After a lean spell, the national team qualified in 1962 and 1966 – a period which saw Real Madrid dominate European football – but they were not quite the match of teams such as Brazil and West Germany.

However, the biggest blow to the fanatical Spanish public was their poor display when, as hosts in 1982, they were considered one of the pre-tournament favourites. In one of the worst performances by a host country, Spain struggled through the first round and despite a highly talented team of individuals they crashed out of the tournament.

In 1986 they produced a sensational display to beat Denmark, the revelation of the finals, 5–1, after which, they were unlucky to lose to Belgium in a penalty shoot-out.

In 1994, Spain cruised through to the quarter-finals and had Salinas converted his golden chance against Italy when the Spanish were dominating, the result could have been different. As it was, Roberto Baggio's last gasp winner saw the Italians pull through.

Finals appearances: 9 (1934, 1950, 1962–66, 1978–94)
Biggest win: 5–1 v Denmark (1986)
Biggest defeat: 1–6 v Brazil (1950)

1934 Eliminated second round
    First round: 3–1 v Brazil;
    second round: 1–1 v Italy, 0–1 v Italy (replay)
1950 Fourth
    Group Two: 3–1 v United States, 2–0 v Chile, 1–0 v England;
    final pool: 2–2 v Uruguay, 1–6 v Brazil, 1–3 v Sweden
1962 Eliminated first round
    Group Three: 0–1 v Czechoslovakia, 1–0 v Mexico,
    1–2 v Brazil
1966 Eliminated first round
    Group Two: 1–2 v Argentina, 2–1 v Switzerland,
    1–2 v West Germany

1978 Eliminated first round

Group Three: 1–2 v Austria, 0–0 v Brazil, 1–0 v Sweden

1982 Eliminated second round

Group Five: 1–1 v Honduras, 2–1 v Yugoslavia,
0–1 v Northern Ireland; Group B: 1–2 v West Germany,
0–0 v England

1986 Quarter-finalists

Group D: 0–1 v Brazil, 2–1 v Northern Ireland, 3–0 v Algeria;
second round: 5–1 v Denmark;
quarter-final: 1–1 v Belgium (4–5 on penalties)

1990 Eliminated second round

Group E: 0–0 v Uruguay, 3–1 v South Korea, 2–1 v Belgium;
second round: 1–2 v Yugoslavia

1994 Quarter-finalists

Group C: 1–1 v Germany, 2–2 v South Korea, 3–1 v Bolivia;
second round: 3–0 v Switzerland; quarter-final: 1–2 v Italy

Nigeria

Federation
Nigeria Football Association

Founded
1945

Strip
Green shirts, white shorts, green socks

Coach
Bora Milutinovic

Qualification
First in African Zone Group One

Since their first appearance in the World Cup at USA '94 Nigeria have made significant progress, winning gold in the 1996 Atlanta Olympics. And they did it the hard way, coming from behind to beat Brazil in the semis and then overcoming a skilful Argentinian side 3–2 in the final.

Nigeria are many people's favourites to be the first African nation to win the World Cup and it's easy to see why. They are undeniably one of the most talented, confident and superbly athletic teams in the world.

With this sort of pedigree, France '98 should mark the point at which Nigeria consolidate and build on what they achieved four years ago but at the start of the year this looked unlikely.

Once again they were without a coach, poorly prepared and forced to miss the African Nations Cup after being banned for refusing to take part in the 1996 tournament in South Africa.

Into this confusion and disarray strode Bora Milutinovic, the highly experienced coach who managed Mexico, Costa Rica and the USA at the last three World Cups. Coping with the demands of the international game is nothing new to him but managing Nigeria will be his biggest test yet.

Coaching Nigeria must be one of the most thankless tasks in the world. It takes just one reversal and the football-mad nation are baying for your dismissal.

Jo Bonfrere, the Dutch coach who led them to such great success in Atlanta left soon afterwards, claiming that he had been badly treated. His assistant Amodu Shaibu took control and Nigeria got off a winning start with star striker Amokachi bagging both goals against Burkina Faso.

But just one match later they struggled to a 1–1 draw in Kenya and the writing was on the wall for Shaibu. True to form he was sacked and replaced by Philippe Troussier. The Super Eagles then beat Guinea 2–1 and scored three superb goals against Kenya to clinch their place in the finals. But there was a final twist. Despite having qualified, a 1–0 defeat against Guinea saw Troussier on his way out.

Milutinovic doesn't have long to organise his talented squad and he will be hindered by the fact that most play overseas but any coach would love to have the resources of talent available to him.

English football fans have already caught a glimpse of what to expect from Nigeria through the performances of Chelsea's Babayaro. A defender with a penchant for overlapping into attack, the 19-year-old Babayaro has scored vital goals for club and country, none more so than the flying header in Nigeria's victory in the Olympic final.

Former Evertonian Amokachi is still a powerful presence up front and has formed a formidable partnership with Amunike. The team's most dangerous player, however, is captain Kanu who has battled back to fitness after a heart defect threatened to end his career. His pace and power in attack will pose problems for the best defenders. Kanu's Inter Milan team-mate, West, is a huge physical presence in defence and is another who has benefited greatly from playing at the very top in Europe while Okocha could well prove to be the player of the tournament.

Nigeria can also boast the presence of the African Footballer of the Year in the attacking midfield talent of Ikpeba, who plays for Monaco.

On top of all that, the experience George has acquired at Real Betis will prove valuable for when Nigeria take on Spain. In fact, such is the spread of Nigerian players throughout Europe that together they could come up with a pretty complete assessment of most European teams competing in France.

At their best, the Nigerians are certainly good enough to get through to the second round. They face a tough opening game against Spain but should be lifted by the way in which they simply tore through Bulgaria four years ago to go on and win their two remaining games.

HOW THEY QUALIFIED

Results: Nigeria 2 Burkina Faso 0; Kenya 1 **Nigeria 1**; **Nigeria 2** Guinea 1; Burkina Faso 1 **Nigeria 2**; **Nigeria 3** Kenya 0; Guinea 1 **Nigeria 0**

	P	W	D	L	F	A	Pts
Nigeria	6	4	1	1	10	4	13
Guinea	6	4	0	2	10	5	12
Kenya	6	3	1	2	11	12	10
Burkina Faso	6	0	0	6	7	17	0

Top goalscorers: 4, Amokachi; 2, Amunike.

WORLD CUP HISTORY

Four years ago, Nigeria made a stunning first appearance in the World Cup finals. They finished top of a group containing Argentina, Bulgaria and Greece and came within two minutes of beating Italy and moving into the quarter-finals. Were it not for Baggio's goals and the greater big-match experience of the Italian players, Nigeria would surely have gone even further.

Finals appearances: 1 (1994)
Biggest win: 3–0 v Bulgaria (1994)
Biggest defeat: 1–2 v Argentina (1994)

1994   Eliminated first round
> Group D: 3–0 v Bulgaria, 1–2 v Argentina, 2–0 v Greece; second round: 1–2 v Italy (aet)

Paraguay

Federation
Liga Paraguaya de Futbol

Founded
1906

Strip
Red and white striped shirts, blue shorts, blue socks

Coach
Paulo Cesar Carpegiani

Qualification
Second in South American Group

We are used to the eccentricities of South American goalkeepers. After the suicidal dribbling and scorpion kick of Colombia's Higuita comes Chilavert of Paraguay, who is better known for scoring goals from penalties and free-kicks than for preventing them.

The captain's value to the national team is not in question. When the 32-year-old Chilavert was suspended during the qualifiers for punching and then spitting at Colombia's Asprilla in an incident that resulted in a full-scale brawl between the sides, Paraguay lost three of the four matches they played without their talismanic keeper. But they still qualified in second place behind Argentina in the South American group.

The highlight of their campaign was the free-kick from which Chilavert secured a 1–1 draw in Buenos Aires. Paraguay trailed when Chilavert strode forward to take the kick on the edge of the Argentine box. Photographers said later that Burgos, Argentina's keeper, was visibly trembling as the giant Paraguayan lined up his shot, which flew round the wall and through the goalkeeper's hands.

That result, together with an unexpected 2–0 win in Uruguay, set the Paraguayans on their way to their fifth World Cup finals and their first since 1986, when they reached the second round before losing 3–0 to England. In the current campaign they were almost invincible in their intimidating Defensores del Chaco Stadium in Asuncion, losing only to Argentina.

Paraguay's Brazilian manager, Paulo Cesar Carpegiani, introduced the 3–5–2 formation to the South American country, and it seems well suited to his team, based on a solid defensive unit and quick counter-attacks aimed at getting the ball to top scorer Rojas and Benitez as quickly as possible. Paraguay have found route one effective, never more so than in a qualifier against Bolivia when another Chilavert free-kick from deep in his own half was headed by Richard Baez into the path of Benitez, who struck it on the half-volley into the Bolivian net.

Drawn in a tough group with Spain, Bulgaria and Nigeria, the Paraguayans may struggle even to emulate their Mexico '86 achievement. Chilavert will take the spotlight in France, but watch out too for Arce, an attacking right-back who was one of the players of the tournament at last year's South American championship. Arce puts a wicked swerve on his corners and free-kicks, and should have the big European clubs flocking to sign him after the World Cup.

HOW THEY QUALIFIED

Results: Colombia 1 **Paraguay 0**; Uruguay 0 **Paraguay 2**; Argentina 1 **Paraguay 1**; **Paraguay 2** Chile 1; **Paraguay 1** Ecuador 0; Bolivia 0 **Paraguay 0**; Venezuela 0 **Paraguay 2**; **Paraguay 2** Peru 1; **Paraguay 2** Colombia 1; **Paraguay 2** Uruguay 1; **Paraguay 1** Argentina 2; Chile 2 **Paraguay 1**; Ecuador 2 **Paraguay 1**; **Paraguay 2** Bolivia 1; **Paraguay 1** Venezuela 0; Peru 1 **Paraguay 0**

	P	W	D	L	F	A	Pts
Argentina	16	8	6	2	23	13	30
Paraguay	**16**	**9**	**2**	**5**	**21**	**14**	**29**
Colombia	16	8	4	4	23	15	28
Chile	16	7	4	5	32	18	25
Peru	16	7	4	5	19	20	25
Ecuador	16	6	3	7	22	21	21
Uruguay	16	6	3	7	18	21	21
Bolivia	16	4	5	7	18	21	17
Venezuela	16	0	3	13	8	41	3

Top goalscorers: 3 Rojas; 2, Rivarola, Benitez, Soto, Gamarra.

WORLD CUP HISTORY

The national side first made their mark on world football in 1953 when they won the South American Championship – a feat they repeated in 1979. But even in the 1950s – considered to be their most successful era – Paraguay failed to progress beyond the first round of the World Cup. However, it has been said that Feola, the coach of the 1958 Brazilians, had been so impressed with the Paraguayan system that he implemented it himself.

On the occasion Paraguay did finally get beyond the first round in 1986, they found an in-form Lineker/Beardsley partnership waiting for them.

Finals appearances: 4 (1930, 1950, 1958, 1986)
Biggest win: 3–2 v Scotland (1958)
Biggest defeat: 3–7 v France (1958)

1930 Eliminated first round
Group Four: 0–3 v USA, 0–1 v Belgium
1950 Eliminated first round
Group Three: 2–2 v Sweden, 0–2 v Italy
1958 Eliminated first round
Group Two: 3–7 v France, 3–2 v Scotland, 3–3 v Yugoslavia
1986 Eliminated second round
Group Two: 1–0 v Iraq, 1–1 v Mexico, 2–2 v Belgium;
second round: 0–3 v England

Bulgaria

Federation
Bulgarian Football Union

Founded
1923

Strip
White shirts, green shorts, and red socks

Coach
Hristo Bonev

Qualification
First in European Zone Group Eight

With no outstanding replacements for the class of 1994, many familiar names will again be on show in France this summer with the notable exception of coach Dimitar Penev. The man who led Bulgaria to their greatest ever success on the world stage was sacked, somewhat harshly considering his record, following the team's first-round flop at Euro '96. He was replaced by Hristo Bonev, a former international and the leading goalscorer in Bulgarian football history (47 goals in 96 games).

Angered at Penev's dismissal, Stoichkov and Penev's nephew Luboslav organised a boycott in an attempt to get Penev reinstated and it has been Bonev's greatest achievement of diplomacy since then to unite the Bulgarian squad and put an end to the boycotts which threatened to destroy their chances of qualifying for this World Cup.

Despite an ageing squad, Bonev intends to stand by the old guard who brought respect to the Bulgarian game after decades of failure. This should mean more of the attacking style which brought them a new group of fans, but even four years ago the Bulgarians physically weakened towards the end of the tournament and, four years on, this would appear to be their major problem.

Bonev introduced a number of young newcomers in the qualifying games including defenders Ivailo Petkov, Milen Petkov and

Zafirov, and strikers Gruev and Georgi Ivanov but they are still relatively inexperienced.

Wrangling within the squad meant that half the qualifying games were boycotted by such experienced players as Stoichkov, Penev and Lechkov. The Bulgarians began their campaign with a 2–1 defeat in Israel but then won six consecutive matches to launch themselves into the finals. They became the tenth team to qualify for France by beating main rivals Russia 1–0 at home. It was two of the heroes of 1994 who combined for the only goal – Stoichkov delivering a perfectly weighted cross for captain Trifon Ivanov to score with the simplest of headers. With qualification secure, the 4–2 defeat in Russia was rendered meaningless.

Moody, arrogant but, above all, wonderfully gifted Stoichkov is still one of the few players who can single-handedly change the course of a game. However, the great man has been struggling to see first-team action for Barcelona and will need to play regular matches if he is to keep fit enough for June.

Kostadinov was one of only two players ever present during the qualifiers and his goals once again proved vital. His probable strike partner Penev only played in four games but he scored a vital goal on his return against Israel and is in prolific form for his club Compostela despite the club languishing near the foot of the Spanish first division.

Contrary to popular opinion, the bald Lechkov hasn't hung up his boots in favour of a free bus pass. The scorer of Bulgaria's World Cup winner against Germany is in fact only 30 years old and is still the creative part of the team and dictates play for Bulgaria in midfield. He has great vision, tactical awareness and can make devastating attacking runs into the area.

Although Stoichkov may be the star, the heart of the team beats in 32-year-old Balakov who plays his club football in Germany. Balakov played every minute of Bulgaria's historic 1994 World Cup campaign and only missed one of their qualification games. He puts in an enormous amount of work all over midfield and is always available to help the more stately Lechkov.

Mikhailov, possessor of the most famous toupee after Burt Reynolds, is still at his eccentric best in goal although Zdravkov is now well-established as the first-choice keeper and played in most of the qualifying matches.

The wild man of Bulgarian football, Ivanov, will no doubt still be prepared to throw his body in front of anything to protect the goal even if it means hospital treatment. However, the fierce and totally committed defender has seemingly tried the patience of his club coach at Rapid Vienna with frequent absences from training and Bonev may not look too kindly on a player who is not performing regularly for his club.

With players of such international quality Bulgaria have the ability to progress to the second round without ever threatening to go all the way. They are unlikely to overcome the strong Spanish squad and may well have to call on all their experience and guile to beat Nigeria who steamrollered them four years ago in the first round.

HOW THEY QUALIFIED

Results: Israel 2 **Bulgaria 1**; Luxembourg 1 **Bulgaria 2**; Cyprus 1 **Bulgaria 3**; **Bulgaria 4** Cyprus 1; **Bulgaria 4** Luxembourg 0; **Bulgaria 1** Israel 0; **Bulgaria 1** Russia 0; Russia 4 **Bulgaria 2**

	P	W	D	L	F	A	Pts
Bulgaria	**8**	**6**	**0**	**2**	**18**	**9**	**18**
Russia	8	5	2	1	19	5	17
Israel	8	4	1	3	9	7	13
Cyprus	8	3	1	4	10	15	10
Luxembourg	8	0	0	8	2	22	0

Top goalscorers: 5, Kostadinov, Balakov.

WORLD CUP HISTORY

Bulgaria played well to qualify for their first World Cup in 1962 at the expense of France who had finished third four years before. But defeats against Argentina and Hungary and a scoreless draw against England set the pattern for the next three finals. Admittedly, they were up against Brazil, Portugal and Hungary in 1966 but they fared no better in 1970.

Bulgaria's captain Bonev was their outstanding player in 1974 and they had chances to beat Sweden and Uruguay before both games were eventually drawn. Bonev scored against Uruguay and Bulgaria were only three minutes away from a first win when Pavoni equalised for the South Americans.

In 1986, Bulgaria did qualify for the second round by virtue of two more drawn games but lost tamely to the hosts Mexico.

In 1994, after an inauspicious 3–0 defeat by the powerful Nigerians, subsequent wins over Greece and a Maradona-less Argentina saw Bulgaria through to the second round where they beat Mexico courtesy of some woeful penalty taking by the Mexicans in the shoot-out.

The quarter-final against Germany was one of the most exciting games in World Cup history as first Stoichkov's brilliant free-kick and then Lechkov's header knocked the Germans out. Sadly, the dream was dashed in the semi-finals by Italy who finally put in a performance worthy of their standing.

But Bulgaria had gone further than even they, in their wildest dreams, could ever have believed possible.

Finals appearances: 6 (1962–74, 1986, 1994)
Biggest win: 4–0 v Greece (1994)
Biggest defeat: 1–6 v Hungary (1962)

1962 Eliminated first round
        Group Four: 0–1 v Argentina, 1–6 v Hungary, 0–0 England
1966 Eliminated first round
        Group Three: 0–2 v Brazil, 0–3 v Portugal, 1–3 v Hungary
1970 Eliminated first round
        Group Four: 2–3 v Peru, 2–5 v West Germany, 1–1 v Morocco
1974 Eliminated first round
        Group Three: 0–0 v Sweden, 1–1 v Uruguay, 1–4 v Holland
1986 Eliminated second round
        Group A: 1–1 v Italy, 1–1 v South Korea, 0–2 v Argentina;
        second round: 0–2 v Mexico
1994 Fourth
        Group D: 0–3 v Nigeria, 4–0 v Greece, 2–0 v Argentina;
        second round: 1–1 v Mexico (3–1 on penalties);
        quarter-final: 2–1 v Germany; semi-final: 1–2 v Italy;
        third-place play-off: 0–4 v Sweden

Group E

Holland, Belgium, South Korea, Mexico

With Holland and Belgium being drawn together in the qualifiers and now the finals they should know each other's strengths and weaknesses by heart. The advantage will lie with the Dutch, however, who beat their European neighbours twice on the way to France. With Holland expected to top the group, Belgium will need to grind out results against Mexico and South Korea to claim second place.

This will be South Korea's fourth consecutive finals and although they have never progressed beyond the first round, they have given established teams a scare in the past. They will be confident of getting their first-ever World Cup finals win.

FIXTURES

Holland v Belgium	13 June, 19.00, Stade de France	**BBC**
South Korea v Mexico	13 June, 15.30, Lyon	**ITV**
Holland v South Korea	20 June, 19.00, Marseille	**ITV**
Belgium v Mexico	20 June, 15.30, Bordeaux	**BBC**
Belgium v South Korea	25 June, 14.00, Parc des Princes	**BBC**
Holland v Mexico	25 June, 14.00, Saint Etienne	**BBC**

Holland

Federation
Koninklijke Nederlandsche Voetbalbond

Founded
1889

Strip
Orange shirts, white shorts, orange socks

Coach
Guus Hiddink

Qualification
First in European Zone Group Seven

Since their less than spectacular World Cup tournament in the USA
– enlivened only by an entertaining 3–2 defeat at the hands of Brazil
– coach Guus Hiddink has developed a good understanding with his
players. This shouldn't really come as a surprise, but at national
level the Dutch game has frequently been hindered by differences
between the players and manager, a situation which certainly undermined their progress eight years ago at Italia '90 and again in the
1994 World Cup under then manager Dick Advocaat.

A measure of how well Giddink has got his team of individuals
to gel was their comfortable canter through qualification. At no
stage did they look in danger of losing grip on their qualifying
group and would surely have remained unbeaten had Seedorf not
insisted on taking – and missing – a crucial penalty.

Although the Dutch finished just one point clear of Belgium,
they demonstrated clear superiority over their European neighbours with two emphatic victories and the advantage should lie
with the Dutch when the two sides meet at the Stade de France on
13 June.

Hiddink, a close friend of Johan Cruyff, has decided to abandon
the typical Dutch 4–3–3 in favour of 4–4–2 and has a talented
squad of players with which to apply his new strategy.

In goal, Van der Sar remains first choice for the national side ahead of Chelsea's De Goey. He may look awkward but Van Der Sar is totally reliable and a good shot-stopper.

The defence is marshalled by his Ajax team-mate and captain Frank de Boer – a key figure in the team. Lining up alongside De Boer in central defence is Stam, a quick, powerful player, with the equally impressive Reiziger at right-back and Numan on the left. All these players are exceptional at coming forward and comfortable on the ball.

In midfield, Jonk is another player to have come through Ajax on his way to Inter and now PSV Eindhoven. He is a creative playmaker and has a wonderful synergy with Bergkamp for whom he creates many chances. The strong midfield line-up also contains Seedorf, still only 22, but another former Ajax star who has made a great impact at Real Madrid. He usually operates to the right of Jonk, leaving Ronald de Boer to tuck in just behind the front pair. Like his twin brother, Ronald is a seasoned member of both Ajax and the national team where he plays a fine supportive role for the strikers.

Cocu appears to have played himself into the left-hand side of midfield although Davids and the swift Overmars are pushing for contention.

Up front, the pairing of Bergkamp and Kluivert will give opposing defenders an absolute nightmare. Both graduated from the youth scheme at Ajax which always seems to find another highly talented youngster capable of stepping into the team once one star has moved on. So when the 'irreplaceable' Van Basten left to join Milan, Bergkamp became the scoring sensation. After Bergkamp came Kluivert. It's almost a production-line mentality.

Bergkamp demonstrated his scoring ability only in short bursts at USA '94 but if his recent form is anything to go by he could make a serious challenge for the Golden Boot award in France. Kluivert, on the other hand, has seemingly lost the form which made him a teenage prodigy at Ajax. He has struggled in the high-pressure surroundings at Milan and also faces accusations of rape.

The two strikers have already developed an understanding lucidly demonstrated in the return fixture against Belgium. First, a smart one-two with Bergkamp enabled Kluivert to fire a crisp drive home. Then Bergkamp scored his 33rd international goal following another clever one-two with Kluivert.

The Dutch remain a talented outfit but doubts persist over their appetite for the big occasion. Their players have experience with Europe's biggest clubs, yet when the orange shirts are pulled on it's frequently a case of unfulfilled potential.

Guus Hiddink has created a good team spirit – something that hasn't always been available to his predecessors – and if the undoubted talent in the squad is free to flourish then the Dutch could go as far as the quarter-finals.

A good Dutch team will enhance the World Cup but one which fails to deliver will be a huge disappointment. It's an enigma that will not be solved until the finals themselves.

HOW THEY QUALIFIED

Results: Wales 1 **Holland 3**; **Holland 7** Wales 1;
Belgium 0 **Holland 3**; **Holland 4** San Marino 0;
Turkey 1 **Holland 0**; San Marino 0 **Holland 6**;
Holland 3 Belgium 0; **Holland 0** Turkey 0

	P	W	D	L	F	A	Pts
Holland	8	6	1	1	26	4	19
Belgium	8	6	0	2	20	11	18
Turkey	8	4	2	2	21	9	14
Wales	8	2	1	5	20	21	7
San Marino	8	0	0	8	0	42	0

Top goalscorers: 7, Bergkamp; 4, Frank de Boer.

WORLD CUP HISTORY

Dutch soccer blossomed spectacularly in the early 1970s. After years of non-qualification for the World Cup the introduction of a professional league system revolutionised the club structure and saw the rise of Feyenoord, PSV Eindhoven and Ajax. Feyenoord won the 1970 European Cup and Ajax won it for the next three years to become the dominant club in Europe. The Ajax team consisted of some of the best players to come out of Holland – Neeskens, Krol, Rep and Haan. And with Johan Cruyff they arguably had the best player in the world.

If ever a team deserved to win a major international title in the 1970s it was the Dutch – they were runners-up to the hosts in consecutive World Cup finals. Cruyff refused to go to Argentina for the 1978 finals. Had he gone, Holland may well have beaten the Argentinians who were desperate for success in front of their home support. As it was, they came close to winning in the last minute when Rensenbrink hit the post but Kempes struck for Argentina in extra-time.

Since then, internal disputes between players and manager have been a familiar story with the Dutch national side at the World Cup. Internal discord has led to below-par performances on the pitch.

Finals appearances: 6 (1934–38, 1974–78, 1990–94)
Biggest win: 5–1 v Austria (1978)
Biggest defeat: 0–3 v Czechoslovakia (1938)

1934 Eliminated first round
First round: 2–3 v Switzerland
1938 Eliminated first round
First round: 0–3 v Czechoslovakia
1974 Runners-up
Group Three: 2–0 v Uruguay, 0–0 v Sweden, 4–1 v Bulgaria;
Group A: 4–0 v Argentina, 2–0 v East Germany,
2–0 v Brazil; final: 1–2 v West Germany
1978 Runners-up
Group Four: 3–0 v Iran, 0–0 v Peru, 2–3 v Scotland;
Group A: 5–1 v Austria, 2–2 v West Germany, 2–1 v Italy;
final: 1–3 v Argentina
1990 Eliminated second round
Group F: 1–1 v Egypt, 0–0 v England,
1–1 v Republic of Ireland; second round: 1–2 v West Germany
1994 Quarter-finalists
Group F: 2–1 v Saudi Arabia, 0–1 v Belgium, 2–1 v Morocco;
second round: 2–0 v Republic of Ireland;
quarter-final: 2–3 v Brazil

Belgium

Federation
Belgian football federation

Founded
1895

Strip
Red shirt, red shorts, red socks

Coach
George Leekens

Qualification
Second in European Group Seven
Beat the Republic of Ireland in play-off

The Belgians must feel there is an unwritten rule that they always have to play Holland. For the second time running, these close European neighbours have been drawn in the same group for the finals – and that after the two countries had come through the same qualifying group.

The advantage will certainly lie with the Dutch when the teams meet on 13 June for Belgium were convincingly beaten in both qualifying games. In the first encounter, on a bitterly cold night in December 1996, Bergkamp evaded the Belgian offside trap to open the scoring and take his tally to within one of equalling the Dutch national record. Seedorf made it two with a rising drive from the edge of the penalty area and after Van de Sar had saved well from Nilis, Jonk completed the scoring from the penalty spot after Albert had brought down the speedy Overmars.

The result ended the tenure of coach Wilfried Van Moer and George Leekens was given the task of ensuring Belgium qualified for the fifth successive time.

Things didn't get much better for Belgium in the return leg in Brussels. Stam scored his first international goal to put the Dutch ahead before a smart one-two with Bergkamp enabled Kluivert to fire a crisp drive home. Belgium fought back and were awarded a penalty after Jonk's clumsy challenge on Oliveira. Staelens brought the score back to within one goal but Bergkamp scored his 33rd international goal following another clever one-two with Kluivert.

However, other than these two defeats, Belgium won their remaining games and finished comfortably ahead of Turkey. They then sent the Republic of Ireland packing with a 2–1 win in their play-off return leg in Brussels, after holding them to a 1–1 draw in Dublin.

After being overshadowed by their Dutch neighbours in the 1970s, Belgian football has earned a respected place on the world map in the last decade. This will be their fifth consecutive finals – a feat their more celebrated neighbours Holland cannot claim. And when the two met in the finals in 1994, it was Albert's goal which split the sides in an entertaining match. However, the victory did the Belgians no favours as two days later they were drawn against Germany and lost 3–2.

Leekens has relied heavily on what can be politely termed 'experienced' players. In midfield, 34-year-old Staelens has been given a central role with freedom to attack. He is a very hard worker and scored five times during the qualifying games. He is joined in midfield by 37-year-old Van der Elst, Belgium's current player of the year, who received an unexpected call-up to the national side after two years on the sidelines. Another, making a welcome if somewhat belated return is 32-year-old Scifo, one of the most talented players of his time and, like Van der Elst, making his fourth World Cup finals appearance.

The defence also contains more than its fair share of 30-somethings although for goalkeeper De Wilde it's not surprising as he has been forced to play patient understudy to the brilliant Preud'homme for the best part of ten years.

Solid in defence, industrious and creative in midfield, Belgium have finally found a consistent strikeforce to complete a useful-looking side. Brazilian-born Oliveira finished as Belgium's top scorer in the qualifying series and Leekens also has the blossoming talent of Nilis – the driving force behind PSV. His international career took some time to take off but he is now a highly respected striker.

De Bilde has struck up an effective partnership with Nilis at club level although ill discipline has let him down. Finally, there's

Wilmots who knows about scoring on the big occasion – his goals won the UEFA Cup for Schalke in 1997.

Only time will tell if the ageing squad can withstand the rigours of top-quality opposition in stifling heat but the Belgians, often underestimated, have progressed quietly through. They should qualify from the group but the second round is likely to be their limit.

HOW THEY QUALIFIED

Results: Belgium 2 Turkey 1; San Marino 0 **Belgium 3**; **Belgium 0** Holland 3; Wales 1 **Belgium 2**; Turkey 1 **Belgium 3**; **Belgium 6** San Marino 0; Holland 3 **Belgium 1**; **Belgium 3** Wales 2. Play-off: Republic of Ireland 1 **Belgium 1**; **Belgium 2** Republic of Ireland 1. Belgium won 3–2 on aggregate.

	P	W	D	L	F	A	Pts
Holland	8	6	1	1	26	4	19
Belgium	**8**	**6**	**0**	**2**	**20**	**11**	**18**
Turkey	8	4	2	2	21	9	14
Wales	8	2	1	5	20	21	7
San Marino	8	0	0	8	0	42	0

Top goalscorers: 6, Oliveira; 5, Staelens; 4, Nilis.

WORLD CUP HISTORY

Belgium, a founder member of FIFA, made little impression on soccer's world stage until the 1970s. But as players moved from semi-professional to professional status the standard at club level improved to such an extent that Anderlecht won the European Cup Winners' Cup in 1976.

The national team were runners-up to West Germany in the 1980 European Championship and qualified for the World Cup two years later. But the team's greatest achievement came in the 1986 finals when they beat the Soviet Union and Spain before losing to Argentina, or more specifically Maradona, in the semi-finals.

In 1994, Belgium thought they had done the hard work in beating Morocco and Holland but a spectacular goal by Saudi Arabia's Owairan resulted in three teams tying on six points each with Belgium getting through in third place.

As a result they were drawn against Germany and lost 3–2 under controversial circumstances. Having gone 3–1 behind, the Belgians had what looked a clear-cut penalty turned down by the referee. It was little consolation that he was later sent home.

Finals appearances: 9 (1930–38, 1954, 1970, 1982–94)
Biggest win: 4–3 v Soviet Union (1986)
Biggest defeat: 2–5 v Germany (1934)

1930 Eliminated first round
Group Four: 0–3 v United States, 0–1 v Paraguay
1934 Eliminated first round
First round: 2–5 v Germany
1938 Eliminated first round
First round: 1–3 v France
1954 Eliminated first round
Group Four: 4–4 v England, 1–4 v Italy
1970 Eliminated first round
Group One: 3–0 v El Salvador, 1–4 v Soviet Union,
0–1 v Mexico
1982 Eliminated second round
Group Three: 1–0 v Argentina, 1–0 v El Salvador,
1–1 v Hungary; Group A: 0–3 v Poland, 0–1 v Soviet Union
1986 Fourth
Group B: 1–2 v Mexico, 2–1 v Iraq, 2–2 v Paraguay;
second round: 4–3 v Soviet Union; quarter-final: 1–1 v Spain
(5–4 on penalties); semi-final: 0–2 v Argentina;
third-place play-off: 2–4 v France
1990 Eliminated second round
Group E: 2–0 v South Korea, 3–1 v Uruguay, 1–2 v Spain;
second round: 0–1 v England
1994 Eliminated second round
Group F: 1–0 v Morocco; 1–0 v Holland; 0–1 v Saudi Arabia;
second round: 2–3 v Germany

South Korea

Federation
Korean Football Association

Founded
1928

Strip
Red shirts, black shorts, red socks

Coach
Cha Bum-kun

Qualification
First in final Asian Zone Group B

Although they have never progressed beyond the first round, South Korea have given established teams a scare in the past. Four years ago, they came from two down against Spain to pull off a draw and despite going three down against Germany they finished the stronger and were unlucky not to level the scores.

For this, their fourth consecutive appearance in the World Cup finals, South Korea's main ambition will be to gain a first-ever victory to add a measure of pride for when they co-host the 2002 World Cup finals with Japan.

South Korea, traditionally the strongest team in the region, coasted through their group and qualified with three games to spare. Their most dramatic match was probably when they beat Japan 2–1 in Tokyo to stun the 60,000 home fans at the National stadium. Yamaguchi gave Japan a 65th-minute lead but two goals in the last seven minutes from Korean substitute Seo and defender Lee turned the game around.

From there on it was plain sailing and the defeat by Japan in the return leg came after the Koreans had already qualified by thrashing Uzbekistan 5–1 in Tashkent two weeks earlier. In fairness, South Korea were not at their strongest in that defeat as playmaker Hong Myung-bo was suspended and prolific striker Choi was forced out through injury.

South Korea completed their programme with a 3–1 win over the United Arab Emirates and that result, plus their defeat by Japan, conspired to lift their co-hosts for the finals of 2002 into second place.

Since his appointment as team coach in early 1997, Cha Bum-kun (who spent ten seasons in the German Bundesliga – at Bayer Leverkusen and Eintracht Frankfurt) has instilled strict discipline as well as working on his players' fitness and mental approach.

South Korea's biggest star and top scorer, Choi, will lead the attack and aim to maintain the prolific run which saw him finish as top scorer during qualification. He extended his tally in Thailand earlier in the year when South Korea lifted the King's Cup in a four-way tournament with the hosts, Egypt and Denmark.

In midfield, Ko is considered to be something of a prodigy of whom a lot is expected, while in defence, Hong was South Korea's representative in the Rest of the World side.

Earlier this year, Paris St-Germain made the unusual step of buying South Korean attacker Seo. Naturally, at first he found it tricky to fit in but he has blinding speed – he has run 100 metres in under 11 seconds – and scored in his opening games for his new club.

Having made it to four previous World Cup finals, South Korea have the experience to know what to expect in a extremely tough opening group. If they can reproduce those second-half efforts against Spain and Germany in USA '94 they could trouble their group rivals. Holland, particularly, may struggle to match their speed in the heat of Marseille but South Korea's greatest triumph looks as though it is still four years away.

HOW THEY QUALIFIED

Results: First round: Hong Kong 0 **South Korea 2**;
Thailand 1 **South Korea 3**; **South Korea 4** Hong Kong 0;
South Korea 0 Thailand 0. Second round: Group B:
South Korea 3 Kazakhstan 0; **South Korea 2** Uzbekistan 1;
Japan 1 **South Korea 2**; **South Korea 3** UAE 0;
Kazakhstan 1 **South Korea 1**; Uzbekistan 1 **South Korea 5**;
South Korea 0 Japan 2; UAE 1 **South Korea 3**

	P	W	D	L	F	A	Pts
South Korea	8	6	1	1	19	7	19
Japan	8	3	4	1	17	9	13
UAE	8	2	3	3	9	12	9
Uzbekistan	8	1	3	4	13	18	6
Kazakhstan	8	1	3	4	7	19	6

Top goalscorers: 9, Choi; 4, Kim.

WORLD CUP HISTORY

South Korea's first appearance on the world stage in 1954 was a sobering one as they faced the mighty Hungarians who had not been beaten since 1950. The Koreans were never going to change the order of things and Hungary ran out easy winners. Things didn't get much better in their second game when Turkey scored seven without reply.

In 1986, the South Koreans became the first Asian side to qualify for two finals and went to Mexico with some optimism. Although they didn't progress beyond the first round they played attacking soccer and gained their first point from a draw with Bulgaria.

It was a shame that in the following tournament they were defensive and uninspiring. Only against Spain did they show a glimmer of attacking spirit before they submitted to sustained pressure.

Four years ago, they put in probably their most consistent displays with Spain and Germany struggling to match their pace in the latter stages of their games.

Finals appearances: 4 (1954, 1986–94)
Biggest win: yet to win a game
Biggest defeat: 0–9 v Hungary (1954)

1954 Eliminated first round
    Pool Two: 0–9 v Hungary, 0–7 v Turkey
1986 Eliminated first round
    Group A: 1–3 v Argentina, 1–1 v Bulgaria, 2–3 v Italy
1990 Eliminated first round
    Group E: 0–2 v Belgium, 1–3 v Spain, 0–1 v Uruguay
1994 Eliminated first round
    Group C: 2–2 v South Korea, 0–0 v Bolivia, 2–3 v Germany

Mexico

Federation
Federacion Mexicana de Futbol

Founded
1927

Strip
Green shirts, white shorts, red socks

Coach
Manuel Lapuente

Qualification
First in CONCACAF Zone

Mexico's advantage, by tradition, is that they are the most powerful football nation in the Central American region.

This has meant, in the past, almost automatic qualification for the World Cup finals but this regional domination has meant that Mexico have never really had to exert themselves and consequently results in the finals have been below what their football-crazy fans would wish for.

Mexico have qualified 11 times for the finals – only Brazil, Germany and Italy can better that – but very little success has come in those appearances. In fact, the only times the ardent fans have had anything to cheer were in 1970 and 1986 when Mexico hosted the competition.

But recent tournaments have seen the other CONCACAF nations improving and although Mexico are still some way ahead, the odd stray result has started to try the public's patience.

Having strolled away with the qualifying group, Mexico failed to win their last two home matches at the Azteca Stadium. First, a ten-man United States, who had lost on every previous visit, held out for a goalless draw. It seemed of little consequence that the result qualified Mexico for the finals. The 114,000-strong crowd started cheering every US touch and demanded the sacking of coach Bora Milutinovic for his over-defensive tactics.

A 3–3 draw against Costa Rica – in a game Mexico led 3–1 – was bad enough, but a subsequent draw with Jamaica was the final straw and Milutinovic was out.

The choice of his successor came as something of a surprise. Not only has Manuel Lapuente coached Mexico before, but he has experienced the humiliation of resigning over a poor result – defeat by the USA in the 1991 Gold Cup.

What possessed him to go through it all again is anyone's guess. Nevertheless, the squad he has inherited looks to have a fine balance of experience and talent with plenty of players from the last World Cup when Mexico probably fielded their best-ever team. Then, the Mexicans beat the Republic of Ireland and drew with Italy before losing out to Bulgaria on penalties in the knock-out phase. The impressive Garcia, who scored both goals against Ireland, will continue to press his claims as the successor to Hugo Sanchez. A quick-thinking, quick-moving forward he is back home with America after an unhappy stay in Spain.

Aspe, outstanding in USA '94, continues as the team's play-maker with Alves, otherwise nicknamed Zaguinho, another to watch for his dribbling skills and powerful shooting.

Hermosillo was a member of the 1986 World Cup squad but the powerful striker has not lost his goalscoring touch – finishing top scorer with 11 goals throughout the qualifiers. If he does struggle for form, it wouldn't be surprising to see goalkeeper-cum-sweeper Campos venturing up into the opponent's penalty area.

With Holland expected to take the top spot, Mexico at least have the opportunity of getting good results against South Korea and Belgium before they meet the Dutch in their final game.

HOW THEY QUALIFIED

Results: Mexico 4 Canada 0; Costa Rica 0 **Mexico 0**;
Mexico 6 Jamaica 0; USA 2 **Mexico 2**; **Mexico 5** El Salvador 0;
Canada 2 **Mexico 2**; **Mexico 0** USA 0; **Mexico 3** Costa Rica 3;
Jamaica 0 **Mexico 0**

	P	W	D	L	F	A	Pts
Mexico	10	4	6	0	23	7	18
USA	10	4	5	1	17	9	17
Jamaica	10	3	5	2	7	12	14
Costa Rica	10	3	3	4	13	12	12
El Salvador	10	2	4	4	11	16	10
Canada	10	1	3	6	5	20	6

Top goalscorers: 11, Hermosillo; 8, Galindo.

WORLD CUP HISTORY

It was not until a 3–1 victory over Czechoslovakia in 1962 that Mexico won their first World Cup game. Mexico's goalkeeper, Antonio Carbajal, was celebrating his 33rd birthday that day so it was a suitable present for the man who was to play in five consecutive World Cups.

Mexico has twice staged the World Cup and reaching the quarter-finals on each occasion represents their best finish. The 1970 team was not especially good but in 1986, with Sanchez and Nagrette in spectacular goalscoring form, they only lost out to West Germany in a penalty shoot-out.

Finals appearances: 10 (1930, 1950–70, 1978, 1986, 1994)
Biggest win: 4–0 v El Salvador (1970)
Biggest defeat: 0–6 v West Germany (1978)

1930 Eliminated first round
   Group One: 1–4 v France, 0–3 v Chile, 3–6 v Argentina
1950 Eliminated first round
   Pool One: 0–4 v Brazil, 1–4 v Yugoslavia, 1–2 v Switzerland
1954 Eliminated first round
   Pool One: 0–5 v Brazil, 2–3 v France
1958 Eliminated first round
   Pool Three: 0–3 v Sweden, 1–1 v Wales, 0–4 v Hungary
1962 Eliminated first round
   Group Three: 0–2 v Brazil, 0–1 v Spain, 3–1 v Czechoslovakia

1966 Eliminated first round
Group One: 1–1 v France, 0–2 v England, 0–0 v Uruguay

1970 Quarter-finalists
Group One: 0–0 v Soviet Union, 4–0 v El Salvador,
1–0 v Belgium; quarter-final: 1–4 v Italy

1978 Eliminated first round
Group Two: 1–3 v Tunisia, 0–6 v West Germany, 1–3 v Poland

1986 Quarter-finalists
Group B: 2–1 v Belgium, 1–1 v Paraguay, 1–0 v Iraq;
second round: 2–0 v Bulgaria;
quarter-final: 0–0 v West Germany (1–4 on penalties)

1994 Eliminated second round
Group E: 0–1 v Norway, 2–1 v Republic of Ireland,
1–1 v Italy; second round: 1–1 v Bulgaria (1–3 on penalties)

Group F

Germany, USA, Yugoslavia, Iran

In pursuit of Brazil's record haul of four World Cups, Germany, the European champions, couldn't have hoped for a kinder first-round draw. There has been much talk of a decline in the national squad but once a tournament starts they really know how to peak at the right time.

Yugoslavia are a good side with a long and distinguished record in the World Cup. They are sure to qualify for the second round but lack of international competition may have blunted their competitive edge come the knock-out stage.

The US certainly earned the right to be in France this summer but they must have wished for something easier than an opening game against Germany at the Parc des Princes.

Still the encounter with Iran on 21 June should prove interesting from a diplomatic, if not a footballing, viewpoint.

FIXTURES

Yugoslavia v Iran	14 June, 15.30, Saint Etienne	**BBC**
Germany v USA	15 June, 19.00, Parc des Princes	**BBC**
Germany v Yugoslavia	21 June, 12.30, Lens	**BBC**
USA v Iran	21 June, 19.00, Lyon	**BBC**
Germany v Iran	25 June, 19.00, Montpellier	**ITV**
USA v Yugoslavia	25 June, 19.00, Nantes	**ITV**

Germany

Federation
German football federation

Founded
1900

Strip
White shirts, black shorts, white socks

Coach
Berti Vogts

Qualification
First in European Zone Group Nine

During Germany's quarter-final match against Bulgaria in the 1994 World Cup, the German defender Wagner was knocked unconcious and substituted shortly after Matthaus had put his team in the lead. When Wagner came round he asked: 'Is it still 1–0?' Told by a coach that the game had finished 2–1, Wagner asked: 'Who scored our second?'

The fact that Stoichkov and Lechkov had put Bulgaria through to the semi-finals was obviously a notion that he had not even remotely considered and highlights the fundamental quality which has brought Germany such phenomenal success. The players have a confidence which, combined with an amazing resilience, has made them such a successful team in world football over the past 30 years.

Since the early 1970s, they have won the World Cup twice and finished runners-up twice. And in the intervening years, just for good measure, they have won the European Championship three times. You can never discount them, no matter what the score, no matter how little time is left to play. They've made more comebacks than Gary Glitter.

Perhaps because of this, Bulgaria's victory in the World Cup was gleefully received worldwide – except of course in Germany. The national side, the pride and joy of the nation, had been beaten at a stage far short of its expected position.

Vogts was in an unenviable position. His four predecessors Sepp Herberger (1936–63), Helmut Schon (1964–1978) Jupp Derwall (1979–1983) and Franz Beckenbauer (1984–1990) had all won either the World Cup, European Championship or both.

Victory in Euro '96 went some way to dispelling the doubters but seldom has the national team approached a World Cup with so much uncertainty surrounding them.

They certainly did not convince the home fans during qualification where they dropped points to Northern Ireland, Ukraine and Portugal. And against lowly Albania, needing only a draw to qualify, they even went behind before a late goal by Bierhoff saved the day.

Bierhoff proved Germany's saviour on more than one occasion. Having been held by Northern Ireland at home, Germany fell behind to a first-half goal from Hughes in Belfast. Bierhoff came on as a substitute in the 69th minute and promptly scored from Hassler's cross. Two more goals from Bierhoff gave him a seven-minute hat-trick and the Germans a precious away win.

Another late strike, this time from former East German striker Kirsten, saved German blushes in Berlin against Portugal in a gripping match. With Bierhoff and Kirsten proving so effective, Klinsmann needed to regain his scoring touch to stay in the side and grabbed two in the 4–0 home win over Armenia. This result effectively sealed qualification but they still needed a draw against Albania to make sure. The extraordinary game started with a bizarre own goal by the normally reliable Kohler. Helmer got an immediate equaliser and when Bierhoff got a second Germany were on their way. But the last ten minutes proved suicidal with the Albanians pulling the score back to 2–2 then 3–3 before Bierhoff got the winning header.

Bierhoff's golden goal against the Czech Republic at Wembley won Germany their third European title and his form in the qualifiers suggests he will be the first-choice striker in France and not just used as a super-sub. Kirsten has been in prolific form for club and country while Bobic is approaching his old form after two injury-hit years. There should still be room for Klinsmann as long as he suffers no further side-effects after breaking his jaw during

Spurs' FA Cup replay against Barnsley. He made a speedy recovery but has not discovered top form. However, Vogts is a great admirer of Klinsmann's leadership qualities and will wait until the last minute for him.

Vogts may have to apply the same criteria to his star *libero* Sammer who may be forced to retire due to persistent knee problems. His career has been plagued by injury and last October he had surgery on his left knee for the fourth time. A few days later, an infection forced a fifth trip to face the surgeon's scalpel.

It would be a great loss if Sammer does not make it to France and even if he does there must be a question mark over his effectiveness after so many injuries. The good news for Vogts is that the experienced Helmer and the indomitable Kohler are still rock-solid in defence while former midfielder Thon has switched to sweeper for his club and may make a reliable substitute for Sammer should he not make it.

At least Vogts still has Moller and the ever-inventive Hassler in midfield so things can't be all bad. Whether the erratic but talented 'Super' Mario Basler lines up alongside them depends very much on his ability to settle down.

Also in midfield, Tarnat played in most of the qualifying games having forced his way into the reckoning in the past two years. The 28 year old was signed by Bayern Munich in 1997 to replace Ziege who joined Milan but it is Ziege who may prove to be Germany's trump card.

Several newcomers have also strenthened Vogts' hand – Hamann in midfield has been in oustanding form with Bayern and Kaiserslautern striker Marschall has regained fitness after injury and looks ready to challenge for a place alongside Bierhoff.

So perhaps it has all been a ruse to lure the rest of the world into thinking that Germany was an ailing force. The team has been criticised before and has nearly always come good.

Not spectacular, just very efficient and once the tournament starts they really know how to get it together to peak at the right time. Never, ever, understimate the Germans. They can play badly and still reach the final.

In pursuit of Brazil's record haul of four World Cups, the European champions couldn't have hoped for a kinder first-round draw.

HOW THEY QUALIFIED

Results: Armenia 1 **Germany 5**; **Germany 1** Northern Ireland 1;
Portugal 0 **Germany 0**; Albania 2 **Germany 3**;
Germany 2 Ukraine 0; Ukraine 0 **Germany 0**;
Northern Ireland 1 **Germany 3**; **Germany 1** Portugal 1;
Germany 4 Armenia 0; **Germany 4** Albania 3

	P	W	D	L	F	A	Pts
Germany	10	6	4	0	23	9	22
Ukraine	10	6	2	2	10	6	20
Portugal	10	5	4	1	12	4	19
Armenia	10	1	5	4	8	17	8
N Ireland	10	1	4	5	6	10	7
Albania	10	1	1	8	7	20	4

Top goalscorers: 6, Bierhoff; 5, Kirsten; 3, Klinsmann, Hassler.

WORLD CUP HISTORY

Three World Cup victories and appearances in six World Cup finals is a record which no other country can match. For sheer consistency, Germany have been the outstanding team since the Second World War.

Despite finishing third in the 1934 tournament, beating the Austrian 'Wunderteam', the Germans began their World Cup campaign quietly. Germany was excluded from the 1950 tournament by FIFA as a result of the war but four years later they were world champions and had completed one of the most amazing turn-arounds in soccer history.

The Hungarian team of 1954 was considered the best in the world and yet the Germans beat them in a scintillating final which saw Hungary take a quick 2–0 lead only for the Germans to reply with a goal from Morlock and two from Rahn. This established a great German tradition of resilience and a never-say-die attitude.

Semi-finalists in 1958 and quarter-finalists in 1962 precluded West Germany's next final appearance in 1966.

In 1974 a team including Muller, Beckenbauer and Maier won the World Cup. Since then the Germans have continued their great tradition by reaching the final in 1982, 1986 and 1990. Each World Cup witnessed new players stepping in to carry on where the last one left off.

Finals appearances: 13 (1934–38 as Germany, 1954–1994 as West Germany)
Biggest win: 7–2 v Turkey (1954)
Biggest defeat: 3–8 v Hungary (1954)

1934 Third
　　　　First round: 5–2 v Belgium; second round: 2–1 v Sweden;
　　　　semi-final: 1–3 v Czechoslovakia;
　　　　third-place play-off: 3–2 v Austria
1938 Eliminated first round
　　　　First round: 1–1 v Switzerland; 2–4 v Switzerland (replay)
1954 Winners
　　　　Group Two: 4–1 v Turkey, 3–8 v Hungary, 7–2 v Turkey
　　　　(play-off); quarter-final: 2–0 v Yugoslavia;
　　　　semi-final: 6–1 v Austria; final: 3–2 v Hungary
1958 Fourth
　　　　Group One: 3–1 v Argentina, 2–2 v Czechoslovakia,
　　　　2–2 v Northern Ireland; quarter-final: 1–0 v Yugoslavia;
　　　　semi-final: 1–3 v Sweden; third-place play-off: 3–6 v France
1962 Quarter-finalists
　　　　Group Two: 0–0 v Italy, 2–1 v Switzerland, 2–0 v Chile;
　　　　quarter-final: 0–1 v Yugoslavia
1966 Runners-up
　　　　Group Two: 5–0 v Switzerland, 0–0 v Argentina, 2–1 v Spain;
　　　　quarter-final: 4–0 v Uruguay; semi-final: 2–1 v Soviet Union;
　　　　final: 2–4 v England
1970 Third
　　　　Group Four: 2–1 v Morocco, 5–2 v Bulgaria; 3–1 v Peru;
　　　　quarter-final: 3–2 v England; semi-final: 3–4 v Italy;
　　　　third-place play-off: 1–0 v Uruguay

1974 Winners
Group One: 1–0 v Chile, 3–0 v Australia, 0–1 v East Germany;
Group B: 2–0 v Yugoslavia, 4–2 v Sweden, 1–0 v Poland;
final: 2–1 v Holland

1978 Eliminated second round
Group Two: 0–0 v Poland, 6–0 v Mexico, 0–0 v Tunisia;
Group A: 0–0 v Italy, 2–2 v Holland, 2–3 v Austria

1982 Runners-up
Group Two: 1–2 v Algeria, 4–1 v Chile, 1–0 v Austria;
Group B: 0–0 v England, 2–1 v Spain;
semi-final: 3–3 v France (5–4 on penalties); final: 1–3 v Italy

1986 Runners-up
Group E: 1–1 v Uruguay, 2–1 v Scotland, 0–2 v Denmark;
second round: 1–0 v Morocco; quarter-final: 0–0 v Mexico
(4–1 on penalties); semi-final: 2–0 v France;
final: 2–3 v Argentina

1990 Winners
Group D: 4–1 v Yugoslavia, 5–1 v United Arab Emirates,
1–1 v Colombia; second round: 2–1 v Holland;
quarter-final: 1–0 v Czechoslovakia;
semi-final: 1–1 v England (4–3 on penalties);
final: 1–0 v Argentina

1994 Quarter-finalists
Group C: 1–0 v Bolivia, 1–1 v Spain, 3–2 v South Korea;
second round: 3–2 v Belgium; quarter-final: 1–2 v Bulgaria

United States of America

Federation
United States Soccer Federation

Founded
1913

Strip
White shirts with blue trim, white shorts, white socks

Coach
Steve Sampson

Qualification
Second in CONCACAF Zone

The United States is viewed by many as a non-footballing country but there is no doubt that they earned the right to be in France this summer. In 1990 they were a little fortunate because Mexico were disqualified from competing and in 1994 they qualified automatically as hosts. However, this appearance is fully deserved.

The USA, for so long an amusing minnow in world football, has made a real improvement in the past ten years and is now the second strongest nation in the CONCACAF region, behind Mexico.

Only two losses in 16 World Cup qualifiers is an indication of the Americans' new-found consistency, and two draws in the final round of CONCACAF qualifying against Mexico proved they could perform when the chips were down.

In fact, the goalless draw in Mexico on 2 November 1997 was a key moment in their qualification campaign. Never in 17 matches going back 60 years had the USA avoided defeat in Mexico. But needing to get their qualification back on track the Americans battled to a valuable draw. In the intimidating atmosphere of the Azteca Stadium, with 114,000 fans cheering on the home team, the Americans never lost their shape or composure despite playing with only ten men for an hour after Agoos was sent off.

Subsequent victories over Canada and El Salvador secured second place in the group and finally gave their beleagured coach, Steve Sampson, something to smile about.

Sampson, assistant to Bora Milutinovic in the 1994 finals, took over in 1995 when Milutinovic left to coach Mexico. So it was something of an unfortunate coincidence when that draw in the Azteca prompted the dismissal of Milutinovic from the Mexican team.

Sampson will rely on many familiar faces from the 1994 side in France such as Keller, the Leicester City goalkeeper. Lalas, the straggly-haired, goatee-bearded guitar player, is easily the most recognisable person in the American squad and he remains a dominant figure in defence although he is somewhat prone to being beaten for speed.

Although John Harkes, the captain and former Sheffield Wednesday player still runs the show the Americans face an uphill task in France. This time there will be no squeaking by in third place and the little matter of of an opening game against Germany in Paris is daunting.

With Yugoslavia also likely to be too strong for them, the USA can only hope that a gutsy performance will not knock the shine off the progress they made in 1994 and that football will continue to develop back home.

HOW THEY QUALIFIED

Results: Semi-finals: **USA 2** Guatemala 0;
USA 2 Trinidad and Tobago 0; Trinidad and Tobago 0 **USA 1**;
Costa Rica 2 **USA 1**; **USA 2** Costa Rica 1; Guatemala 2 **USA 2**.
Final group: Jamaica 0 **USA 0**; **USA 3** Canada 0;
Costa Rica 3 **USA 2**; **USA 2** Mexico 2; El Salvador 1 **USA 1**;
USA 1 Costa Rica 0; **USA 1** Jamaica 1; Mexico 0 **USA 0**;
Canada 0 **USA 3**; **USA 4** El Salvador 2

	P	W	D	L	F	A	Pts
Mexico	10	4	6	0	23	7	18
USA	**10**	**4**	**5**	**1**	**17**	**9**	**17**
Jamaica	10	3	5	2	7	12	14
Costa Rica	10	3	3	4	13	12	12
El Salvador	10	2	4	4	11	16	10
Canada	10	1	3	6	5	20	6

Top goalscorers: 5, Wynalda; 4, McBrid.

WORLD CUP HISTORY

In the first World Cup, the United States beat Belgium and Paraguay to qualify for the semi-finals. In a tough encounter they lost 6–1 to Argentina.

Four years later they made the long trip to Italy only to return shortly after having lost their first game. But this was compensated for in the 1950 World Cup in Brazil. This time, the team was composed almost entirely of American-born players and after an unlucky defeat against Spain, they produced the single greatest shock in the history of the World Cup. In Belo Horizonte, Larry Gaetjens scored a goal that humbled the mighty English side.

It was not until Italy 1990 that the United States managed to qualify for the finals again. Despite a strong team spirit the Americans were brought down to earth by Czechoslovakia but showed great resolve as they tightened up their game for the match against Italy. They lost 1–0 but came out of the game and the tournament with credit and respect.

The States' finest moment came in the 1994 World Cup when they beat the much-vaunted Colombia 2–1 to get to the second round of the competition before going out, honour intact, to Brazil.

Finals appearances: 5 (1930–34, 1950, 1990–94)
Biggest win: 3–0 v Belgium (1930); 3–0 v Paraguay (1930)
Biggest defeat: 1–7 v Italy (1934)

1930 Semi-finalists
   Group Four: 3–0 v Belgium, 3–0 v Paraguay;
   semi-final: 1–6 v Argentina
1934 Eliminated first round
   First round: 1–7 v Italy
1950 Eliminated first round
   Pool Two: 1–3 v Spain, 1–0 v England, 2–5 v Chile
1990 Eliminated first round
   Group A: 1–5 v Czechoslovakia, 0–1 v Italy, 1–2 v Austria
1994 Eliminated second round
   Group A: 1–1 v Switzerland, 2–1 v Colombia, 0–1 v Romania;
   second round: 0–1 v Brazil

Yugoslavia

Federation
Fudbalski Savez Jugoslavije

Founded
1919

Strip
Blue shirts, white shorts, red socks

Coach
Slobodan Santrac

Qualification
Defeated Hungary in play-off having finished second
in European Zone Group Six

In many ways, being back amongst the international fold is an achievement worth celebrating in its own right. Shortly after a game against Holland in the spring of 1992, Yugoslavia were expelled from the European Championship finals and excluded from the 1994 World Cup competition as part of the UN sanctions imposed on the country.

But they were invited back by FIFA in 1994 and the finals this summer will provide a measure of whether Yugoslavia can rebuild the footballing reputation which was so cruelly destroyed by the war.

The campaign to reach France '98 began quietly with a struggle to overcome the Faeroe Islands and although they never looked like troubling group winners Spain, the Yugoslavs collected maximum points against the Czech Republic to earn second place. Under the continued guidance of coach Slobodan Santrac, Yugoslavia booked their place in spectacular fashion with a staggering 12–1 aggregate win over Hungary in the European play-offs.

As a nation Yugoslavia were often called the 'Argentina of Europe' for the way in which they exported fine players and coaches all over the world. In their forward line of Mijatovic and

Savicevic, Yugoslavia possess two players who have continued this tradition.

Mijatovic started his career at Partizan Belgrade before moving to Valencia. His 28 goals in one season took the Spanish club to the runners-up spot in the Spanish Primera Liga and earned him the 1995/96 Footballer of the Year award. His ability in front of goal was such that the then Real Madrid boss Fabio Capello splashed out a cool £6 million on him to partner Suker in attack and his goals helped Real land the title.

Mijatovic's prolific scoring continued for the national side as he netted vital goals throughout qualification as well as helping himself to seven of the 12 scored against Hungary.

The 29-year-old is joined up front by the wily Savicevic who has given Milan such superb service while Milosevic's ten goals in qualifying must have had Aston Villa fans cursing in frustration that he couldn't reproduce the same form for his club.

The forward line is one any coach would be delighted to have – Capello memorably claimed that he wouldn't swap Mijatovic for Ronaldo – and Santrac can also boast a classy midfield comprising of Lazio's Jurgovic and the ever-present Stojkovic while Sampdoria's Mihajlovic is a world-class defender.

Many of these players are graduates of the brilliant Red Star Belgrade side that won the 1991 European Cup. That team might have gone on to even greater things but many left to join foreign clubs at the end of the season. But such was the strength and quality of the youth system at Red Star – on a par with that at Ajax – that they replaced those stars with yet more talented players. However, the long-term impact of the war in Yugoslavia may have had a detrimental effect on this process and could weaken the national side in future.

As for this summer, Yugoslavia are a good side with a long and distinguished record in the World Cup. They are sure to qualify for the second round but lack of international competition may have blunted their competitive edge in the knockout stage.

HOW THEY QUALIFIED

Results: Yugoslavia 3 Faeroe Islands 1; **Yugoslavia 6** Malta 0;
Faeroe Islands 1 **Yugoslavia 8**; **Yugoslavia 1** Czech Republic 0;
Spain 2 **Yugoslavia 0**; Czech Republic 1 **Yugoslavia 2**;
Yugoslavia 1 Spain 1; **Yugoslavia 2** Slovakia 0;
Slovakia 1 **Yugoslavia 1**; Malta 0 **Yugoslavia 5**.
Play-off: Hungary 1 **Yugoslavia 7**; **Yugoslavia 5** Hungary 0

	P	W	D	L	F	A	Pts
Spain	10	8	2	0	26	6	26
Yugoslavia	**10**	**7**	**2**	**1**	**29**	**7**	**23**
Czech Rep	10	5	1	4	16	6	16
Slovakia	10	5	1	4	18	14	16
Faeroe Isles	10	2	0	8	10	31	6
Malta	10	0	0	10	2	37	0

Top goalscorers: 14, Mijatovic; 10, Milosevic.

WORLD CUP HISTORY

Having reached the semi-finals of the first ever World Cup,
Yugoslavia fell into the habit in 1954 and 1958 of reaching the
quarter-finals before losing to Germany. However, at the same
stage in 1962, they finally beat the Germans but having done the
hard part they subsequently lost to a weaker Czech side.

Despite inconsistent form in the World Cup qualifiers, it was a
different story in the European Championship as Yugoslavia played
in two of the first three finals, losing 2–1 after extra-time to the
Soviet Union in 1960 and 2–0 in a replay to the hosts Italy in 1968.

The 1990 World Cup team was probably one of Yugoslavia's
finest and had they been able to convert just one chance against the
unadventurous Argentines it would have set up a mouthwatering
semi-final tie with Italy.

They displayed the more attacking football and looked the more
likely to score but this was the year that Argentina stifled their way

to the finals and the Yugoslavs lost out in the inevitable penalty shoot-out.

Finals appearances: 8 (1930, 1950–62, 1974, 1982, 1990)
Biggest win: 9–0 v Zaire (1974)
Biggest defeat: 1–6 v Uruguay (1930)

1930 Semi-finalists
> Group Two: 2–1 v Brazil, 4–0 v Bolivia;
> semi-final: 1–6 v Uruguay
1950 Eliminated first round
> Group One: 3–0 v Sweden, 4–1 v Mexico, 0–2 v Brazil
1954 Quarter-finalists
> Group One: 1–0 v France, 1–1 v Brazil;
> quarter-final: 0–2 v Germany
1958 Quarter-finalists
> Group Two: 1–1 v Scotland, 3–2 v France, 3–3 v Paraguay;
> quarter-final: 0–1 v Germany
1962 Fourth
> Group One: 0–2 v Soviet Union, 3–1 v Uruguay,
> 5–0 v Colombia; quarter-final: 1–0 v West Germany;
> semi-final: 1–3 v Czechoslovakia;
> third-place play-off: 0–1 v Chile
1974 Eliminated second round
> Group Two: 0–0 v Brazil, 9–0 v Zaire, 1–1 v Scotland;
> Group B: 0–2 v West Germany, 1–2 v Poland, 1–2 v Sweden
1982 Eliminated first round
> Group Five: 0–0 v Northern Ireland, 1–2 v Spain,
> 1–0 v Honduras
1990 Group D: 1–4 v West Germany, 1–0 v Colombia, 4–1 v UAE;
> second round: 2–1 v Spain (aet),
> quarter-final: 0–0 v Argentina (2–3 on penalties)

Iran

Federation
Iran Football Federation

Founded
1920

Strip
Red shirts, white shorts, green socks

Coach
Tomislav Ivic

Qualification
Beat Australia in Asia-Oceania play-off having lost to Japan in Asia Zone play-off after finishing second in Asia Zone Group A

It was a real rollercoaster of a ride but the Iranians scraped into France '98 as the 32nd and final qualifier thanks to an amazing comeback in Australia.

With just 14 minutes left of the last qualifying match for the 1998 World Cup finals, Australia were 2–0 ahead and the issue seemed to have been settled. But within three minutes, goals from Bagheri and Asia's Player of the Year, Azizi, turned the whole game around. With the aggregate scores now 3–3, Iran qualified for the finals on the away goals rule.

Celebrations broke out all across Iran with millions of people flocking on to the streets and motorists turning their stereos to full blast in a massive display of jubilation. On balance, Iran deserved to qualify, having overcome internal conflicts and a run of bad results which plagued them after a strong start in the final round of qualifiers.

Under coach Majeli Kohan, Iran won their first qualifying group and appeared well on their way to France after shooting to the top of Group A following three wins and two draws in the first five matches of the second round. But as newspapers reported serious differences between Kohan and key players, Iran hit a slump. They lost to Saudi Arabia, drew with Kuwait and as the vital game against Qatar approached the row between players and coach resurfaced.

Iranian football officials moved in and Kohan was sacked and replaced by Brazilian Valdeir Vieira. Hired to manage the Olympic team, Vieira found himself in charge of the senior squad but could do nothing to stop them losing 2–0 to Qatar.

Saudi Arabia took the only automatic qualification place from the Asian Group A which left Iran to play-off against Group B runners-up Japan. A heartbreaking 3–2 defeat by the golden goal followed but a place in France was finally claimed by that dramatic comeback in Melbourne.

However, it wasn't enough to keep Vieira in his job. Before he could get his feet under the table he was succeeded by Tomislav Ivic – a hugely experienced international coach.

The nature of their qualification suggests that Iran will struggle to match Germany and Yugoslavia in the first phase. They scored more goals in qualification than any other country, but with 26 of those going past the Maldives alone that shouldn't be taken as a reliable guide.

They do possess three players who their group rivals would be wise to respect. In fact, the Germans should be well aware of the talents of Bagheri, Daei and Azizi as all play in the Bundesliga.

Bagheri, an attacking midfielder, was the leading goalscorer in the qualifying rounds, thanks largely to his seven goals in the 17–0 thrashing of the Maldives. He's strong in the air and has a good nose for the goal.

Daei plays alongside Bagheri at Armenia Bielefeld and is also a prolific striker while Azizi, a talented attacking midfielder, is the Asian Footballer of the Year and was worshipped by the Iranian football fans even before he snatched that all important second goal against Australia.

Iran do not possess enough strength in depth to challenge Yugoslavia and Germany for a place in the second round but the encounter with the USA should prove most interesting.

HOW THEY QUALIFIED

Results: First round: Maldives 0 **Iran 17**; Kirghizstan 0 **Iran 7**;
Syria 0 **Iran 1**; **Iran 3** Kirghizstan 1; **Iran 9** Maldives 0;
Iran 2 Syria 2; second round Group A: China 2 **Iran 4**;
Iran 1 Saudi Arabia 1; Kuwait 1 **Iran 1**; **Iran 3** Qatar 0;
Iran 4 China 1; Saudi Arabia 1 **Iran 0**; **Iran 0** Kuwait 0;
Qatar 2 **Iran 0**. Asia Zone play-off: **Iran 2** Japan 3 (aet).
Oceania-Asia Zone play-off: **Iran 1** Australia 1; Australia 2 **Iran 2**.
Aggregate 3–3, Iran won on away goals rule.

	P	W	D	L	F	A	Pts
Saudi Arabia	8	4	2	2	8	6	14
Iran	**8**	**3**	**3**	**2**	**13**	**8**	**12**
China	8	3	2	3	11	14	11
Qatar	8	3	1	4	7	10	10
Kuwait	8	2	2	4	7	8	8

Top goalscorer: 17, Bagheri.

WORLD CUP HISTORY

Iran's only previous appearance in the finals was in 1978 in
Argentina where they held Scotland to a 1–1 draw but finished last
in their first-round group after defeats by Holland and Peru.

Finals appearances: 1 (1978)
Biggest win: yet to win a game
Biggest defeat: 0–3 v Holland (1978)

1978 Eliminated first round
Group Four: 0–3 v Holland, 1–1 v Scotland, 1–4 v Peru

Group G

Romania, Colombia, England, Tunisia

This is a tight first-round group for England with three tricky customers to overcome. Each will play very differently but if England have aspirations of winning the tournament they should take control of this group. They should take advantage of the fact that they play the weakest team, Tunisia, in their opening game. Anything but a win will make the seven days before their next match seem like an eternity.

When Romania met Colombia at the same stage in 1994, the much-fancied Colombians were destroyed by the genius of Hagi in the first half-hour. The Maradona of the Carpathians is still providing the inspiration for Romania who qualified easily for the finals.

Colombia are a talented team and should not be underestimated. Nor are they burdened with a favourite's tag like last time. But they rely overly on Asprilla and an ageing squad suggests they lack the necessary edge to reach the second stage.

FIXTURES

England v Tunisia	15 June, 12.30, Marseille	**BBC**
Romania v Colombia	15 June, 15.30, Lyon	**ITV**
Colombia v Tunisia	22 June, 15.30, Montpellier	**BBC**
Romania v England	22 June, 19.00, Toulouse	**ITV**
Romania v Tunisia	26 June, 19.00, Stade de France	**BBC**
Colombia v England	26 June, 19.00, Lens	**BBC**

Romania

Federation
Federatia Romana de Fotbal

Founded
1908

Strip
Yellow shirts, blue shorts, red socks

Coach
Anghel Iordanescu

Qualification
First in European Zone Group Eight

Romania dropped only two points in reaching their seventh World Cup finals, and that 1–1 draw in their final group tie in Dublin came long after they had become the first European team to qualify for France.

The bare statistics – six successive clean sheets and a final 37–4 goalscoring record – suggest that Anghel Iordanescu's cultured side may have recovered the sort of form that took them to the quarter-finals of USA '94. However, they were drawn in by far the easiest of the nine European qualifying groups, with Macedonia, Lithuania and Iceland among their opponents, and will be mindful of their pitiful performance at Euro '96 when they suffered three consecutive defeats and scored only one goal.

Whatever happens this summer, France '98 will mark the swan-song for a number of Romania's established stars such as Hagi, Petrescu, Popescu and Lacatus, not to mention Iordanescu himself, who has already agreed a lucrative contract to manage the Greek national team in qualifying for the 2000 European Championship.

Iordanescu's disciplinarian approach – he holds the rank of army general – has led to clashes with several squad members, including Raducioiu, the team's leading scorer in 1994, who was unhappy after being left out of the squad. Worse still, Lupescu has vowed never to play for the national team again after Iordanescu repeatedly kept him on the bench.

Yet a number of younger talents have broken into the team, including Moldovan of Coventry City, who will carry the main striking burden and who disputes the conventional wisdom that Romania may be a spent force. 'We are not given enough credit,' he said. 'Many people seem to think of us as second raters, a team whose golden years are over. It will be a pleasure to prove them wrong.' Iordanescu has also given two talented teenagers, Munteanu and Stoica, a chance to stake their claim in the squad.

Romania's chances of reaching the knock-out stages in France may depend on the group match with Colombia. When the two sides met at the same stage in 1994, the much fancied Colombians were destroyed by the genius of Hagi in the first half-hour. Romania must hope that their little midfield general, who has had something of a footballing resurgence with Galatasaray, will not be running on empty this summer.

HOW THEY QUALIFIED

Results: Romania 3 Lithuania 0; Iceland 0 **Romania 4**; Macedonia 0 **Romania 3**; **Romania 8** Liechtenstein 0; Lithuania 0 **Romania 1**; **Romania 1** Republic of Ireland 0; **Romania 4** Macedonia 2; Liechtenstein 1 **Romania 8**; **Romania 4** Iceland 0; Republic of Ireland 1 **Romania 1**

	P	W	D	L	F	A	Pts
Romania	**10**	**9**	**1**	**0**	**37**	**4**	**28**
Ireland	10	5	3	2	22	8	18
Lithuania	10	5	2	3	11	8	17
Macedonia	10	4	1	5	22	18	13
Iceland	10	2	3	5	11	16	9
Lichenstein	10	0	0	10	7	20	0

Top goalscorers: 8, Popescu; 6, Moldovan; 5, Hagi.

WORLD CUP HISTORY

Romania embraced football before most of her Balkan neighbours, mainly owing to the influence of the country's sovereign, King Carol, a football fanatic. He instigated the formation of a federation in 1908 and in 1930 he was determined that Romania should enter the first World Cup. He selected the team himself and persuaded their employers to allow them three months' leave to travel to South America. King Carol didn't make a bad job of picking the team either as they opened with a 3–1 victory over Peru. In their next game they lost to eventual champions Uruguay.

Having played in the first three World Cup finals, being eliminated in the first round of each, Romania failed to qualify or did not even enter the competition again until 1970. Once more they failed to survive the opening round although their group contained England and Brazil who at the time, were everyone's favourites to reach the final itself.

They failed to qualify for the next four finals but headed their qualification group in 1990. In the finals, they faced defending champions, Argentina, Cameroon and the Soviet Union in Group B. Victory over Russia and a draw against Argentina was sufficient to get them through to the second phase despite losing to the surprise team of the tournament, Cameroon. In the second round they faced the Republic of Ireland and were unlucky to lose in a penalty shoot-out.

Better was to come in 1994. With a side built around Hagi, Romania almost made it to the semi-finals. Before losing to Sweden on penalties in the quarter-finals they put on two of the finest displays in the competition to beat South American opponents Colombia and Argentina with a breathtaking counter-attacking style.

Finals appearances: 6 (1930–38, 1970, 1990–94)
Biggest win: 3–1 v Peru (1930); 3–1 v Colombia (1994)
Biggest defeat: 0–4 v Uruguay (1930)

1930 Eliminated first round
Group Three: 3–1 v Peru, 0–4 v Uruguay
1934 Eliminated first round
First round: 1–2 v Czechoslovakia
1938 Eliminated first round
First round: 3–3 v Cuba, 1–2 v Cuba (replay)
1970 Eliminated first round
Group Three: 0–1 v England, 2–1 v Czechoslovakia,
2–3 v Brazil
1990 Eliminated second round
Group B: 2–0 v Soviet Union, 1–2 v Cameroon,
1–1 v Argentina;
second round: 0–0 v Republic of Ireland (4–5 on penalties)
1994 Quarter-finalists
Group A: 3–1 v Colombia, 1–4 v Switzerland, 1–0 v USA;
second round: 3–2 v Argentina;
quarter-final: 2–2 v Sweden (4–5 on penalties)

Colombia

Federation
Colombian football federation

Founded
1924

Strip
Yellow shirts, blue shorts and red socks

Coach
Hernan Dario Gomez

Qualification
Third in South American Group

There will be a large proportion of familiar faces on view when Colombia trot out to face their 1994 opening group rivals Romania on 15 June in Lyon. Some, like Rincon and Alvarez are veterans of the 1990 World Cup and for those people who were writing Valderrama off before the start of even the last World Cup, the flame-haired captain will still be strolling the park and cutting open defences at the age of 36.

The 1994 finals were disastrous for the Colombians. They arrived as one of the favourites – an assessment based mainly on a stunning 5–0 win over Argentina in the qualifying games. In the finals themselves, the Colombians were first taken apart by Romania, then beaten by the United States and the 2–1 win over Switzerland was not enough to prevent them making an ignominious exit at the bottom of their group.

The performances, however, were overshadowed by the murder of the defender Escobar when he returned to the town of Medellin. The drug barons were linked to his killing and other members of the team also received death threats on their return.

Hernan Dario Gomez took up his duties as Colombian team coach after the 1994 World Cup finals and saw his charges get off to a flying start in their qualifying campaign with five wins and two draws from the first seven games. Just as they appeared to be cantering off with the group they hit a run of four defeats but got back on the rails with a slender home victory against Ecuador.

This time, Colombia are not considered among the favourites and this can only benefit the team. Gomez was assistant coach to Francisco Maturana in the 1990 and 1994 World Cups and he has stayed loyal to many of the players who featured in those finals, although he has tightened up the Colombians' game.

This is based on a typically South American attacking plan. They retain possession in defence, play the ball through midfield with short, close passing, and quicken the tempo as they hit the opposition's penalty area. Players are constantly running into space and creating plenty of attacking options.

Without doubt the most recognisable of the Colombians is the midfield playmaker Valderrama who strolls around the park laying off inch-perfect passes. He was the only player to feature in every qualifier and proved that he hasn't lost the scoring touch either – his three goals made him second top scorer.

The player who could make the biggest impression in the finals is likely to be Asprilla. A gifted, controversial and unpredictable player he was the Colombians' main danger in qualifying and continues to baffle defenders with his on-the-limit-of-control style.

De Avila filled in well for Asprilla when he missed or was suspended from games but it is in partnership with Aristizabal that Asprilla shines. With his intelligent movement, running off the ball and accurate passes, Aristizabal provides the ammunition for Asprilla to fire.

In midfield, Alvarez and Rincon are vastly experienced but look beyond their best although Gomez has at least introduced young players in defence such as Ivan Cordoba and Galeano.

With Oscar Cordoba looking like the first-choice goalkeeper there may not be the opportunity to see the multi-talented Higuita in action – either taking the ball upfield or attempting anything along the lines of his outrageous scorpion kick at Wembley in 1995.

Colombia remain dark horses and cannot be underestimated. The meeting with England in the final group qualifier in Lens on 26 June could be a key game. But Asprilla aside, this Colombian side lacks the necessary edge to progress beyond the first round.

HOW THEY QUALIFIED

Results: Colombia 1 Paraguay 0; Peru 1 **Colombia 1;**
Colombia 3 Uruguay 1; **Colombia 4** Chile 1;
Ecuador 0 **Colombia 1**; Bolivia 2 **Colombia 2;**
Venezuela 0 **Colombia 2; Colombia 0** Argentina 1;
Paraguay 2 **Colombia 1; Colombia 0** Peru 1;
Uruguay 1 **Colombia 1**; Chile 4 **Colombia 1;**
Colombia 1 Ecuador 0; **Colombia 3** Bolivia 0;
Colombia 1 Venezuela 0; Argentina 1 **Colombia 1**

	P	W	D	L	F	A	Pts
Argentina	16	8	6	2	23	13	30
Paraguay	16	9	2	5	21	14	29
Colombia	**16**	**8**	**4**	**4**	**23**	**15**	**28**
Chile	16	7	4	5	32	18	25
Peru	16	7	4	5	19	20	25
Ecuador	16	6	3	7	22	21	21
Uruguay	16	6	3	7	18	21	21
Bolivia	16	4	5	7	18	21	17
Venezuela	16	0	3	13	8	41	3

Top goalscorers: 7, Asprilla; 3, De Avila, Valderrama.

WORLD CUP HISTORY

Colombia made their World Cup debut in 1962 and after a scrappy
defeat against Uruguay pulled off the surprise of the tournament
with a 4–4 draw against the Soviet Union. Trailing 4–1 with only
35 minutes of the game remaining, they decided to throw everything into attack. After such a tremendous fightback, the
Colombians were understandably exhausted and couldn't put up
such stern opposition to an efficient Yugoslavian side.

Colombia made a welcome return to the World Cup in 1990
with victory against the United Arab Emirates, their first in the
finals. Defeat by Yugoslavia meant that a draw was needed against

West Germany to see them through to the second round. This led to Colombia displaying one of the less attractive aspects of South American football – time-wasting – which was very nearly their undoing as Littbarski scored in the 89th minute for West Germany. Spurred into action Valderrama split the German defence with an accurate pass to Rincon who equalised two minutes into injury time.

The second round tie against Cameroon belonged to the 38-year-old African Milla, who scored two goals in extra time to see his team through to the quarter-finals.

Four years ago, Colombia failed to reproduce their form in the qualifiers, losing to Romania and the USA.

Finals appearances: 3 (1962, 1990–94)
Biggest win: 2–0 v United Arab Emirates (1990)
Biggest defeat: 0–5 v Yugoslavia (1962)

1962 Eliminated first round
> Group One: 1–2 v Uruguay; 4–4 v Soviet Union;
> 0–5 v Yugoslavia
1990 Eliminated second round
> Group D: 2–0 v United Arab Emirates; 0–1 v Yugoslavia;
> 1–1 v West Germany; second round: 1–2 v Cameroon
1994 Eliminated first round
> Group A: 1–3 v Romania; 1–2 v USA, 2–0 v Switzerland

England

Federation
The Football Association

Founded
1883

Strip
White shirts, blue shorts, white socks

Coach
Glenn Hoddle

Qualification
First in European Zone Group Two

If the general mood after England had qualified ahead of Italy for the World Cup finals was one of euphoria and confidence for the main event in June, the arrival of Chile at Wembley in January soon threw a bucket of icy water over proceedings.

In one game, England were taught a sobering lesson in how to pass and move with cohesion and penetration – and this from a team purpose-picked as a poor man's Colombia. On the plus side, it was best to suffer this type of reverse when only pride was at stake but Hoddle's decision to experiment revealed glaring inadequacies which must be put right.

Much of the excitement surrounding England's chances in the finals rested on the manner of their qualification for France but also a scintillating performance in Euro '96 and last summer's Tournoi.

First, there has seldom been a better England performance than the one which annihilated the Dutch at Wembley in the European Championship. It seemed so easy that the 4–1 scoreline could have been even more embarrassing for the shell-shocked Dutch.

And in the summer diversion that was the Tournoi, England's victories over Italy and France gave them an unassailable lead in the table so that even a 1–0 defeat by Brazil could not prevent Shearer from lifting the trophy. Spirits were justifiably high.

But it was the style of the qualifying games that impressed most. Having lost to Italy at Wembley, Hoddle went out to get positive results in Poland, Moldova and Georgia where his predecessors might have played for the draw. By the time of the final showdown with Italy in Rome, it was the Italians who had to go out and win the game and England's gutsy performance was enough to get the necessary point to top the group.

Under Hoddle, England have persevered with the 3–5–2 system – one with which they are comfortable but which sometimes lacks penetration.

In defence, Adams and Campbell are the preferred centre-backs and are solidly dependable when their backs are against the wall. But given the room and time, they lack the confidence and inventiveness to carry the ball out of defence and rely too much on the safe ball square across the line.

Of the other central defenders, Gary Neville is the first choice who, when playing for his club, regularly makes penetrating runs down the line to deliver accurate balls into the box. His club teammate Pallister has been overlooked by Hoddle despite being arguably the best centre-half in the country.

Le Saux appears to have made the left wing-back position his own but is stonger going forward than defensively and his temperament can be a liability. If Beckham isn't given a more central midfield role he is likely to occupy the right wing-back position.

It seems remarkable that Hoddle of all people has lined his midfield with defensively minded players like Ince and Batty. Neither will shirk a tackle and Ince is an awesome driving force but with Gascoigne's participation remaining in doubt, where is the inspiration and creativity coming from to feed the striking partnership of Shearer and Sheringham?

Of late, Gascoigne has only treated us to his full range of talents in tantalisingly brief spells. There are doubts concerning his effectiveness and stamina and, as hard as it is to come to terms with, the best of the virtuoso is behind him. Gascoigne still possesses skills which other players can only dream about but those explosive spurts which would propel him deep into the heart of the opponent's area are seldom seen. But Gascoigne is still the one player who can seriously be described as a genius and the World Cup is as good a stage to prove it as any.

Gascoigne is determined to be fit and involved in what will be his last major tournament but Scholes is ready and waiting to make his mark. The young Manchester United midfielder was the star of the Tournoi and has managed to move through the ranks at Old Trafford without attracting the attention heaped on Beckham and Giggs.

Scholes is England's dark horse and, given the opportunity, could prove to be the revelation of the tournament. Like the other Manchester United youngsters, he is unlikely to be overawed by the responsibility having gained so much experience in such a short time thanks to his club's success in the Premiership and Europe.

This leaves Scholes' team-mate Butt competing for the remaining midfield slot alongside the cultured Redknapp and McManaman.

With the return of Shearer, there are fewer problems up front. His form and fitness will be more closely monitored than share prices in the City but he gives England something that even Spain and France lack – a world-class striker. And history shows that this commodity is one which any team with aspirations to win the World Cup must possess.

Sheringham's partnership with Shearer has been a tremendous find for England. The Manchester United player lacks a sprinter's acceleration but has more subtlety to his game. He's a clever, flexible striker capable of dropping deep to link the play.

Considering that so many countries are experiencing difficulty in finding a top striker, it seems bizarre that England have several to call on. Michael Owen has been in prolific form and that one performance against Chile where his startling pace was the only thing to trouble the defenders has fired him right past the likes of Ferdinand, Wright and even Cole in many people's estimation.

At the other end, Seaman is still the first-choice guardian and his calming influence is a bonus for defenders who have had reason to be grateful for his terrific agility, command of the penalty area and penchant for saving crucial penalties.

The World Cup is the biggest stage of all and Hoddle knows that experience will be vital next summer. But he also believes in the power of youth and claims that players like Scholes and Beckham don't know fear as they haven't experienced failure.

This is a tight first-round group with three tricky customers to overcome. Each will play very differently but if England have aspirations of winning the tournament they should win this group convincingly.

RECORD AGAINST WORLD CUP OPPONENTS

Games against Tunisia (England's score listed first)
2 June 1990 (Tunis) 1–1

Games against Romania
24 May 1939 (Bucharest) 2–0; 6 November 1968 (Bucharest) 0–0;
15 January 1969 (Wembley) 1–1; 2 June 1970 (Guadalajara) 1–0
(WC); 15 October 1980 (Bucharest) 1–2 (WC); 29 April 1981
(Wembley) 0–0 (WC); 1 May 1985 (Bucharest) 0–0 (WC);
11 September 1985 (Wembley) 1–1 (WC); 12 October 1994
(Wembley) 1–1

Games against Colombia
20 May 1970 (Bogota) 4–0; 24 May 1988 (Wembley) 1–1;
6 September 1995 (Wembley) 0–0

HOW THEY QUALIFIED

Results: Moldova 0 **England 3**; **England 2** Poland 1;
Georgia 0 **England 2**; **England 0** Italy 1; **England 2** Georgia 0;
Poland 0 **England 2**; **England 4** Moldova 0; Italy 0 **England 0**

	P	W	D	L	F	A	Pts
England	8	6	1	1	15	2	19
Italy	8	5	3	0	11	1	18
Poland	8	3	1	4	10	12	10
Georgia	8	3	1	4	7	9	10
Moldova	8	0	0	8	2	21	0

Top goalscorers: 5, Shearer; 3, Sheringham.

WORLD CUP HISTORY

Having deigned to rejoin FIFA in 1946, England won the British Championship to qualify for the 1950 finals. A fine team including Wright, Finney, Matthews, Mortensen and Ramsey somehow managed to lose to the USA – Gaetjens, a Haitian, scoring the goal.

Four years later, England fans were able to watch the World Cup on television where a bizarre 4–4 draw with Belgium followed by a 2–0 win over Switzerland secured a quarter-final slot. Up against the holders Uruguay, goalkeeper Merrick had a nightmare game – three of the four goals being down to him. Matthews hit the post at 3–2 down but England could not rally further.

In 1958, the only occasion all four British teams have qualified, only Scotland were automatically eliminated at the pool stage. England drew all their pool games and lost out to the Soviet Union in the play-off.

In 1962, a 2–1 defeat to Hungary, at the group stage, was offset by a 3–1 triumph over Argentina, that enabled an unconvincing team to progress to the last eight and a meeting with reigning champions, Brazil. Pelé was injured but in came Garrincha and his long-range shooting accounted for England.

Not since Italy in 1934 had the hosts won the World Cup so England's achievement in 1966 should not be undervalued. Greaves was the crowd favourite but injury against France let in Hurst who scored the only goal in the second half of the ill-tempered win over Argentina to book England's semi-final place. The 3–1 win over Eusebio's Portugal was a classic but proved merely an appetiser for the main event and England's greatest hour.

England set out for Mexico 1970 with a squad that was considered fully capable of retaining the Cup they had won four years earlier. A 1–0 defeat by Brazil was thought to be just a precursor for when the teams met in the final but England met their nemesis in the quarter-finals. Without Banks in goal England squandered a 2–0 lead to lose to West Germany in extra-time.

In 1982, After a lengthy 12-year stretch, Bryan Robson heralded England's return by scoring the World Cup's quickest goal after 27 seconds in the 3–1 win over France. But it was an inability to score against West Germany or Spain that saw Greenwood's men slip out of the tournament unbeaten but unadventurous.

After a poor start to the 1986 campaign, losing to Portugal and managing only a draw against Morocco, England made several important changes which suddenly transformed them into a team of confidence and enthusiasm. From being on the brink of an early exit, Lineker scored three goals to beat Poland and take them through to the second phase. He got two more against Paraguay but in the Azteca England lost to eventual winners, Argentina. God's hand thumped the ball past Shilton for the first while Maradona scored a truly brilliant goal for the second. Lineker's sixth goal couldn't haul England back into it.

Paul Gascoigne's tears at Italia '90 will always sum up the nation's memories of a wonderful tournament that saw England go their furthest on foreign territory. Gazza flowered at exactly the right time to make an ordinary team, overly dependent on Lineker's goals, into a very good one. Platt also emerged, scoring vital goals against Belgium and Cameroon.

Only some dodgy penalty-taking from Stuart Pearce and Chris Waddle prevented England from beating eventual winners Germany.

Finals appearances: 9 (1950–70, 1982–90)
Biggest win: 3–0 v Poland and Paraguay (1986)
Biggest defeat: 2–4 v Uruguay (1954)

1950 Eliminated first round
　　　Group Two: 0–2 v Chile, 0-1 v USA, 0–1 v Spain
1954 Quarter-finalists
　　　Group Four: 4–4 v Belgium, 2–0 v Switzerland, 2–4 v Uruguay
1958 Eliminated first round
　　　Group Four: 2–2 v Soviet Union, 0–0 v Brazil, 2–2 v Austria;
　　　play-off: 0–1 v Soviet Union
1962 Quarter-finalists
　　　Group Four: 1–2 v Hungary, 3–1 v Argentina, 0–0 v Bulgaria;
　　　quarter-final: 1–3 v Brazil
1966 Winners
　　　Group One: 0–0 v Uruguay, 2–1 v France, 2–0 v Mexico;
　　　quarter-final: 1–0 v Argentina; semi-final: 2–1 v Portugal;
　　　final: 4–2 v West Germany (aet)

1970 Quarter-finalists
Group Three: 1–0 v Romania, 0–1 v Brazil,
1–0 v Czechoslovakia;
quarter-final: 2–3 v West Germany (aet)

1982 Eliminated second round
Group Four: 3–1 v France, 2–0 v Czechoslovakia,
1–0 v Kuwait; Group B: 0–0 v West Germany; 0–0 v Spain

1986 Quarter-finalists
Group F: 0–1 v Portugal, 0–0 v Morocco, 3–0 v Poland;
second round: 3–0 v Paraguay;
quarter-final: 1–2 v Argentina

1990 Fourth
Group F: 1–1 v Republic of Ireland, 0–0 v Holland,
1–0 v Egypt; second round: 1–0 v Belgium (aet);
quarter-final: 3–2 v Cameroon (aet);
semi-final: 1–1 v Germany (3–4 on penalties)

Tunisia

Federation
Tunisia football federation

Founded
1957

Strip
Red shirts, white shorts, red socks

Coach
Henry Kasperczak

Qualification
First in African Zone Group Two

Twenty years ago in Argentina, Tunisia made their first appearance in the World Cup finals. When they lost 1–0 to Poland in their group game, it is doubtful they would have considered that one of their opponents, Henry Kasperczak, would one day lead them to another World Cup finals.

Twenty years on, Kasperczak is the Tunisian coach and one of the most celebrated people in the country after taking Tunisia to their second finals.

Kasperczak was a key player in the great Polish teams of the 1970s, competing in the 1974 World Cup in Germany, where Poland finished third, and again in 1978 in Argentina when Poland reached the quarter-finals.

After a successful coaching career with various French clubs, Kasperczak signed a five-month contract with the Ivory Coast national team, which he led to the semi-finals of the African Nations Cup in 1994.

The Tunisians had flopped in the same tournament and decided that Kasperczak was the right man to re-organise Tunisian football. He was appointed national team coach in 1994 and he led them to the final of the African Nations Cup in 1996 where they narrowly lost to South Africa.

In good heart, Tunisia began their World Cup qualifying campaign in November 1996 with a 1–0 win over Liberia in neutral Ghana thanks to a last-minute goal from Jlassi.

They then scored a vital 1–0 win over Egypt at home and with group rivals dropping points, Tunisia took advantage with two further wins. With a growing conviction in their own ability they travelled to Cairo where, despite losing their perfect record, the goalless draw was enough to qualify for France. Tunisia's impressive qualifying campaign had yielded five wins and a draw in their six matches and a goal tally of 10–1.

Kasperczak has helped to bring to Tunisia some of the determination and discipline all successful sides need. All but a handful of players are based in the domestic league but the outstanding player is the midfielder Sellimi who plays for Nantes and who finished as Tunisia's top scorer during qualification.

On paper, it looks a soft opener for England, but Tunisia will not be goal fodder in the heat of Marseille and Kasperczak could prove to be a jinx. It was his ball from defence which set up the goal at Wembley that destroyed England's chances of qualifying for the World Cup finals in 1974 and he will be looking to exploit any further frailties.

Even so, a place in the second round looks beyond them.

HOW THEY QUALIFIED

Results: Preliminary round: Rwanda 1 **Tunisia 3**;
Tunisia 2 Rwanda 0. Group 2: Liberia 0 **Tunisia 1**;
Tunisia 1 Egypt 0; Namibia 1 **Tunisia 2**; **Tunisia 2** Liberia 0;
Egypt 0 **Tunisia 0**; **Tunisia 4** Namibia 0

	P	W	D	L	F	A	Pts
Tunisia	**6**	**5**	**1**	**0**	**10**	**1**	**16**
Egypt	6	3	1	2	15	5	10
Liberia	6	1	1	4	2	10	4
Namibia	6	1	1	4	6	17	4

Top goalscorer: 4, Sellimi.

WORLD CUP HISTORY

Tunisia were not disgraced when they reached the 1978 World Cup, becoming the first African side to win a match in the finals when they beat Mexico 3–1. They also held West Germany to a 0–0 draw and narrowly lost 1–0 to Poland, who eventually finished third.

Finals appearances: 1 (1978)
Biggest win: 3–1 v Mexico (1978)
Biggest defeat: 0–1 v Poland (1978)

1978   Eliminated first round
      Group Two: 3–1 v Mexico, 0–1 v Poland, 0–0 v West Germany

Group H

Argentina, Japan, Jamaica, Croatia

With Japan and Jamaica both making their World Cup debuts, the path to the second round could not be simpler for Argentina and Croatia. The only question will be which team finishes top of the group.

Argentina struggled in the early stages of the mammoth South American qualifying tournament but came through strongly and appear to have a team which could progress to the quarter-finals, if not the semis.

Croatia also made hard work of reaching France, relying on the play-offs to secure their place. But they are developing as one of Europe's strongest footballing countries and made an impressive debut in the 1996 European Championship, narrowly losing to the eventual winners, Germany.

For Japan, this should provide valuable experience for when they host the finals in four years' time while Jamaica should enjoy the support of every football neutral.

FIXTURES

Argentina v Japan	14 June, 12.30, Toulouse	**ITV**
Jamaica v Croatia	14 June, 19.00, Lens	**ITV**
Japan v Croatia	20 June, 12.30, Nantes	**ITV**
Argentina v Jamaica	21 June, 15.30, Parc des Princes	**ITV**
Japan v Jamaica	26 June, 14.00, Lyon	**ITV**
Argentina v Croatia	26 June, 14.00, Bordeaux	**ITV**

Argentina

Federation
Asociacion del Fulbol Argentino

Founded
1893

Strip
Blue and white striped shirts, black shorts,
white socks with blue trim

Coach
Daniel Passarella

Qualification
First in South American group

Argentina were one of the countries to complain about the long
South American qualifying tournament of 16 matches. Coach
Daniel Passarella was particularly concerned about getting his
European-based players for 16 games spaced over 18 months but
in the end it worked out in his favour. The 1978 and 1986 champions got better as the qualifying competition progressed and by
the closing stages appeared to be a team shaping up to make a
serious challenge for the title in France.

There was little doubt that Argentina struggled in the early
stages and it took Passarella, captain of the 1978 World Cup
winning team, around ten games before he found his ideal side. In
an effort to find the right mix, the coach used nearly 50 players,
including six goalkeepers.

Argentina eventually qualified comfortably, making sure of their
place with two matches to spare, but at one stage the outlook
looked bleak.

A 2–1 defeat away to Bolivia in their ninth game actually left
Argentina out of the qualifying places with only seven matches
remaining. Although they had previously been beaten 2–0 away by
Ecuador, four draws, including a lucky 0–0 escape from Peru after

a bad-tempered display which saw Balbo sent off for an awful tackle, left them struggling.

Both of Argentina's defeats came at high altitude – Ecuador's capital Quito lies at 2,800 metres above sea level and the Bolivian capital La Paz at 3,600 metres.

Argentina complained bitterly about having to play in La Paz and their fear of heights became so apparent that Chile considered moving their home game with Argentina to the mining town of Calama, 2,800 metres up in a bleak windswept desert.

The defeat in Bolivia also saw the re-appearance of Argentina's ugly side. Two Argentines were sent off, goalkeeper Ignacio Gonzalez head-butted an opponent in an incident missed by officials and near the end of the game the entire team became involved in a massive brawl that held up play for ten minutes. Riot police were needed to stop the trouble as fighting held up play.

This, however, appeared to be the turning point in Argentina's campaign. Three players were suspended but Argentina could consider themselves extremely lucky to have escaped more severe disciplinary measures.

The team took full advantage of their let-off as they won their next five games, a run which included impressive away wins against Paraguay and Chile, both of whom had 100 per cent home records in the group at the time.

Passarella caused amazement with his continued omission of Batistuta. The Fiorentina centre-forward, a prolific scorer for club and country, played six times and was then left out for nearly ten months until Passarella, reportedly under pressure, recalled him for the final match against Colombia. Bati-gol, as he is known, did not score but it would be amazing if Passarella left him out of the eventual World Cup team. Passarella has argued that Batistuta is incompatible with Crespo but others claim that he prefers Crespo because he knows him from his time as coach of River Plate.

In midfield they have the gifted Ortega – one of the revelations of the last World Cup – and Veron, another outstanding newcomer who has a fierce right-foot shot. Simeone, the most capped player in the team, resurrected his international career and re-established himself as a regular during the qualifiers.

The coach has failed to solve his differences with midfielder Redondo, whose absence from the World Cup could make a huge difference to Argentina's chances. Redondo has not played since Passarella took over as coach in 1995 and the differences between the two – over such issues as the length of Redondo's hair and the position he favours, look insurmountable.

The experience of Chamot, Diaz and Sensini, who all played in 1994, will be invaluable and Argentina at least have some stability in defence. Passarella was one of the most effective attacking defenders ever. He was appointed coach after the last World Cup having made his name in coaching with Buenos Aires club River Plate, leading them to two national championship titles and unearthing several new talents on the way such as Ortega, Crespo and Gallardo. He is known as a strict disciplinarian and has banned long hair, earrings and homosexuals from the national team. However, he has agreed that players can take wives and girlfriends to the World Cup, but not the training camp.

HOW THEY QUALIFIED

Results: Argentina 3 Bolivia 1; Ecuador 2 **Argentina 0**; Peru 0 **Argentina 0**; **Argentina 1** Paraguay 1; Venezuela 2 **Argentina 5**; **Argentina 1** Chile 1; Uruguay 0 **Argentina 0**; Colombia 0 **Argentina 1**; Bolivia 2 **Argentina 1**; **Argentina 2** Ecuador 1; **Argentina 2** Peru 0; Paraguay 1 **Argentina 2**; **Argentina 2** Venezuela 0; Chile 1 **Argentina 2**; **Argentina 0** Uruguay 0; **Argentina 1** Colombia 1

	P	W	D	L	F	A	Pts
Argentina	16	8	6	2	23	13	30
Paraguay	16	9	2	5	21	14	29
Colombia	16	8	4	4	23	15	28
Chile	16	7	4	5	32	18	25
Peru	16	7	4	5	19	20	25
Ecuador	16	6	3	7	22	21	21
Uruguay	16	6	3	7	18	21	21
Bolivia	16	4	5	7	18	21	17
Venezuela	16	0	3	13	8	41	3

Top goalscorers: 5, Ortega; 4, Batistuta; 3, Crespo.

WORLD CUP HISTORY

Argentina has maintained a proud tradition of producing great players. It was a tragedy that so many were persuaded to leave the country and play in the Italian and Spanish leagues, leaving the national team below strength for many years. After finishing runners-up to their great rivals Uruguay in the 1930 World Cup final, Argentina sent a weakened team to Italy for the 1934 competition because they were afraid that they would lose more of their star players to the Italian league. As if to prove their point, three Argentinians, Orsi, Guaita, and Monti all played for the victorious Italian team.

It was for this reason and the fact that Argentina were always overlooked as hosts that it was not until 1958 that they sent another team to the World Cup. Argentina had won the South American Championship the year before with a strong side but again refused to recall their foreign-based players and fielded a weakened side. They were promptly eliminated after the first round.

The country was finally awarded the World Cup in 1978 and their manager, Cesar Menotti, built an impressive team to take the title for the first time. Only Mario Kempes, the tournament's top scorer, played abroad.

Since then, Argentina have been at the forefront of world soccer, appearing in the 1986 and 1990 finals, both against West Germany. The side that won in 1986 was more than a one-man team but there was no denying that Maradona was the inspiration behind a popular success. Four years later the contrast could not have been more marked. Criticised for their negative tactics and reliance on penalty shoot-outs to reach the final, Argentina and a less effective Maradona were beaten by West Germany in one of the poorest finals ever seen.

In 1994, Argentina, with Maradona back in the fold, crushed Greece and overcame the powerful Nigerians. But just as they were developing as a team Maradona failed a drugs test. Without him and Cannigia they were unable to match the Romanians' quick counter-attacking moves.

Finals appearances: 11 (1930–34, 1958–66, 1974–98)
Biggest win: 6–0 v Peru (1978)
Biggest defeat: 1–6 v Czechoslovakia (1958)

1930 Runners-up
Group One: 1–0 v France, 6–3 v Mexico, 3–1 v Chile;
semi-final: 6–1 v United States; final: 2–4 v Uruguay
1934 Eliminated first round
First round: 2–3 v Sweden
1958 Eliminated first round
Group One: 1–3 v West Germany, 3–1 v Northern Ireland,
1–6 v Czechoslovakia
1962 Eliminated first round
Group Four: 1–0 v Bulgaria, 1–3 v England, 0–0 v Hungary
1966 Quarter-finalists
Group Two: 2–1 v Spain, 0–0 v West Germany,
2–0 v Switzerland; quarter-final: 0–1 v England
1974 Eliminated second round
Group Four: 2–3 v Poland; 1–1 v Italy, 4–1 v Haiti;
Group A: 0–4 v Holland, 1–2 v Brazil, 1–1 v East Germany
1978 Winners
Group One: 2–1 v Hungary, 2–1 v France, 0–1 v Italy; Group
B: 2–0 v Poland, 0–0 v Brazil, 6–0 v Peru; final: 3–1 v Holland
1982 Eliminated second round
Group Three: 0–1 v Belgium, 4–1 v Hungary,
2–0 v El Salvador; Group C: 1–2 v Italy, 1–3 v Brazil
1986 Winners
Group A: 3–1 v South Korea, 1–1 v Italy, 2–0 v Bulgaria;
second round: 1–0 v Uruguay; quarter-final: 2–1 v England;
semi-final: 2–0 v Belgium; final: 3–2 v West Germany
1990 Runners-up
Group B: 0–1 v Cameroon, 2–0 v Soviet Union,
1–1 v Romania; second round: 1–0 v Brazil; quarter-final:
0–0 v Yugoslavia (3–2 on penalties); semi-final: 1–1 v Italy
(4–3 on penalties); final: 0–1 v West Germany
1994 Eliminated second round
Group D: 4–0 v Argentina, 2–1 v Nigeria, 0–2 v Bulgaria;
second round: 2–3 v Romania

Japan

Federation
Football Association of Japan

Founded
1921

Strip
Blue shirts, white shorts, blue socks

Coach
Takeshi Okada

Qualification
Second in Asian zone Group B. Beat Iran 3–2 in play-off.

There was a collective sigh of relief when Okano scored the winning goal with just one minute remaining of extra-time to put Japan through to the finals of the World Cup for the first time in their history.

The 3–2 win over Iran earned Japan their first World Cup finals place and, perhaps more importantly for football's administrators, avoided the embarrassment of having a country host a World Cup before having qualified for one.

With Asia's representation increased from two to a minimum of three teams for the finals, Japan had expected a straightforward route to France '98. But after cruising through the first round, they were drawn in the same group as South Korea – for some time the leading football power in the region.

Japan started with a 6–3 victory over lightweights Uzbekistan, drew two of their next three games and lost the other 2–1 at home to South Korea. The sequence of poor results led to Shu Kamo's dismissal as national coach and he was replaced by his assistant, Takeshi Okada.

Immediate results did not inspire much hope but a vital and unexpected 2–0 victory over Korea in Seoul followed by a 5–1 drubbing of Kazakstan lifted the Japanese into second place. South Korea won the group convincingly and with Saudi Arabia topping the other Asian group it was left to the runners-up from each,

Japan and Iran, to play-off for the third automatic Asian World Cup qualifying place. In the play-off, Japan went 2–1 behind and it was only a 'golden goal' in extra-time which brought the 3–2 victory. Four years ago, Japan, despite being the favourites to qualify, had missed out on USA '94 when they conceded a last-minute equaliser in their match with Iraq during the play-offs.

Okada has managed to instil new confidence in the Japanese team, while at the same time introducing a new fast-moving and attacking style. In Ihara they have a wealth of experience – the sweeper has more than 100 caps – and Nakata in midfield is one of the blossoming, talented youngsters. Miura, the top scorer in qualification, has played for Genoa but it is hard to see the Japanese, as technically capable as they are, having the resilience to trouble either Argentina or Croatia.

Their meeting with Jamaica in the final group game, will probably decide who finishes bottom of the group but at least the tournament should provide valuable experience for when they host the finals, along with South Korea, in four years' time.

HOW THEY QUALIFIED

Results: First round: Oman 0 **Japan 1**; Macao 0 **Japan 10**; Nepal 0 **Japan 6**; **Japan 10** Macao 0; **Japan 3** Nepal 0; **Japan 1** Oman 1; second round, Group B: **Japan 6** Uzbekistan 3; UAE 0 **Japan 0**; **Japan 1** South Korea 2; Kazakhstan 1 **Japan 1**; Uzbekistan 1 **Japan 1**; **Japan 1** UAE 1; South Korea 0 **Japan 2**; **Japan 5** Kazakhstan 1; Play-off: **Japan 3** Iran 2 (aet)

	P	W	D	L	F	A	Pts
South Korea	8	6	1	1	19	7	19
Japan	**8**	**3**	**4**	**1**	**17**	**9**	**13**
UAE	8	2	3	3	9	12	9
Uzbekistan	8	1	3	4	13	18	6
Kazakhstan	8	1	3	4	7	19	6

Top goalscorers: 14, Miura; 7, Tagaki.

WORLD CUP HISTORY

This is Japan's first appearance in the finals.

Jamaica

Federation
Jamaica Football Federation

Founded
1910

Strip
Green shirt, black shorts, yellow socks

Coach
Rene Simoes

Qualification
Third in CONCACAF zone

'We're not going there to advertise tourism, we're going to play soccer.' Those were the words of Jamaica's Brazilian-born coach Rene Simoes after his team's surprise qualification for the World Cup finals. 'The other teams had better be prepared for us,' he warned.

France '98 will be Jamaica's first-ever appearance in the World Cup finals, and when the national side qualified following the draw at home to Mexico, the Prime Minister generously declared a public holiday in recognition of their success. The scale of celebration was almost unprecedented as the Reggae Boyz became the first team from the Caribbean to qualify for the finals since Haiti in 1974.

The inspiration behind their success is Simoes, who has brought discipline and organisation to the side. He has been technical director of Jamaica's national football programme since 1994 and is also responsible for Jamaica's national youth sides. He has over 20 years' coaching experience and led Brazil's national Under-17, Under-20 and Under-23 squads for several years.

Jamaica got off to a strong start in the preliminary round – including a home win against Mexico – which was enough to put them at top of the group and lift them into the final CONCACAF qualifying round.

However, it was at this point that the team began to falter, and after their opening four matches they sat bottom of the six-team group with just two points and a humbling 6–0 away defeat by Mexico. France '98 was looking a very remote possibility and pressure began to build on Simoes with rifts between him and the team's two main strikers, Boyd and Lowe. Boyd had scored five goals from 12 qualifying matches and many felt his inclusion was critical to Jamaica's chances.

Simoes made himself unpopular with many locals by dropping them from the team and introducing four England-based players, Burton of Derby County, Hall and Simpson of Portsmouth and Earle of Wimbledon.

Burton proved a crucial addition, emerging as the third-leading goalscorer in the final round, with four goals from as many games, but the four players' experience proved vital. The team was suitably revitalised. Victories over Costa Rica and Canada put the Reggae Boyz back in contention, then goals by Burton earned his team valuable points away to the United States and El Salvador.

This meant Jamaica needed only another draw against Mexico at home in their final match in November, a game they could even afford to lose if El Salvador lost to the United States the same day – which, in fact, they did.

With Earle, Burton, Hall and Simpson happy in the team, other England based players have been considering staking their claims, including Chelsea's Frank Sinclair and Wimbledon's Marcus Gayle.

Further good news for Simoes came in the shapes of Boyd and Lowe who publicly declared that they wanted to be brought back into the team. Simoes will need all the firepower he can muster as seven goals in ten qualifying games was a poor return.

Although the main focus may fall upon the likes of Burton and Gayle who have injected a much-needed professionalism, players such as Whitmore, Messam and Williams have shown good skill and ability on the ball. It has been the influence of those sort of players which has raised the level of Jamaican football and led to FIFA awarding the title of World's Most Improved Team to Jamaica in 1995.

At best, Jamaica might display the impact shown by Cameroon eight years ago and it is interesting that they are drawn in Argentina's group – the first team to be humbled by the Africans at Italia '90.

The support is also likely to match the samba style of Brazil in vibrancy, colour and spectacle. Although the second round might be an ambitious target, just becoming one of the more romantic qualifying stories is achievement enough.

HOW THEY QUALIFIED

Results: Jamaica 0 USA 0; Mexico 6 **Jamaica 0**; Canada 0 **Jamaica 0**; Costa Rica 3 **Jamaica 1**; **Jamaica 1** El Salvador 0; **Jamaica 1** Canada 0; **Jamaica 1** Costa Rica 0; USA 1 **Jamaica 1**; El Salvador 2 **Jamaica 2**; **Jamaica 0** Mexico 0

	P	W	D	L	F	A	Pts
Mexico	10	4	6	0	23	7	18
USA	10	4	5	1	17	9	17
Jamaica	**10**	**3**	**5**	**2**	**7**	**12**	**14**
Costa Rica	10	3	3	4	13	12	12
El Salvador	10	2	4	4	11	16	10
Canada	10	1	3	6	5	20	6

Top goalscorers: 5, Whitmore, Boyd; 4, Burton.

WORLD CUP HISTORY

This is Jamaica's first appearance in the finals.

Croatia

Federation
Croatian Football Federation

Founded
1912

Strip
Red and white checked shirts, white shorts, white socks

Coach
Miroslav Blazevic

Qualification
Second in European Zone Group One. Beat Ukraine in play-off.

Croatia arrived at Euro '96 as one of the outsiders to win the tournament on the basis of a superb victory against the Italians in Palermo during qualification. They were fiercely proud and motivated to do well in their first finals as a new nation and hoped that success would raise the morale of a war-weary population that had suffered during the break-up of the former Yugoslavia.

Croatia successfully negotiated the first round and looked poised for a major upset against Germany in the quarter-finals before they lost their composure and the game. That performance highlighted Croatia's dramatic emergence as a major international football power. It was an impressive debut from the proud Croatians and considering the wealth of talent at the call of coach Miroslav Blazevic they were expected to qualify comfortably for the World Cup finals.

Yet despite the presence of the likes of Boban, Suker and Bilic, Croatia only made the finals by the skin of their teeth. They started the campaign well enough with victory over Bosnia but then three drawn home games in succession led to calls for the coach's resignation. A late Suker strike gave Croatia an important away win in Greece to ease their position and an even later strike by Boban completed a 3–2 win over Bosnia.

However, a 3–1 defeat in Copenhagen meant that their fate now lay in Danish hands. Croatia beat Slovenia to go second in the table but could only wait to see if Denmark could hold Greece to a draw in Athens. The resulting 0–0 scoreline was enough for Croatia to qualify for the play-off positions where first-leg goals from Bilic and Vlaovic were enough to see off Ukraine.

The player who exemplifies Croatian football is Boban – the heart, soul and captain of the team. The Milan midfielder has donated thousands of pounds to help aid organisations in his country and few Croatians will forget the day some eight years ago when, outraged at seeing Serbian police attacking Croatian supporters at the Yugoslav Cup final between Red Star Belgrade and his team, Dinamo Zagreb, he defended a young fan by kicking out at a policeman.

Boban moved to Milan in 1992 and has become an influential figure in the midfield for club and country with his surging runs and excellent distribution. He is joined in midfield by the sublimely talented Prosinecki who won a European Cup medal with Red Star Belgrade in 1991 before joining Real Madrid the following year. He had a disappointing spell with Barcelona but has since returned to Croatia Zagreb where he has rediscovered the brilliant form that had some people back in the early 1990s claiming that he was the best player in the world. This is his chance to prove them right.

Bilic is still the first-choice central defender but Blazevic has replaced the experienced Jerkan and Stimac with youngsters from Croatia Zagreb. Of these, Juric has quickly established himself as one of the new stars of the team while Simic is held in such high regard that Milan are reportedly after his signature.

The fleet-footed Jarni, who was part of Juventus' league-winning side several seasons back, is still one of the most effective and quickest left-sided wing-backs around.

The attacking pair of Boksic and Suker should strike fear into the most experienced of defences. Although Boksic may not always repeat his club form for his country he can still create chances which Suker will unerringly put away. Suker came to prominence somewhat late but has since become one of Europe's most formidable goalscorers.

Having reached the finals, Croatia have been drawn in a comfortable group with Argentina posing the only threat.

HOW THEY QUALIFIED

Results: Bosnia 1 **Croatia 4**; **Croatia 1** Greece 1;
Croatia 1 Denmark 1; **Croatia 3** Slovenia 3; Greece 0 **Croatia 1**;
Croatia 3 Bosnia 2; Denmark 3 **Croatia 1**; Slovenia 1 **Croatia 3**.
Play-off: **Croatia 2** Ukraine 0; Ukraine 1 **Croatia 1**

	P	W	D	L	F	A	Pts
Denmark	8	5	2	1	14	6	17
Croatia	**8**	**4**	**3**	**1**	**17**	**12**	**15**
Greece	8	4	2	2	11	4	14
Bosnia	8	3	0	5	9	14	9
Slovenia	8	0	1	7	5	20	1

Top goalscorers: 5, Suker; 4, Boksic; 3, Bilic, Boban.

WORLD CUP HISTORY

This is Croatia's first appearance in the finals.

THE VENUES

BORDEAUX: PARC LESCURE

Capacity: 36,500
Club: Girondins de Bordeaux

FIXTURES

First round
11 June: Italy v Chile
16 June: Scotland v Norway
20 June: Belgium v Mexico
24 June: South Africa v Saudi Arabia
26 June: Argentina v Croatia

Second round
30 June: Winner Group G v Runner-up Group H

The Lescure stadium is a fine example of 1930s architecture and is one of Bordeaux's major landmarks. It was originally built for the 1938 World Cup when its first game was the ill-tempered quarter-final match between Czechoslovakia and Brazil. The game, which later became known as the Battle of Bordeaux, ended 1–1 with two players sent off and more nursing broken limbs. The milder replay went Brazil's way and they returned to the stadium for the third-place play-off, beating Sweden 4–2.

The stadium has since staged many memorable football matches, as well as top athletics and cycling events. In preparation for the World Cup, it has undergone a huge revamp which will reduce the capacity from nearly 47,000 to an all-seated 36,500, including 15,000 under cover. However, it remains a national heritage and protected monument.

The region itself has been influenced by many different cultures and has been a busy commercial centre since Roman times. Bordeaux underwent a boom period between the 12th and 15th centuries when it was occupied by the English. In the 18th century, its harbour and maritime activities brought further prosperity. This was the golden age of opulent fortunes and much of the architectural splendour of the time can still be seen in the city today, particularly in the quartier St. Pierre.

But it is for wine production that the region is justly famous. The surrounding countryside may be a little flat and uninteresting but it enjoys almost perfect climatic and soil conditions. It is the largest quality wine district in the world and turns out around 500 million bottles a year, including such prestigious names as Saint-Emilion, Margaux, Pomerol and Saint-Estèphe.

If you are interested in buying wines, it is possible to find bargains at the châteaux but the main advantage is that you can try before you buy and get expert advice about the different vintages. The Bordeaux tourist office holds details of the places that allow visits and wine tasting.

'Welcome to the World' is the message Bordeaux hopes to convey to the thousands of fans and tourists arriving there during the summer. The city has set up a dedicated team with a view to involve the entire population so there should be something to entertain everyone.

The city intends to host its own version of the World Cup for 32 teams of young players from the Aquitaine region with the final due to be played during the World Cup competition.

Bordeaux will also host a huge show during the tournament. The 'Welcome to the World' village will be at the heart of the celebrations. This will showcase local culinary specialities, craftsman-ship and cultural highlights.

At night, the party is set to continue with bands playing music typical of the region in the city's main squares.

Tourist Office: 12 cours du 30 juillet, 33080 Bordeaux

LENS: STADE FELIX BOLLAERT

Capacity: 42,000
Club: Racing Club de Lens

FIXTURES

First round
12 June: Saudi Arabia v Denmark
14 June: Jamaica v Croatia
21 June: Germany v Yugoslavia
24 June: Spain v Bulgaria
26 June: Colombia v England

Second round
28 June: Winner Group C v Runner-up Group D

The northern mining city of Lens has a population of just 35,000, yet its stadium will host six World Cup matches. Thankfully, the people of Lens are obsessed with the game and the entire popula-tion gets behind its leading football club. Several times during the year, the Felix Bollaert stadium holds more spectators than the city has inhabitants.

The stadium, named after a local mine owner, has had a FF100 million refit in preparation for the finals. This will reduce the capacity from nearly 50,000 to an all-seated limit of 42,000. It's only a gentle 15-minute walk from the city centre – the best area for bars and restaurants.

Situated in the heart of the Artois, the city of Lens has been the subject of bitter battles over the centuries, and was completely destroyed during the First World War.

The discovery of coal in 1849 led to unprecedented expansion for Lens, where the largest and most productive mines were to be found. For a century, the city lived on the proceeds of coalmining. But when recession hit the industry in the 1960s, Lens embarked on an ambitious modernisation programme and has expanded in the fields of information technology, farm produce, distribution and construction.

The huge offices that used to house the coalmining headquarters were given back to the people in 1992 to create the Jean Perrin College of Science, which is home to some 3,000 students.

The inhabitants of Lens are famed for their hospitality and the city aims to make up for being the smallest of the World Cup host cities by making their visitors extremely welcome.

Tourist Office: 26 rue de la Paix, 62300 Lens

LYON: STADE GERLAND

Capacity: 44,000
Club: Olympique Lyonnais

FIXTURES

First round
13 June: South Korea v Mexico
15 June: Romania v Colombia
21 June: USA v Iran
24 June: France v Denmark
26 June: Japan v Jamaica

Quarter-final
4 July: Winner 6 v Winner 7

The second largest city in France, Lyon sits on two rivers, the Rhône and the Saône. Across the Saône is the old town at the foot of the Fourvière on which the Romans built their capital of Gaul. To the north of the Presqu'île is the old silk-weavers' district, La Croîx-Rousse. Silk-weaving was the city's main industry from the 16th century until the present domination of commerce and industry.

The stadium is just south of the city centre and around FF90 million has been spent on its redevelopment. Built in 1924, Stade Gerland, along with Parc Lescure in Bordeaux, is one of the two French World Cup stadiums listed as historic monuments. Inspired by Roman architecture, the stadium is surrounded by a gallery set on a grass embankment with four great symbolic gateways.

After many alterations over the years, Gerland is undergoing a further youthful facelift in readiness for the World Cup. By completion it will hold 44,000 – all seated – and the north corner will be covered and moved closer to the pitch.

The stadium is within easy reach of the city centre which boasts several of the finest restaurants in the world. It is a great gastronomic centre where you will find specialities from every region of France and abroad, prepared by a galaxy of internationally renowned chefs.

Lyon owes its distinctive character to its surroundings, which include two steep hills, a vast plain and two rivers. During the last decade, the city has become even more handsome. It has transformed and improved its squares and gardens, and implemented a lighting strategy to show off its finest features: 150 points of interest are now illuminated each night.

In fact, Lyon offers everything you would expect of a big city – good food, hundreds of bars, music, movies and cultural festivals.

Tourist Office: Place Bellecour, 69002 Lyon

MARSEILLE: STADE VELODROME

Capacity: 60,000
Club: Olympique Marseille

FIXTURES

First round
12 June: France v South Africa
15 June: England v Tunisia
20 June: Holland v South Korea
23 June: Brazil v Norway

Second round
27 June: Winner Group B v Runner-up Group A

Quarter-final
4 July: Winner 5 v Winner 8

Semi-final
7 July: Winner A v Winner C

Home to the best-supported team in France and located on the Mediterranean coast, this busy port will host seven games in all – including one semi-final. It may not be the most beautiful city and has a somewhat seedy reputation but it boasts a great cosmopolitan ambience and the whole city is football-mad.

The Velodrome Stadium, situated in the heart of the city, will have its capacity raised from 46,000 to 60,000 in time for the finals and there is sure to be a fantastic atmosphere when the stadium hosts France's opening game in their World Cup campaign, against South Africa.

Marseille is a vibrant city. When it comes to eating, fish and seafood are, not surprisingly, the main ingredients. There is also a strong North African influence on cooking. Bouillabaise is the local speciality, made with rock fish and cooked in a broth with onions,

eddy Sheringham demonstrates his acute positioning sense – both for the
ame and a lovely back-lit portrait. He's enhanced his reputation at Manchester
nited and is now the main support in a first-class striking duo with Shearer.

If Dennis Bergkamp carries his outstanding league form into the finals then the Dutch could be major contenders. Internal disputes withstanding, of course.

Youri Djorkaeff has been the inspiration for Inter's resurgence. Alongside Zinedine Zidane, he could work the same magic for France.

We qualified? Jamaica's Dean Burton and Fitzroy Simpson seconds before they realise they're on their way to France.

Veteran Argentinian midfielder Diego Simeone remembers that players can take wives and girlfriends to the World Cup.

Marcelo Salas' two goals at Wembley brought
England crashing back down to earth. And that
was without his prolific partner Ivan Zamorano.

The rising star of Spanish football, we may see the best of Raul in 2002.

Stoitchkov: moody and arrogant, but sublimely gifted.

is goal won Euro '96. Now Bierhoff is ermany's main man.

Georghe Hagi can still make opposing defences look stupid.

Paolo Maldini, the pin-up of
Italian football and the best
defender around. His dad's
also the boss.

The goal-scoring heroics of
Blackburn striker Kevin
Gallacher have been one of
the most pleasing aspects of
Scotland's progress.

'Will Ronaldo be the star of the finals?
s he the best player in the world? Probably.

What all the fuss is about. Brazil won the World Cup
for a record fourth time in 1994 and who will bet
against them making it five this summer?

garlic, olive oil, tomatoes and saffron. It's served with garlic crou-
tons and a spicy sauce called *rouille* and well worth a try.

The port is the life centre of the city. Two fortresses guard the
harbour entrance and the whole area is overlooked from a height
of 162 metres by the Basilica of Notre-Dame-de-la-Garde which is
capped by a golden statue of the Virgin, known as the 'Good
Mother'. The Virgin is the symbol of the city.

Tourist Office: 4 la Canebière, 13001 Marseille

MONTPELLIER: STADE DE LA MOSSON

Capacity: 35,500
Club: Montpellier

FIXTURES

First round
10 June: Morocco v Norway
12 June: Paraguay v Bulgaria
17 June: Italy v Cameroon
22 June: Colombia v Tunisia
25 June: Germany v Iran

Second round
29 June: Winner Group F v Runner-up Group E

Montpellier is a young, lively city and rivals Toulouse and Nîmes
as the most dynamic city in the south.

The Stade de la Mosson is six kilometres from the city centre.
The stadium was built in 1988 and has undergone a series of reno-
vations since – the latest increasing the capacity to 35,500.

Montpellier's central focus is the Place de la Comédie – a huge
oblong square, paved with cream marble with a fountain in the
middle and cafes on either side. One end is closed by the Opera

while the other opens on to the Esplanade, a tree-lined promenade. The square is an entertaining place to eat, drink and watch the day's activities.

As a university city, Montpellier has a young and dynamic population – in fact, one out of every four inhabitants is under 25 years old – and as a result, it's a great city for culture and entertainment.

The city and the surrounding area have been preparing for the World Cup for a long time – in 1996, the Mayor of Montpellier and the President of the Languedoc-Roussillon Football League embarked on a vast regional tour to spread the word about the World Cup among the population.

Today, the Place de la Comédie is ready for the Football World Cup: the France '98 mascot, Footix, an integral part of the countdown to the big event, crows Buuuuuuut! (goal!) every hour on the hour from his perch.

Tourist Office: 78 avenue du Pirée, 34000 Montpellier

NANTES: STADE DE LA BEAUJOIRE

Capacity: 40,000
Club: FC Nantes

FIXTURES

First round
13 June: Spain v Nigeria
16 June: Brazil v Morocco
20 June: Japan v Croatia
23 June: Cameroon v Chile
25 June: Yugoslavia v USA

Quarter-final
3 July: Winner 1 v Winner 4

The Nantes club, which has won the French Championship seven times, had a new football stadium built in 1984 to host the European Championship. Alhough it is a relatively recent construction, further improvements have been made – including making it a 40,000 all-seated venue – in preparation for the six World Cup matches.

In the 17th and 18th centuries Nantes became France's leading commercial port, building its fortune on the trade with Africa and the West Indies. Today, the Loire estuary, which includes Nantes and Saint-Nazaire, is the fourth most important industrial site in France with maritime engineering and food production providing the major industries.

The city launched a Supporters' Charter programme for school-children of the ten cities in the World Cup programme: a charter based on the principle of tolerance, a key rule in sport and, in particular, football.

Nantes is also host to a theatre troupe named the Royal de Luxe who will be providing the creative input to make the giant, a huge ten-metre tall puppet that will walk through the city acting out a series of scenes.

As Nantes will be host to Brazil during the first stages of the competition, the authorities have decided to build a replica of Copacabana beach in the heart of the city. Tons of sand will transform the former home of the Dukes of Brittany into a citadel for football.

Tourist Office: 7 rue de Valmy, 44041 Nantes

PARIS: PARC DES PRINCES

Capacity: 49,500
Club: Paris Saint-Germain

FIXTURES

First round
15 June: Germany v USA
19 June: Nigeria v Bulgaria
21 June: Argentina v Jamaica
25 June: Belgium v South Korea

Second round
27 June: Winner Group A v Runner-up Group B

Third-place play-off
11 July

The home of Paris Saint-Germain and just a short journey to the south-west of the city, this grand all-seated stadium is well known to all sports fans. The Parc des Princes holds a special place in the hearts of the French people. Ever since its renovation in 1972, it has been the stage for the triumphs of French rugby and football teams and has undergone several improvements in preparation for the World Cup.

As for the city itself, what more can one say? So much has been written about Paris which occupies a special place in the social and cultural history of the world. There is its history, its monuments, the secret Paris with its gardens and the lively, imaginative, creative and fashionable element.

The list of good restaurants and bars is endless. There is no problem finding a meal, whether it be five star or fast food, to suit your pocket. The one rule to bear in mind is not to drink outside at a Parisian cafe unless you want to spend your entire budget in one hit. There is also an increasing number of Irish bars springing up around the city which have the useful bonus of satellite television.

Paris is well versed in hosting international events. With more trade fairs and conventions than anywhere else in the world it is not surprising that events held here are so successful.

Not only will Paris be welcoming spectators for all the matches played at the Parc des Princes and Stade de France, it will also be the place through which most fans will be passing to reach the other World Cup cities.

Nevertheless, the organisers say they won't be forgetting the hundreds of thousands of other tourists, who will be coming just to visit the capital, nor will it ignore Parisians themselves, whom it would like to involve in the great celebration.

A huge party to get the 16th World Cup off to a roaring start is to be laid on for everyone on 9 June. The day before the opening match, Paris and all of France will welcome the world with a vast celebration in the heart of the capital.

Tourist Office: 127 avenue des Champs-Elysées, 75008 Paris

PARIS: SAINT-DENIS – STADE DE FRANCE

Capacity: 80,000

FIXTURES

First round
10 June: Brazil v Scotland
13 June: Holland v Belgium
18 June: France v Saudi Arabia
23 June: Italy v Austria
26 June: Romania v Tunisia

Second round
28 June: Winner Group D v Runner-up Group C

Quarter-final
3 July: Winner 2 v Winner 3

Semi-final
8 July: Winner B v Winner D

Final
12 July

Le Stade de France at Saint-Denis was built specially for the World Cup and will seat 80,000. It was inaugurated on 28 January 1998 with a friendly between France and Spain which France won 1–0, thanks to a goal by Zidane. The stadium will host the opening ceremony and the competition's first game on 10 June.

The futuristic stadium cost a large fortune to build but it is a triumph of design and construction. The elliptical roof stands 42 metres above the pitch while a sliding stand allows the Stade de France to be converted into an athletics stadium – the lower stand will be able to retract 15 metres beneath the middle stand to reveal a running track.

The ability to vary its capacity is one of the stadium's chief assets. The circle of mobile stands closest to the sports area, which contains 25,000 seats, is an amazing technical achievement.

Saint-Denis is one of the most heavily industrialised areas in the region but it has managed to preserve some of its architectural splendour. The town's main feature is its magnificent cathedral, Basilique St. Denis, which many consider to be the birthplace of the Gothic style. Once the place where the kings of France were crowned, it houses 70 royal tombs – those of nearly all the kings of France since Hugues Capet.

Saint-Denis plays an important role in the economic life of Paris. For the last 100 years it has been the home of large business concerns, including Siemens, Panasonic, the Gaz de France research centre, the TGV (high-speed train) workshops and numerous audio-visual companies.

Ever since the announcement that it was to be one of the host cities, Saint-Denis has embraced the World Cup. Students and schoolchildren have been thoroughly involved – some schools have corresponded with children in Barcelona, Milan, Paris and Manchester, in order to get to know other supporters' clubs better. Their work will culminate in 1998 with a grand meeting on the theme of sport and citizenship.

The World Cup programme includes a grand carnival procession, a *son-et-lumière* show, a fairground set up for the duration of the event, a literary voyage around all the 32 countries qualifying for the World Cup, a rock concert venue, a multi-section exhibition put on throughout the city, dance cafes along the canal and much, much more.

Tourist Office: 1 rue de la Republique, 93200 Saint-Denis

SAINT ETIENNE: STADE GEOFFREY GUICHARD

Capacity: 36,000
Club: AS Saint Etienne

FIXTURES

First round
14 June: Yugoslavia v Iran
17 June: Chile v Austria
19 June: Spain v Paraguay
23 June: Scotland v Morocco
25 June: Holland v Mexico

Second round
30 June: Winner Group H v Runner-up Group G

Saint Etienne used to be one of the best teams in France but that was back in the 1970s and the club has since fallen on hard times. The stadium is just north of the city centre and will seat 36,000 by the time the tournament starts.

Saint Etienne is the capital of the Forez region and, owing to its long manufacturing experience in the heart of a coalmining area, was one of the first cities to be affected by the French industrial revolution. This turned the city into one of France's leading centres. Since the 1960s the city has converted to information technology and there is not a huge amount to entertain or enthral the visitor.

However, the Modern Art Museum houses the second largest public collection of French contemporary art in the country. The Museum of Art and Industry is about to receive a unique collection of weapons, while the Coalmining Museum and the Planetarium are among the cultural landmarks in a city that also welcomes nearly 400 authors every year to its Book Fair.

The city is proving highly creative in the run-up to the finals. The day before renovation work started on the Stade Geoffrey Guichard, the old pitch was cut up and segments were offered to the club's supporters, enabling them to take home a piece of the sacred turf. Shortly before the World Cup kick-off, Saint-Etienne's citizens will be invited to a huge show organised for the inauguration of the new stadium.

A village set up in the downtown area is to host a continous celebration, with activities, meetings with well-known personalities and exclusive shows, while the city's neighbourhoods will be adorned with the colours of the qualifying countries.

Tourist Office: 3 place Roannelle, 42029 Saint Etienne

TOULOUSE: STADE MUNICIPAL

Capacity: 37,000
Club: Toulouse FC

FIXTURES

First round
11 June: Cameroon v Austria
14 June: Argentina v Japan
18 June: South Africa v Denmark
22 June: Romania v England
24 June: Nigeria v Paraguay

Second round
29 June: Winner Group E v Runner-up Group F

Built on the River Garonne, Toulouse is the fourth largest city in France and one of its most exciting centres. It has now acquired a reputation for both intellect and industry, making it one of the major cities in south-western France.

It has a beautiful historic centre but its prominence lies in the fact that the city has developed into a centre of aviation. From the early pioneers such as Jean Mermoz and Antoine de Saint-Exupéry, to the Airbus aircraft and the Ariane rockets, Toulouse has played an important part in Europe's aeronautical history and continues to do so. It also has a 60,000 student population, making it second only to Paris as a university centre.

The heart of the city is the huge town hall – a great meeting place with numerous cafes in the city square. The town hall is surrounded by a labyrinth of old city alleyways, beautifully constructed almost exclusively from rosy-coloured brick. The colour gives the city its nickname, 'Ville Rose'.

The Stade Municipal, erected on an island between two branches of the Garonne, is conveniently close to the city centre and by the time the tournament starts the capacity will be 37,000, all-seated.

Toulouse offers a cosmopolitan mix of food – Japanese, Italian and Indian – as well as traditional French cuisine. It's a great city for bars – thanks to the large number of students which make up 25 per cent of the population. In addition to cassoulet – the main ingredients of which are goose, duck, poultry, game and beans, the city is also famous for other culinary specialities such as the local sausage.

Sixty years after first hosting a World Cup, Toulouse is once again to be the stage for the celebration of football in 1998. Although the city is more familiar as a venue for rugby, there is still a big following for football.

The Garonne is the focus of the city, and will be even more so during the World Cup, serving as a thoroughfare, a games area and a stage for shows. Its embankments will become a permanent fairground offering gastronomical and cultural specialities from the area. River shuttles will take visitors to the Ile du Ramier, home to the stadium, and further celebrations, including a huge parade, are to be staged on the water.

Tourist Office: Donjon du Capitole, BP 0801, 31080 Toulouse

HISTORY

URUGUAY 1930

The idea of a World Cup was considered as early as 1904 – the year FIFA was formed – but it was to be 26 years before it came to fruition. There didn't seem to be any real need for the tournament as in most countries football was played by amateurs and there was therefore no problem of eligibility for the Olympic tournament – the winners of which were regarded as world champions.

However, in the 1920s, some of the major powers in football, notably Czechoslovakia, Austria and Hungary, introduced professionalism to their national game and were unable to send their strongest teams to the Olympic competition. There were also growing doubts concerning the amateur status of some of the South American teams – all of which served to reduce the credibility of the Olympic tournament.

At FIFA's congress in Amsterdam in 1928 a motion was proposed by Jules Rimet, FIFA's president, that another world tournament should be held, also every four years, and open to any FIFA member. The motion was passed 25 votes to 5 and the Jules Rimet Trophy was commissioned.

Uruguay, Holland, Hungary, Italy, Spain and Sweden all put their names forward but the honour of hosting the inaugural tournament fell to Uruguay – they were the current Olympic champions, it was the centenary of their independence and, perhaps overgenerously, they had offered to pay all the visiting teams' travel and accommodation expenses. Besides, the other bidding countries had done their maths and, realising how much of a financial burden they would have to take on, had systematically withdrawn.

Thirteen countries made the trip to Montevideo. Europe was represented by a poor showing of just four teams – Romania, France, Belgium and Yugoslavia. None of these could have been described as footballing powers. Even those countries which had put their names forward as potential hosts decided not to enter.

However, at least some people got into the spirit of the occasion. Romania was not supposed to be sending a team but the young King Carol, a keen football fan, requested employers to give three months' leave to any employees picked for the team. They agreed, and King Carol selected the team himself.

France, although realising their team was not up to the standard of the South Americans, felt obliged to send a team since they had been instrumental in getting the World Cup tournament off the ground. Some wondered why Belgium and Yugoslavia bothered to make the long trip.

The worthy favourites were Uruguay and Argentina, who had dominated the South American Championship since the first official tournament in 1916, and were fancied to contest the final. They were the seeded countries in Pools 1 and 3 with Brazil and the USA heading the other pools.

On Sunday 13 July 1930, France faced Mexico in front of just 1,000 spectators in the very first World Cup match. The honour of scoring the first World Cup goal fell to Lucien Laurent and the French went on to win the game 4–1 despite playing most of the game with just ten men after their goalkeeper had been forced off following a kick in the head (substitutions were not introduced until 1970).

Misfortune followed the French into their second match against Argentina. Although they had fallen a goal behind in the 81st minute, the French were outplaying their more celebrated opponents and looking certain to equalise when the Brazilian referee blew for full-time, ending the match six minutes early. The spectators invaded the pitch and France protested. The remaining time was eventually played but France never got back into the game.

Right from the start of the World Cup the words 'Argentina' and 'controversy' have been indelibly linked. Following their victory over France they brought in Guillermo Stabile who kicked off with three goals in Argentina's 6–3 win over Mexico – a game in which the referee awarded five penalties. Even their final group game, against Chile, was not without incident as a foul by Luisito Monti turned into a brawl with the police called in to separate the players.

The United States were the surprise team of the competition. They had been beaten 11–2 by Argentina in the 1928 Olympics but since then many British professionals had emigrated to the States and were now members of the national side. They were probably past their best in footballing terms as some of them were rather overweight – a detail the French were quick to pick up on, nicknaming them the shot-putters. Despite this, the so-called has-beens boasted considerable stamina and enthusiasm, and beat Belgium and Paraguay on the way to the semi-finals without conceding a goal.

Yugoslavia beat Brazil and Bolivia to reach the last four but it was only in Pool Three, containing Uruguay, Romania and Peru, that the crowds turned out in any number. Even so, in the group's opening game just 300 saw King Carol's Romania beat Peru 3–1 but when the home nation first took to the field in the newly completed Centenary Stadium over 70,000 saw their heroes nervously beat Peru 1–0. The deciding game of the group four days later was played before a crowd of 80,000 and this time Uruguay effectively finished the contest with four goals in the opening 35 minutes, to win 4–0.

The USA succumbed to Argentina in a bruising encounter in the first semi-final. The USA's centre half, Raphael Tracy, had his leg broken after only ten minutes and their goalkeeper suffered numerous injuries. One up at half-time, Argentina ran away with the second half, winning 6–1.

Uruguay also won their semi-final against Yugoslavia 6–1 so the final became a re-run of the 1928 Olympic final. Relations were strained between the host nation and Argentina. It didn't help when Argentine supporters, who arrived in boats across the River Plate, were searched for weapons at the docks and before entering the ground. In a close match, the Argentinians had the better of the first half, leading 2–1 at the interval. But with the majority of the

93,000 crowd cheering for the home side, Uruguay breached the Argentine defence four times to take the title 4–2 – their final goal being scored in the closing minute by Castro, a centre-forward who had the lower half of one arm missing.

Montevideo erupted into celebration – their team's win being the crowning glory in such a significant year in their country's history.

RESULTS

Pool One
France 4 Mexico 1; Argentina 1 France 0; Chile 3 Mexico 0; Chile 1 France 0; Argentina 6 Mexico 3; Argentina 3 Chile 1

Final table	P	W	D	L	F	A	Pts
Argentina	3	3	0	0	10	4	6
Chile	3	2	0	1	5	3	4
France	3	1	0	2	4	3	2
Mexico	3	0	0	3	4	13	0

Pool Two
Yugoslavia 2 Brazil 1; Yugoslavia 4 Bolivia 0; Brazil 4 Bolivia 0

Final table	P	W	D	L	F	A	Pts
Yugoslavia	2	2	0	0	6	1	4
Brazil	2	1	0	1	5	2	2
Bolivia	2	0	0	2	0	8	0

Pool Three
Romania 3 Peru 1; Uruguay 1 Peru 0; Uruguay 4 Romania 0

Final table	P	W	D	L	F	A	Pts
Uruguay	2	2	0	0	5	0	4
Romania	2	1	0	1	3	5	2
Peru	2	0	0	2	1	4	0

Pool Four

USA 3 Belgium 0; USA 3 Paraguay 0; Paraguay 1 Belgium 0

Final table	P	W	D	L	F	A	Pts
USA	2	2	0	0	6	0	4
Paraguay	2	1	0	1	1	3	2
Belgium	2	0	0	2	0	4	0

Semi-finals

Argentina 6 USA 1; Uruguay 6 Yugoslavia 1

Final

Uruguay (1) 4	Argentina (2) 2;
Dorado	Peucelle
Cea	Stabile
Iriarte	
Castro	

Top goalscorers: 8 Stabile (Argentina); 5 Cea (Uruguay); 4 Subiabre (Chile), Preguinho (Brazil); 3 Anselmo (Uruguay), Beck (Yugoslavia), Patenaude (United States), Peucelle (Argentina).

Fastest goal: 1 minute, Desu (Romania v Peru).

Most goals scored: 18 (Argentina).

Total goals scored: 70 (average 3.88 per game).

Total attendance: 434,500 (average 24,139 per game).

Final attendance: 93,000.

ITALY 1934

It took several lengthy meetings before FIFA confirmed Italy as the host venue for the 1934 tournament. It was a strange choice of venue as Italy was under the dictatorial control of Mussolini, who viewed the competition as a great propaganda opportunity. However, government backing ensured that it would be a well-funded and well-organised event and this probably swung the decision Italy's way.

For the first and only time in the history of the competition the holders did not defend their title. Uruguay stayed at home, upset that so few European teams had agreed to compete in their tournament four years earlier.

The second World Cup established the number of finalists at 16, which was considered sufficient until 1982. As the number of entrants had risen to 32, qualifying rounds were needed to reduce the number of teams to 16 for the final tournament which was to be played on a purely knock-out basis. Even the host nation, Italy, had to qualify, which they did comfortably. They were installed as one of the eight seeded nations – a system devised to prevent the strongest nations meeting in the first round.

The Republic of Ireland were the only British representatives but were eliminated in the qualifying rounds by virtue of losing 5–2 to Holland. They had previously drawn 4–4 with Belgium. But it was Belgium who qualified as they had only lost 4–2 to the Dutch.

The United States were late entrants and missed the qualifying round but FIFA decided that they should play Mexico, the winners of Group One, in Rome. Hence both teams had to make the long trip fully aware that they might be eliminated after only one game. This unhappy fate fell to Mexico.

On 27 May 1934, Italy got the competition underway in the magnificent Rome Stadium with an impressive 7–1 victory over the United States.

After dominating the first World Cup, the South American contingent this time failed to get past the first round. Brazil lost to Spain while Argentina couldn't match the industry of the Swedes. To be fair, Argentina fielded a much weakened team as they had lost many of their finest players to the Italian league and had decided to keep their star players at home. The South Americans could feel justifiably aggrieved as Guaita, Orsi, and Monti (who had played in the 1930 final) now turned out for Italy.

Egypt became the first African nation to compete in the World Cup and were far from disgraced in defeat by Hungary – one of Europe's strongest teams.

Of the remaining teams, Germany were uninspiring in their victory over Belgium, Czechoslovakia struggled against Romania and even the powerful Austrians, nicknamed the 'Wunderteam' and one of the favourites, were fortunate to beat the French.

In the second round, Italy were drawn to play Spain. In a bruising encounter Regueiro put the Spanish into the lead but shortly after half-time Ferrari equalised for Italy, much to the delight and relief of the home supporters. The score remained level after extra-time and both teams had to make dramatic changes as a result of injuries for the replay the following day. Despite fielding a depleted team, Spain did well to limit Italy to one goal, scored by Meazza in the 12th minute, and were unlucky to have two goals disallowed in controversial circumstances.

Czechoslovakia and Switzerland were involved in one of the games of the finals – the Czechs swinging the game 3–2 – while Germany beat Sweden 2–1 in the other tie.

Austria defeated old rivals Hungary in a game their manager Hugo Meisl described as 'a brawl not a football match', which set up a semi-final against Italy – a meeting many people had hoped would be the final. In a game played on a heavy pitch, Italy were thankful for Guaita, one of their three Argentinian players, when he scored the decisive goal in the first half. The Italian manager, Vittorio Pozzo, had moulded a great side but he still felt the need to field the three Argentinians. He did point out that all three had Italian fathers and said: 'if they can die for Italy, they can play football for Italy'.

Austria failed to have a shot on target for most of the first half but applied sustained pressure after the interval, only to be thwarted by the Italian goalkeeper, Combi. The home crowd, which included Mussolini, were delighted.

For the other semi-final, in front of only 10,000 spectators, Czechoslovakia, with three goals from Nejedly, outplayed a well-organised but uninspired German side to book their place in the final. Three days before the final Germany beat a clearly tired Austrian team in the third-place play-off – a match which has always been considered dubious. The Italian public shared that view as only 7,000 turned out to watch.

And so to an intriguing final. The Italians had proved they were a strong, powerful team but the stylish Czechs were looking capable of producing an upset. Despite both sides showing a positive approach to the game, it was 70 minutes before the Czechs took the lead through Puc, who had only just returned to the field after suffering from cramp. Czechoslovakia had two more golden opportunities to make the game safe but with only eight minutes remaining Italy scored a spectacular equaliser. Orsi received the ball from his fellow Argentinian, Guaita, ran through the Czech defence and struck a swerving shot past the goalkeeper's desperate dive into the net, taking the final into extra-time. (Next day, Orsi tried to repeat the shot for photographers but failed.)

The teams had been evenly matched but the stamina of the Italians now held them in good stead. The Czech defence neglected to mark Meazza, who was limping through injury, but he played a telling ball to Guaita who, in turn, found Schiavio. With a final effort Schiavio beat a defender and then the goalkeeper for what proved to be the winning goal.

Italy were world champions and their captain, goalkeeper Combi, received the trophy from Mussolini who hailed it as a victory for Fascism. Even though the tournament had been used as a political tool, the number of participants and interest in the competition had been considerable. The Italian team had also set new standards of teamwork and professionalism.

RESULTS

First round
Italy 7 USA 1; Czechoslovakia 2 Romania 1; Germany 5 Belgium 2; Austria 3 France 2 (aet); Spain 3 Brazil 1; Switzerland 3 Holland 2; Sweden 3 Argentina 2; Hungary 4 Egypt 2

Second round

Germany 2 Sweden 1; Austria 2 Hungary 1; Italy 1 Spain 1 (aet);
Italy 1 Spain 0 (replay); Czechoslovakia 3 Switzerland 2

Semi-finals

Italy 1 Austria 0; Czechoslovakia 3 Germany 1

Third-place play-off

Germany 3 Austria 2

Final

Italy (0) 2   Czechoslovakia (0) 1 (aet)
Orsi   Puc
Schiavio

Top goalscorers: 5 Nejedly (Czechoslovakia); 4 Conen (Germany),
Schiavio (Italy); 3 Kielholz (Switzerland), Orsi (Italy).
Fastest goal: 30 seconds, Lehner (Germany v Austria).
Most goals scored: 12 (Italy).
Total goals scored: 70 (average 4.12 per game).
Total attendance: 395,000 (average 23,235 per game).
Final attendance: 55,000.

FRANCE 1938

Only two years after Hitler had used the Berlin Olympics as a political statement and with Europe in turmoil and on the brink of war, FIFA were left with a difficult choice of host country for the third World Cup.

The decision went to France, a popular choice as it was the home country of Jules Rimet whose dream it had been to stage a World Cup tournament. As a result, Argentina refused to take part, upset at not being selected as hosts. The South Americans did have a point as they had believed that the venue for the finals would alternate between Europe and South America. It would be another 20 years before they entered a team again.

It was a traumatic time in Europe. Spain was forced to withdraw on account of the civil war and the Austrians, their country having been taken over by the Nazis in the *Anschluss*, found themselves unable to compete. Germany took advantage by recruiting some of Austria's best players. Only three non-European teams entered – Brazil, Cuba and the Dutch East Indies (now Indonesia) – and despite pleas by FIFA, the British quartet still refused to enter.

This was the first tournament that both holders and hosts were exempt from the qualifying competition but, as in 1934, the finals were played as a straight knock-out competition.

In the opening round of matches Switzerland refused to give the Nazi salute during the national anthem and defeated Germany in a replay while Cuba, making their first and, to date, only World Cup appearance, beat the shocked Romanians 2–1, also in a replay.

Czechoslovakia, with some of the same players who had finished runners-up to Italy in 1934, were one of the fancied sides but made heavy weather of beating Holland – it was not until extra-time that they exerted their superiority. Even the world and Olympic champions, Italy, found their opening game against Norway tough going and left it until the 83rd minute before Brustad equalised. The game went into extra-time and Italy were relieved to see Piola snatch the winner.

France, the home nation, safely negotiated Belgium. The strong Hungarian team, who had beaten Greece 11–1 in the qualifying tournament, netted six against the Dutch East Indies.

However, the most remarkable match of the tournament was the game between Brazil, the sole South American team, and Poland. In a pulsating match, Brazil took control in the first half to lead 3–1 with Leonidas scoring all three of Brazil's goals. After the interval, Poland hit back to level the scores at 3–3; Brazil regained the lead but with only two minutes remaining Willimowski completed his hat-trick for Poland to make the score 4–4. In extra time, Leonidas scored his fourth and Romeo extended Brazil's lead to make it 6–4. Willimowski also scored his fourth but it was too late and Brazil went into the second round.

After such an entertaining and good-natured game, it was sad that Brazil's next, against Czechoslovakia, should turn into such a disgraceful and bad-tempered affair. Three players were sent off and two Czech players suffered broken limbs. Leonidas (who else) scored for Brazil but Nejedly equalised from the penalty spot. Despite losing Nejedly with a broken leg and with goalkeeper Planicka playing with a broken arm, the Czechs held out to force a replay.

Both teams made sweeping changes for the replay which was as docile as the first had been violent. Leonidas equalised for Brazil after Kopecky had given the Czechs the lead, and Roberto volleyed the South American's winner only one minute from time.

Italy met their French hosts in Paris and although the teams were well-matched, France having held the world champions to a goalless draw only seven months before, it was Italy's goalscoring sensation Piola who took control in the second half, scoring two goals. Meanwhile, the Swedes annihilated Cuba and Hungary eased past Switzerland and into the semi-finals.

Brazil's Leonidas and Italy's Piola, two of the game's most prolific goalscorers, were set to meet in the semi-final but, in a curious decision, Brazil's coach, Pimenta, left Leonidas out of the side, claiming he was saving him for the final. This self-assurance proved to be Brazil's undoing as first Colaussi and then Meazza from the penalty spot scored for Italy. Peracio, the replacement for Leonidas, missed two chances for Brazil and Romeo's 87th minute goal came too late for the South Americans.

Hungary had looked an impressive side from the start of the tournament but Sweden were hoping that the fact that the game was being played on the 80th birthday of their monarch King

Gustav V might prove a lucky omen for their semi-final.

Sweden scored within the first minute but this did nothing to deter the Hungarians who had full control of the game by half-time. Zsengeller completed his hat-trick in the 5–1 victory and so dominant were Hungary that a bird apparently sat undisturbed on the pitch near their goal for much of the second half.

In the third-place play-off, Sweden again took an unexpected lead, this time against Brazil who had recalled Leonidas to the team. They went two goals ahead before Romeo pulled one back for Brazil just before half-time. In the second half, Leonidas burst into life, scoring two goals in a 4–2 win which made many people wonder whether the result against Italy might have been reversed if Leonidas, the tournament's top scorer, had been on the field.

So, Italy had reached their second successive final and the crowd was eager to see how they would cope against the Hungarians who had scored 13 goals in only three matches with a classical passing game.

The crowd did not have to wait long. Only six minutes into the game Colaussi scored for the Italians following a fantastic run by Biavati. But Titkos equalised minutes later. Piola then restored Italy's lead and Colaussi extended it before half-time. With 20 minutes remaining Sarosi reduced the deficit to just one goal but eight minutes from time Piola scored a fourth for Italy as Hungary were forced into attack.

No one could deny that Italy were worthy winners. Their manager, Vittorio Pozzo, had thus disproved those sceptics who had suggested Italy could only have won on home soil. To take two different World Cup teams to victory was a great achievement.

After the World Cup the Italian team were received by Mussolini – who followed all the games – in the Palazzo Venezia in Rome where he gave them all medals, not gold in those days but bronze.

The Second World War started just over 12 months later and it would be 12 long years before the next tournament would take place.

RESULTS

Round one
Germany 1 Switzerland 1 (aet); Switzerland 4 Germany 2 (replay);
Cuba 3 Romania 3 (aet); Cuba 2 Romania 1 (replay);
Czechoslovakia 3 Holland 0 (aet); France 3 Belgium 1; Hungary 6
Dutch East Indies 0; Italy 2 Norway 1 (aet); Brazil 6 Poland 5 (aet)

Round two
Italy 3 France 1; Sweden 8 Cuba 0; Hungary 2 Switzerland 0;
Brazil 1 Czechoslovakia 1 (aet); Brazil 2 Czechoslovakia 1 (replay)

Semi-finals
Italy 2 Brazil 1; Hungary 5 Sweden 1

Third-place play-off
Brazil 4 Sweden 2

Final
Italy (3) 4	Hungary (1) 2
Coloussi (2)	Titkos
Piola (2)	Sarosi

Top goalscorers: 8 Leonidas (Brazil); 7 Zsengeller (Hungary); 5 Piola
(Italy); 4 Coloussi (Italy), Sarosi (Hungary), Wetterstrom (Sweden),
Willimowski (Poland).
Fastest goal: 35 seconds, Nyberg (Sweden v Hungary).
Most goals scored: 15 (Hungary).
Total goals scored: 84 (average 4.67 per game).
Total attendance: 483,000 (average of 26,833 per game).
Final attendance: 55,000.

BRAZIL 1950

With Europe still in disarray after the war, FIFA took the decision to stage the fourth World Cup tournament in South America. The choice of Brazil, with its fanatical support and enthusiasm for the game, was a popular one.

However, qualification for the finals proved farcical and was plagued by withdrawals. From a total of 73 FIFA members, 33 teams, including the holders Italy and hosts Brazil, entered the tournament.

The British associations had returned to FIFA in 1946 and the World Cup Committee generously designated the British Championship a qualifying group for two teams. However, although Scotland were guaranteed a place as they had come second in the group, they decided that as they had not finished top they would not enter.

There were other surprising absentees. Argentina withdrew because of 'differences' with the Brazilian FA, Germany was excluded from FIFA as a result of the war and Austria felt their team was not yet strong enough. Ecuador, Peru and Belgium also withdrew.

The decision was made to play the tournament in pools rather than the previous system of straight knock-out. Each group winner then would go through to a final pool, also played on a league basis.

The 15 qualifying teams were divided into four groups but India subsequently pulled out and France, themselves a replacement, felt that the travelling would be too arduous and also decided not to go. It was too late for FIFA to make another draw so the tournament got under way with uneven groups. This left Uruguay with only Bolivia in their group although it seems extraordinary now that a team from one of the two pools with four teams could not have been moved into their pool.

For some obscure reason, the pool matches were not played at a single venue and some teams were obliged to travel huge distances to play their games. Brazil, however, played all but one of their games in Rio.

The competition got under way at the unfinished but impressive Maracana Stadium. Brazil took to the field accompanied by a 21-

gun salute and an ecstatic crowd saw them beat Mexico 4–0 with two goals by the brilliant Ademir. However, a nervous draw against the Swiss meant that Brazil had to beat Yugoslavia to progress to the final stage. Although Ademir scored early on it was not until just after the hour that Zizinho scored Brazil's deciding second – much to the relief of a fanatical crowd of 142,000.

The second pool provided one of the biggest surprises in World Cup history. Both Spain and England had started with victories over the USA and Chile respectively and the much-fancied English now travelled to face the United States, who admittedly had been only ten minutes away from beating Spain. Even the most star-spangled American supporter could not have predicted what was to happen. As expected, England spent most of the first half attacking but excellent goalkeeping by Borghi and the resilience of the defence kept the USA in the game – despite hitting the post and crossbar England could not find the decisive breakthrough. But it just seemed a matter of time.

Then eight minutes from half time Gaetjens, an American-Haitian who was later to disappear, presumed murdered, in Haiti, scored the only goal of the game with a header, bringing about the biggest upset in World Cup history. England continued the onslaught but failed to convert any of their chances.

Harry Keough, an American defender, later recalled his vivid memories of the incident. 'Walter Bahr, our star player, took a shot at the England goal from 25 to 30 yards out. He hit the ball well but I expected the goalkeeper to stop it. It was then that Gaetjens lunged at the ball and I thought, gee, what's Joe trying to do? He didn't make full contact and he just singed it with his head. Once it touched Joe's head, nobody saw it until it was in the goal. We were just a bunch of amateurs playing against a bunch of professionals and nobody in our team had the wildest hope that we would beat England.'

It was such an unlikely result that some British newspapers assumed a mistake had been made and printed the score as 10–1. For America, it was their greatest result – particularly as unlike 1930 their team was composed primarily of American-born players.

England then had to beat Spain and gave a much improved performance. England's Milburn had what appeared a good goal disallowed for offside but it was the Spanish who snatched a 49th minute winner to take them through to the final pool.

The holders, Italy, competed even though they had suffered a tragic blow when an aeroplane carrying the brilliant Torino team crashed into the wall of the Superga Basilica on a hillside near Turin in 1949. Every Torino player was killed; eight of the team played for the national team.

The Italian squad travelled by boat to Brazil and although the long journey would have had a detrimental effect on the players, everything appeared to be going well when they opened the scoring against a strong Swedish side. However, three goals stunned the Italians and although they pulled the score back to 3–2 the equaliser remained elusive. It was their first World Cup defeat.

Sweden drew with Paraguay and although Italy beat Paraguay 2–0, it was to no avail. Sweden were through to join Spain, Brazil and Uruguay, who had enjoyed the easiest qualification, beating Bolivia 8–0 to reach the last four. There was to be no final in this competition – the four semi-finalists playing each other in a final pool.

Brazil trounced the Swedes 7–1 in their first final pool game and put another six past Spain. They were turning on an exhibition of irresistible footballing skills with the trio of Ademir, Jair and Zizinho proving themselves players of genius.

Whilst Brazil were in such splendid form, Uruguay, the only team thought to pose a serious challenge to the hosts, were surprisingly held in a bad-tempered draw against Spain. Indeed, in their next match against Sweden, Uruguay had to come from a goal down and only scored the winner with five minutes remaining. But they were now the only team capable of taking the Jules Rimet Trophy off Brazil. The scene was set and although there had been no provision for a final as such, the Brazil v Uruguay match was to be a final in all but name.

And what a match it turned out to be. A record crowd of nearly 200,000 gathered in the Maracana Stadium to see the game with everyone confident of a Brazilian victory – perhaps too confident. Needing only a draw to win the trophy they relied on attack as the best form of defence and the first half saw the Brazilians moving forward with their now familiar flair. But they were up against sturdy and tactically aware opponents and for all their superiority the Brazilians were playing a team well-versed in soaking up pressure.

Time and again a timely interception or acrobatic save by Maspoli, the Uruguayan goalkeeper, thwarted the Brazilian attack and the game remained delicately balanced at half-time. Two minutes into the second half and the vast crowd erupted as Friaca closed in from the wing, shot and scored for Brazil. But having survived for so long, Uruguay had made their point and were not demoralised. They responded by attacking and the talented Schiaffino equalised with a powerful drive.

The Brazilians continued to press forward when they could have fallen back into defence, but about ten minutes from the end the unthinkable happened as Ghiggia put Uruguay ahead with a great individual effort. Uruguay held out until the referee blew the final whistle, confirming an impossible victory. After 20 years, Uruguay were once again world champions and the highly talented Brazilians would have to wait their turn.

RESULTS

Pool One
Brazil 4 Mexico 0; Yugoslavia 3 Switzerland 0; Brazil 2 Switzerland 2; Yugoslavia 4 Mexico 1; Brazil 2 Yugoslavia 0; Switzerland 2 Mexico 1

Final table	P	W	D	L	F	A	Pts
Brazil	3	2	1	0	8	2	5
Yugoslavia	3	2	0	1	7	3	4
Switzerland	3	1	1	1	4	6	3
Mexico	3	0	0	3	2	10	0

Pool Two
Spain 3 USA 1; England 2 Chile 0; USA 1 England 0; Spain 2 Chile 0; Spain 1 England 0; Chile 5 USA 2

Final table	P	W	D	L	F	A	Pts
Spain	3	3	0	0	6	1	6
England	3	1	0	2	2	2	2
Chile	3	1	0	2	5	6	2
USA	3	1	0	2	4	8	2

Pool Three

Sweden 3 Italy 2; Sweden 2 Paraguay 2; Italy 2 Paraguay 0

Final table	P	W	D	L	F	A	Pts
Sweden	2	1	1	0	5	4	3
Italy	2	1	0	1	4	3	2
Paraguay	2	0	1	1	2	4	1

Pool Four

Uruguay 8 Bolivia 0

Final table	P	W	D	L	F	A	Pts
Uruguay	1	1	0	0	8	0	2
Bolivia	1	0	0	1	0	8	0

Final pool matches

Brazil 7 Sweden 1; Spain 2 Uruguay 2; Brazil 6 Spain 1; Uruguay 3 Sweden 2; Sweden 3 Spain 1; Uruguay 2 Brazil 1

Final table	P	W	D	L	F	A	Pts
Uruguay	3	2	1	0	7	5	5
Brazil	3	2	0	1	14	4	4
Sweden	3	1	0	2	6	11	2
Spain	3	0	1	2	4	11	1

Top goalscorers: 9 Ademir (Brazil) 5 Basora (Spain), Schiaffino (Uruguay); 4 Chico (Brazil), Ghiggia (Uruguay), Miguez (Spain), Zarra (Spain); 3 Cremaschi (Chile), Palmer, Sundqvist (Sweden), Tomasevic (Yugoslavia).
Fastest goal: 2 minutes, Santos (Brazil v Sweden).
Most goals scored: 22 (Brazil).
Total goals scored: 88 (average 4 per game).
Total attendance: 1,337,000 (average 60,772 per game).
Final attendance: 199,854.

SWITZERLAND 1954

The World Cup in Switzerland produced some of the finest attacking football in the tournament's history. It was no surprise that Hungary, the 1952 Olympic champions, were favourites as for the past few years they had been, quite simply, unbeatable. They were the finest attacking team seen up to then – and possibly even to this day – based on a deep-lying centre forward, Nandor Hidegkuti, who controlled much of the build-up and could make and score goals, a tenacious midfield dynamo, Josef Bozsik, and two great strikers, Ferenc Puskas and Sandor Kocsis.

Such was the skill of the Hungarian team, that, in 1953, they became the first side to beat England at Wembley and by a sensational 6–3 margin. England fared no better in the return match in Budapest, losing 7–1.

Football's governing body devised a new eliminating scheme for the finals, reverting to a pool system followed by knock-out. The 16 participants were divided into four groups with two teams in each group seeded to keep the supposedly stronger teams apart in the early stages. However, the seeded teams in each group did not play each other. At the end of the pool matches, the four group winners were to play each other on a knock-out basis as were the four runners-up. To complete a complicated system, it was decided that in the pool matches, extra-time would be played if the scores were level after 90 minutes.

West Germany returned as did the Eastern European bloc with the exception of the Soviet Union and Poland. Argentina continued their boycott of the finals.

In Pool One, there was a shock on the opening day when Yugoslavia beat seeded France 1–0 with a goal from Milos Milutinovic. Although they were somewhat underrated, the Yugoslav team was an impressive blend of youth and experience and their match against Brazil, who had easily beaten Mexico in their opening game, was a very even game. A draw was sufficient for both to progress and that's how it ended.

In Pool Two, the Hungarians served notice by routing South Korea 9–0 and West Germany 8–3. Sepp Herberger, the German manager, took a big gamble for the game against Hungary. He knew that if his team lost they would have to play off against either Turkey or Korea to qualify for the second phase. He also realised that the winners of the group would meet Brazil – a daunting prospect. Confident of beating Turkey or South Korea, he completely changed his team for the game against Hungary.

Despite the onslaught of goals the plan worked, as Germany, back to full strength, next beat Turkey 7–2 to set up a quarter-final clash with Yugoslavia. Perhaps the most important aspect of the game against Hungary was the injury to the Hungarian captain, Puskas, who was to miss the next two games and struggle to regain fitness for the final.

In Pool Three, Uruguay, still inspired by Schiaffino, ended Scotland's first World Cup venture with a 7–0 annihilation and qualified to meet England in the quarter-finals. This proved to be a tight and eventful game with Matthews and Wright shining for England and Schiaffino and Varela outstanding for the South Americans. Both teams created a lot of good scoring chances but Uruguay's superior all-round qualities, coupled with a series of bad errors from the English goalkeeper, swung the game in their favour.

The host nation, Switzerland, had made a successful start against Italy in the opening round but a subsequent defeat by England meant that they had to play Italy again in a decider. A second victory took them through to face Austria and a 12-goal bonanza ensued. Roared on by the home crowd, the Swiss scored three times in the first 20 minutes only for Austria to score five in the next ten minutes. At half-time the score was an amazing 5–4 to Austria who increased their lead to two goals shortly after the restart. Not to be outdone, Switzerland came back again but could find no answer to Austria's seventh. The 12-goal extravaganza established a World Cup record.

Having avoided Brazil, Sepp Herberger's West Germany now faced a useful Yugoslavian team. West Germany took an early lead, withstood everything their opponents could throw at them and sealed victory with a second goal, against the run of play, shortly before the end.

The fourth quarter-final between Brazil and Hungary, pitching two great footballing sides against each other, promised to be the game of the tournament. The match, since referred to as the Battle of Berne, witnessed some dreadful tackles and niggling fouls and the only person to emerge with any credit was referee Arthur Ellis – he of *It's A Knockout* fame – who sent three players off.

Even without Puskas, Hungary started briskly and were two goals up inside the first ten minutes, seemingly well on their way to the semi-finals. But Brazil started to find their form and a first-half penalty reduced the deficit to 2–1. The second half started with more bad fouls and dangerous tackling as tempers frayed. Hungary were themselves awarded a penalty from which Lantos scored but then Julinho struck a marvellous goal for Brazil. Soon after, Bozsik and Nilton Santos came to blows after another dangerous challenge and both were sent off.

Brazil were desperately chasing an equaliser and came close to levelling the match several times. However, pushing forward left them exposed in defence and in the last minute Kocsis scored Hungary's fourth to put the result beyond doubt. Humberto was also sent off for Brazil but the fighting continued even after the game had finished with the teams scuffling in the dressing rooms.

After this disgraceful episode, the semi-final between Hungary and Uruguay turned out to be one of the greatest matches seen – even though both teams were without influential players, Puskas and Varela respectively.

Hungary led 1–0 at the interval and extended their lead early in the second half. Uruguay looked on their way out but they had never been beaten in a World Cup match and once again they mounted a determined comeback. With 15 minutes to go, Schiffiano put Hohberg through to score and, with only three minutes remaining, they combined again to level the score and force the game into extra-time. It nearly began without Hohberg who had been knocked out during the celebrations by his teammates. He recovered in time to drive a shot against the Hungarian post but it was not to be a fairy-tale ending for Uruguay. Their midfield inspiration, Andrade, was hurt in a tackle and while he was still having treatment off the field Kocsis headed Hungary back into the lead. There was no coming back from that and Kocsis rose majestically again to score another superb header.

Most people expected Austria to join Hungary in the final but the Germans were now a very effective team. Austria recalled Walter Zeman – a goalkeeper previously left out because of poor form. Unfortunately for Zeman, it was not a happy return as he and his defence struggled to combat the German attackers who swept into the final with a 6–1 victory.

Even though West Germany had proved themselves shrewd and worthy finalists, victory was surely a formality for Hungary, particularly once Puskas and Czibor had given them a 2–0 lead by the eighth minute of play. But then the Germans showed those battling, never-say-die qualities which have since become a World Cup tradition. Morlock and Rahn quickly levelled the scores and five minutes from the end, Rahn put West Germany in front. A reply by Puskas, who was still struggling from injury, was controversially disallowed for offside and West Germany had pulled off an amazing comeback to become world champions. For the second successive tournament the favourites had been beaten.

RESULTS

Pool One

Yugoslavia 1 France 0; Brazil 5 Mexico 0; France 3 Mexico 2; Brazil 1 Yugoslavia 1

Final table	P	W	D	L	F	A	Pts
Brazil	2	1	1	0	6	1	3
Yugoslavia	2	1	1	0	2	1	3
France	2	1	0	1	3	3	2
Mexico	2	0	0	2	2	8	0

Pool Two

Hungary 9 South Korea 0; West Germany 4 Turkey 1; Hungary 8 West Germany 3; Turkey 7 South Korea 0

Final table	P	W	D	L	F	A	Pts
Hungary	2	2	0	0	17	3	4
Turkey	2	1	0	1	8	4	2
W. Germany	2	1	0	1	7	9	2
South Korea	2	0	0	2	0	16	0

Play-off: West Germany 7 Turkey 2

Pool Three

Austria 1 Scotland 0; Uruguay 2 Czechoslovakia 0; Austria 5
Czechoslovakia 0; Uruguay 7 Scotland 0

Final table	P	W	D	L	F	A	Pts
Uruguay	2	2	0	0	9	0	4
Austria	2	2	0	0	6	0	4
Czechoslovakia	2	0	0	2	0	7	0
Scotland	2	0	0	2	0	8	0

Pool Four

England 4 Belgium 4; Switzerland 2 Italy 1; England 2
Switzerland 0; Italy 4 Belgium 1

Final table	P	W	D	L	F	A	Pts
England	2	1	1	0	6	4	3
Italy	2	1	0	1	5	3	2
Switzerland	2	1	0	1	2	3	2
Belgium	2	0	1	1	5	8	1

Play-off: Switzerland 4 Italy 1

Quarter-finals

Austria 7 Switzerland 5; Uruguay 4 England 2; Hungary 4 Brazil 2;
West Germany 2 Yugoslavia 0

Semi-finals

Hungary 4 Uruguay 2; West Germany 6 Austria 1

Third-place play-off

Austria 3 Uruguay 1

Final

West Germany (2) 3   Hungary (2) 2
Morlock   Puskas
Rahn (2)   Czibor

Top goalscorers: 11 Kocsis (Hungary); 6 Hugi (Switzerland), Morlock (West Germany); 5 Probst (Austria).
Fastest goal: 2 minutes, Suat (Turkey v West Germany).
Most goals scored: 27 (Hungary).
Total goals scored: 140 (average 5.38 per game).
Total attendance: 943, 000 (average of 36,270 per game).
Final attendance: 60,000.

SWEDEN 1958

For the first time in its history the World Cup received international television coverage. It will be remembered as one of the friendliest tournaments and although a number of players shone, this competition was highlighted by the outstanding skills of the Brazilians and in particular the debut of a 17-year-old genius, Pelé. In the Brazilian team, the world witnessed a stunning brand of football which was to become very familiar over the next decade.

The hosts, Sweden, were coached by an Englishman, George Raynor, who astounded everyone by confidently predicting, long before the tournament began, that his team would reach the final. Few took him seriously, and even the Swedish public displayed little patriotism.

In their opening game, Sweden made light work of Mexico, disposing of them 3–0 before beating the once mighty Hungary 2–1. After a convincing victory over the Soviet Union in the quarter-finals the Swedish fans started to believe in their team. Initially sceptical, this traditionally dispassionate nation reached levels of patriotic euphoria when Sweden beat an unsettled West Germany, the 1954 champions, 3–1. George Raynor's prediction had been spot on.

Argentina had qualified for the finals after a 24-year absence and were one of the favourites as they had won the South American Championship the year before. However, they were continuing to lose many of their best players to Italian football and consequently were a much ravaged side by the time they reached the finals. One win and two losses, including a crushing defeat by Czechoslovakia, resulted in them catching the first plane back home where they were greeted with garbage and stones by disappointed fans.

Two of the remaining South American teams, Paraguay and Mexico, also returned home after the first round of games – leaving Brazil as the sole representative from South America.

This was the only time all four British associations have been represented in the finals. Neither of the two more fancied teams, England and Scotland, survived the opening round. England had sadly lost three of its most influential players – Duncan Edwards,

Roger Byrne and Tommy Taylor – in the Munich air crash only a few months earlier but still fielded a side good enough to hold the mighty Brazilians to a goalless draw. Surprisingly, this was the first such scoreline in the history of the competition.

Northern Ireland, who had qualified ahead of Italy, enjoyed an excellent first round. They beat the Czechs 1–0, lost to Argentina and drew with West Germany – against whom they had been just ten minutes away from a famous victory.

In the play-offs for the group qualifying games, Wales, a surprising but deserving qualifier, did well to overcome the Hungarians 2–1 while Northern Ireland beat Czechoslovakia by the same margin. However, hopes of having three British countries in the quarter-finals were dashed when England were beaten by the Soviet Union (competing for the first time) in a play-off – the superb goalkeeping of Lev Yashin thwarting England's best efforts.

Wales gave probably their finest performance against Brazil. Their well-disciplined defence held the likes of Garrincha, Pelé and Didi until the 73rd minute when a goal by Pelé, his first in the World Cup, sealed victory for the South Americans.

France ended Northern Ireland's hopes in the quarter-finals with the prolific Juste Fontaine adding two more goals to the six he had scored in the opening round. Yugoslavia, runners-up behind France in their group, faced their old nemesis West Germany in the quarter-finals and again lost out.

In the first semi-final, Sweden faced the holders, West Germany. Schafer gave the Germans the lead midway through the first half but with the crowd finally getting behind the home team Sweden pressed forward and equalised after 30 minutes. Angry scenes developed when the German defender Juskowiak was sent off after nearly an hour but Sweden exploited their numerical advantage and nine minutes from time Gren put them in front. Hamrin still had time to make it 3–1 and the crowd went wild with excitement – well, as wild as a Swedish crowd can go.

In the other semi-final, favourites Brazil faced France. The French had so far delighted the crowds with the outstanding goalscoring achievements of Fontaine who finished top scorer with a record 13 goals.

Brazil's supremacy was undisputed. They had arrived with a fresh, exciting team and new stars Garrincha, Vava and Pelé joined the great Santos and Didi. Vava joined the team for Brazil's second game with Garrincha (who had been born with a deformed leg) and Pelé was selected for the third. But it was in the semi-final that Pelé came into his own. On the way to a 5–2 victory he scored a hat-trick in the space of just over 20 minutes – the last of which was a perfect volley from just outside the penalty area.

In the final, Brazil met the determined Swedes in front of a 50,000 crowd. George Raynor predicted that an early Swedish goal would throw Brazil into panic but after Liedholm had indeed put the Swedes into a fourth-minute lead Raynor's predictive powers were proved wrong. Within six minutes, Vava equalised and Brazil turned on the samba magic. Vava scored a second and then, ten minutes into the second half, Pelé controlled a difficult ball, flicked it over a defender's head and then volleyed it into the net. The Swedes went further behind before pulling a goal back but it was only a matter of time before Zagalo (who was to manage Brazil in 1970 and 1998) found the net again, to make the final score 5–2.

Orvar Bergmark, the Swedish right-back who went on to coach the national team later recalled that there was a general feeling of complacency in the Swedish team. He felt that for most it was good enough that they should have reached the final. Amazingly, they had not even seen the Brazilians play and only knew that they were very quick and technical. 'They were just an incredible team – maybe the best ever – with young Pelé and Garrincha making us look like fools,' was his forthright and honest assessment. 'Yes, we lost. But we had made it to the final which nobody had expected.'

The World Cup was Brazil's at last. They became the only country to win the tournament outside their own continent and, as if to sum up the great spirit of the competition, they did a lap of honour around the stadium carrying the Swedish flag.

RESULTS

Pool One
Northern Ireland 1 Czechoslovakia 0; West Germany 3 Argentina 1; Argentina 3 Northern Ireland 1; Czechoslovakia 2 West Germany 2; Northern Ireland 2 West Germany 2; Czechoslovakia 6 Argentina 1

Final table	P	W	D	L	F	A	Pts
West Germany	3	1	2	0	7	5	4
Czechoslovakia	3	1	1	1	8	4	3
Northern Ireland	3	1	1	1	4	5	3
Argentina	3	1	0	2	5	10	2

Play-off: Northern Ireland 2 Czechoslovakia 1

Pool Two

Scotland 1 Yugoslavia 1; France 7 Paraguay 3; Paraguay 3 Scotland 2;
Yugoslavia 3 France 2; France 2 Scotland 1; Paraguay 3 Yugoslavia 3

Final table	P	W	D	L	F	A	Pts
France	3	2	0	1	11	7	4
Yugoslavia	3	1	2	0	7	6	4
Paraguay	3	1	1	1	9	12	3
Scotland	3	0	1	2	4	6	1

Pool Three

Sweden 3 Mexico 0; Hungary 1 Wales 1; Mexico 1 Wales 1;
Sweden 2 Hungary 1; Sweden 0 Wales 0; Hungary 4 Mexico 0

Final table	P	W	D	L	F	A	Pts
Sweden	3	2	1	0	5	1	5
Hungary	3	1	1	1	6	3	3
Wales	3	0	3	0	2	2	3
Mexico	3	0	1	2	1	8	1

Play-off: Wales 2 Hungary 1

Pool Four

England 2 Soviet Union 2; Brazil 3 Austria 0; Soviet Union 2 Austria 0;
Brazil 0 England 0; Austria 2 England 2; Brazil 2 Soviet Union 0

Final table	P	W	D	L	F	A	Pts
Brazil	3	2	1	0	5	0	5
England	3	0	3	0	4	4	3
Soviet Union	3	1	1	1	4	4	3
Austria	3	0	1	2	2	7	1

Play-off: Soviet Union 1 England 0

Quarter-finals
France 4 Northern Ireland 0; West Germany 1 Yugoslavia 0;
Sweden 2 Soviet Union 0; Brazil 1 Wales 0

Semi-finals
Sweden 3 West Germany 1; Brazil 5 France 2

Third-place play-off
France 6 West Germany 3

Final
Brazil (2) 5	Sweden (1) 2
Vava (2)	Liedholm
Pelé (2)	Simonsson
Zagalo	

Top goalscorers: 13 Fontaine (France); 6 Pelé (Brazil), Rahn (West Germany); 5 McParland (Northern Ireland), Vava (Brazil).
Fastest goal: 90 seconds, Vava (Brazil v France).
Most goals scored: 23 (France).
Total goals scored: 126 (average 3.60 per game).
Total attendance: 868,000 (average of 24,800 per game).
Final attendance: 49,737.

CHILE 1962

It was remarkable that Chile should successfully host the 1962 tournament as earthquakes had devastated the country at the time FIFA were considering the various candidates. But a desperate plea from Carlos Dittborn, the Chilean FA president, saying: 'We must have the World Cup because we have nothing' seemed to do the trick and the Chileans quickly started work on a magnificent new stadium in Santiago. Sadly, Dittborn died a month before the tournament he had done so much to organise; it was thanks to him that Chile proved to be such worthy hosts.

The format of the finals was similar to 1958 with four groups of four countries each playing one another and the top two progressing to the second round.

Winners in 1958 and now playing on South American soil, Brazil were inevitably the favourites. The side had changed very little in the four intervening years but Pelé's tournament was to be cut cruelly short through injury. Amarildo proved a marvellous stand-in for the irreplaceable but these finals belonged to his teammate Garrincha whose dribbling skills, speed and accuracy were a thorn in the side of every opposing defence.

Brazil's strongest challengers were expected to be the Soviet Union who opened their campaign with a 2–0 win over Yugoslavia in Group One. This was the first of several violent games to mar the tournament yet both teams still managed to produce some skilful football.

The Soviets were then involved in an extraordinary game against newcomers Colombia. They raced into a 3–0 lead after just 11 minutes but the South Americans staged an exciting comeback to level the score 4–4. Soviet qualification to the next round was ensured with victory over Uruguay, who were no longer such a dominant force in world soccer.

The hosts got off to a dreadful start in Group Two, conceding a goal to Switzerland inside the opening ten minutes of their first game. The crowd had to wait until just before half-time before Chile equalised, eventually winning the game 3–1. Chile's next match, against Italy, was probably one of the darkest chapters in the history of the World Cup. Dubbed the Battle of Santiago it was reminiscent of the infamous Battle of Berne in 1954.

The root of the trouble was newspaper features written by Italian journalists criticising the organisation of the tournament and the squalor of Chile and Santiago in particular. From the start, the Italian players were booed by the crowd and spat at and fouled by the Chilean players. After only eight minutes Ferrini of Italy was sent off for retaliating after a bad tackle but for ten minutes he refused to leave the pitch. With both teams trading vicious fouls it was only a matter of time before the millions of viewers around the world witnessed more ugly scenes. After a bad tackle by the Italian Maschio on Sanchez, the Chilean responded by breaking the Italian's nose. Amazingly, neither player was sent off. The catalogue of disasters continued as David became the second Italian to be given his marching orders. Even reduced to nine men, Italy held out until 15 minutes before time when two late goals saw them effectively out of the finals.

Brazil and Czechoslovakia qualified comfortably from Group Three although it was in their game that Pelé sustained the muscle injury which ruled him out of the rest of the tournament. In the same group, Mexico finally broke their World Cup duck after 14 matches, against Czechoslovakia. Spain, such a dominant force in European club football, failed to emulate their domestic success and finished bottom of the group.

Brazil's quarter-final opponents were England who had qualified behind the Hungarians thanks chiefly to a 3–1 victory over Argentina. It was England's misfortune to be drawn against the favourites with Garrincha in such devastating form. Even so, the teams ended the first half all square at 1–1 but two goals in six minutes secured the game for Brazil in the second half. Garrincha, who had scored Brazil's first, provided the powerful shot which was blocked only for Vava to convert and Garrincha stitched up the game with his second.

The Soviet Union's progress was halted, surprisingly, by the hosts. Both goals in Chile's 2–1 victory were long-range shots and Lev Yashin, the Russian goalkeeper and one of the best in the world, if not of all time, would normally have saved both efforts comfortably. Not that this mattered to the jubilant Chileans who had progressed further than even they could possibly have hoped.

While Yashin was having a torrid time, Czechoslovakia's goalkeeper, Schroiff, was in brilliant form against the mighty

Hungarians. After going a goal down early in the first half, the Hungarians threw everything at the Czechs, inflicting serious damage to the woodwork. But the Czechs, the surprise team of the tournament, were well organised and remained solid in defence.

The fourth quarter-final pitched Yugoslavia against West Germany for the third time in succession at this stage. The Germans had won both previous encounters and with the game heading inexorably towards extra-time one felt that they would steal the tie in the dying seconds as is tradition. But the Yugoslavs had obviously not read the script and Radakovic, his head bandaged following a collision, scored from the edge of the penalty area with three minutes on the clock left.

Naturally, the most emotional of the semi-finals involved the hosts and holders. Chile had surprised many people by reaching the semi-finals but now they had to face Garrincha who took it upon himself to win the game. In the ninth minute he rifled in a fierce left-foot shot and added a second with a header. To their credit, Chile fought back and scored from a free-kick only for Vava to restore Brazil's two-goal advantage. Chilean hopes were again raised when Sanchez scored from the penalty spot but Brazil were not to be denied their second successive final as Vava once again headed in. In the final few minutes the game deteriorated and Garrincha was sent off for retaliating and kicking Rojas. He faced suspension from the final.

The semi-final game between Yugoslavia and Czechoslovakia attracted less than 6,000 people. The Czech goalkeeper, Schroiff, again made important saves, but the Czechs took their chances well to run out 3–1 winners.

After Chile had won the third-place play-off, world attention turned to the final. Needless to say, Brazil were the hot favourites but the Czechs were used to the underdog status by now. They were a fine athletic side inspired by the all-round excellence of Masopust.

After his dismissal in the semi-final, Garrincha could count himself lucky that FIFA only issued a warning and he was allowed to play in the final.

As in 1958, Brazil conceded the first goal, this time to the excellent Masopust who calmly scored in the 16th minute after receiving a long pass from Scherer. It took only two minutes for

Brazil to level the score with Amarildo beating the previously reliable Schroiff with a swerving shot from an acute angle. The Czechs were proving sturdy opposition for the favourites until the 68th minute when Amarildo crossed the ball for Zito to score with a powerful header and Schroiff's personal misery was compounded when he misjudged a high cross, lost control of the ball, and watched Vava tuck the ball into the net for the third.

Even without Pelé, Brazil could not be matched and were worthy winners.

RESULTS

Group One

Uruguay 2 Colombia 1; Soviet Union 2 Yugoslavia 0; Yugoslavia 3 Uruguay 1; Soviet Union 4 Colombia 4; Soviet Union 2 Uruguay 1; Yugoslavia 5 Colombia 0

Final table	P	W	D	L	F	A	Pts
Soviet Union	3	2	1	0	8	5	5
Yugoslavia	3	2	0	1	8	3	4
Uruguay	3	1	0	2	4	6	2
Colombia	3	0	1	2	5	11	1

Group Two

Chile 3 Switzerland 1; Italy 0 West Germany 0; Chile 2 Italy 0; West Germany 2 Switzerland 1; West Germany 2 Chile 0; Italy 3 Switzerland 0

Final table	P	W	D	L	F	A	Pts
West Germany	3	2	1	0	4	1	5
Chile	3	2	0	1	5	3	4
Italy	3	1	1	1	3	2	3
Switzerland	3	0	0	3	2	8	0

Group Three

Brazil 2 Mexico 0; Czechoslovakia 1 Spain 0; Brazil 0
Czechoslovakia 0; Spain 1 Mexico 0; Brazil 2 Spain 1; Mexico 3
Czechoslovakia 1

Final table	P	W	D	L	F	A	Pts
Brazil	3	2	1	0	4	1	5
Czechoslovakia	3	1	1	1	2	3	3
Mexico	3	1	0	2	3	4	2
Spain	3	1	0	2	2	3	2

Group Four

Argentina 1 Bulgaria 0; Hungary 2 England 1; England 3 Argentina 1;
Hungary 6 Bulgaria 1; Argentina 0 Hungary 0; Bulgaria 0 England 0

Final table	P	W	D	L	F	A	Pts
Hungary	3	2	1	0	8	2	5
England	3	1	1	1	4	3	3
Argentina	3	1	1	1	2	3	3
Bulgaria	3	0	1	2	1	7	1

Quarter-finals

Chile 2 Soviet Union 1; Yugoslavia 1 West Germany 0; Brazil 3
England 1; Czechoslovakia 1 Hungary 0

Semi-finals

Brazil 4 Chile 2; Czechoslovakia 3 Yugoslavia 1

Third-place play-off

Chile 1 Yugoslavia 0

Final

Brazil (1) 3   Czechoslovakia (1) 1
Amarildo   Masopust
Zito
Vava

Top goalscorers: 4 Albert (Hungary), Garrincha (Brazil), Ivanov (Soviet Union), Jerkovic (Yugoslavia), Sanchez (Chile), Vava (Brazil).
Fastest goal: 1 minute, Albert (Hungary v Bulgaria), Masek (Czechoslovakia v Mexico).
Most goals scored: 14 (Brazil).
Total goals scored: 89 (average of 2.78 per game).
Total attendance: 776,000 (average of 24,250 per game).
Final attendance: 68,679.

ENGLAND 1966

The 1966 World Cup was awarded to England and the tournament was to prove full of excitement and incident as well as lay claim to two superlatives – the most controversial goal and the biggest upset in World Cup history.

Yet despite meticulous organisation by the English Football Association the 1966 tournament got off to a farcical start – four months before a ball was kicked. On 20 March 1966 the Jules Rimet Trophy was stolen whilst on display at an exhibition at Westminster's Central Hall. Faced with the prospect of starting the tournament without a trophy, the FA called in Scotland Yard. But it was a black and white mongrel, Pickles, sniffing out the cup in a South London garden one week later, who saved the FA from further embarrassment.

In the early stages, the tournament was not distinguished by the overall quality of its football. In Group One, England, despite drawing a dull opening game against Uruguay, went on to beat Mexico and France to top their group without ever really showing what they could do.

West Germany safely negotiated a tough Group Two with the talented 20-year-old Franz Beckenbauer scoring two goals against Switzerland. Argentina filled the runners-up place with Spain, once again, failing to live up to their club promise.

Group Three was the best of the World Cup openers with Brazil, Hungary, Portugal and Bulgaria. Brazil had stayed faithful to their experienced players including Pelé who, at 25, was at the peak of his career. Having beaten Bulgaria 2–0, Brazil faced Hungary who had lost their opening game to the Portuguese. The teams served up a classic encounter with the Hungarians displaying the sort of football that had made them such a powerful team in the 1950s. In fact, the game went a long way to dispel the ugly memories from the last time these teams had met in the so-called Battle of Berne 12 years previously. Again the Hungarians came out on top, inflicting the first defeat in 13 World Cup games on the South Americans.

Facing the prospect of not qualifying for the next stage, Brazil made wholesale changes for their match against Portugal, including the return of Pelé who was not fully fit from a knee injury sustained against Bulgaria in the opening match. However, the Portuguese were superior in most areas of the field and, once again, Pelé was subjected to some harsh tackling which left him a hobbling spectator for much of the game. Afterwards, Pelé threatened never to play in another World Cup game because, he said, he didn't want to finish his life as an invalid.

But as one great player left the arena another emerged. Eusebio was instrumental in Portugal's 3–1 victory, scoring twice, and his influence was to achieve even greater heights as the tournament progressed.

The team that captured the hearts of the crowds was undoubtedly the brave appearance of underdogs North Korea in Group Four. Hugely popular, they caused a sensation by beating Italy thanks to Pak Doo Ik's goal and went on to qualify with the Soviet Union. For Italy it was the ultimate humiliation. Twice winners of the trophy, the disgraced team were greeted on their return home with a bombardment of rotten vegetables from disappointed fans.

Having produced the shock of the tournament the Koreans seemed intent on making life hard for another of the tournament favourites, Portugal, in the quarter-finals. No one could have dreamt that after only 22 minutes the scoreline would read Portugal 0 North Korea 3, but it did. The Koreans were waltzing around the Portuguese at will, and continued to play attacking football. This turned out to be their downfall and eventually Eusebio took charge and almost single-handedly demolished the Koreans, scoring two goals before half-time and another two before Augusto added a fifth to see them safely into the semi-final – but not before they had had the fright of their lives.

England met Argentina in an eventful game. From the start Argentina dealt out a number of nasty and deliberate fouls and it was only a matter of time before the referee would send someone off. After a fierce tackle, the Argentinian captain Rattin was ordered off the field but refused to go. It was about ten minutes before he finally left and the match could be restarted. Hurst scored the only goal in the second half of the ill-tempered match to book England's semi-final place.

Send-offs were also Uruguay's undoing in their quarter-final tie against West Germany. Despite Held giving the Germans an early lead, the South Americans looked the better side but a penalty appeal late in the first half was turned down and their composure went. Shortly after the interval, first Troche and then Silva were sent off and with just nine men the Uruguayans conceded three more goals.

Two errors gave the Soviet Union a 2–0 lead over Hungary and despite Bene pulling one back the Soviet defence held out with Yashin back to his imperious best.

West Germany and the Soviet Union met in the first semi-final and in a tough, physical match the otherwise excellent Soviet team lost their discipline. Chislenko was sent off and his team-mate Sabo spent most of the second half injured as first Haller then Beckenbauer scored before Porkujan pulled a goal back for the Russians.

By contrast the other semi-final was full of attacking play with two memorable goals from Bobby Charlton – the second of which was even applauded by some of the Portuguese players. Nobby Stiles shadowed Eusebio and prevented him from exerting the sort of deadly influence which had brought the Portuguese this far. Eusebio did manage to score from the penalty spot but England survived an anxious final few minutes to win their first appearance in a World Cup final.

And what a final it was. It became one of the most televised, photographed and discussed matches in football history.

West Germany took the lead in the 12th minute when a poor clearance fell to Haller who drove his shot past Banks. Hurst equalised with a header six minutes later, after which the game remained in deadlock. Beckenbauer's influence was reduced as he had specific orders to mark Bobby Charlton. This seemed decisive when England took the lead through Martin Peters. The whole of Wembley stadium willed the referee to end the game but in a last-minute scramble from a German free-kick Weber stabbed the ball into the England net. The whole country was stunned.

The England manager, Alf Ramsey, inspired his team to greater efforts. He came out onto the field and told the team that they had won the World Cup once and that they could win it again. Seeing Alan Ball place the ball back on the centre spot again and being so keen was an inspiration and it was Ball, tireless as ever, who provided the cross for Hurst to strike.

With his back to goal Hurst spun and fired his shot. The ball hit the underside of the crossbar and bounced straight down before spinning away from the goal. The England players appealed that it was a goal; the Germans insisted that it had not crossed the line. The referee was not sure but after consulting his Soviet linesman, Bakhramov, he pointed to the centre spot and England were 3–2 ahead. England's victory was sealed in the very last minute of the match when Hurst latched on to Moore's long throughball to become the only man to score a hat-trick in a World Cup final.

Controversy over England's third goal has raged ever since and will no doubt continue as long as the game is played. England striker Hunt was certain the ball had gone over the line; he later recalled that he had expected it to bounce up into the roof of the net. For him, it was a shock when it came out again. It would have ended all arguments if Hunt had netted the rebound but having watched the replays he said that he didn't think he would have got to it first. The ball bounced off to the left and Weber, who was marking him, would probably have got there first.

England had deservedly won the World Cup – the first time in 32 years that the host nation had done so. They were a strong, defensively sound and durable team and the sight of Moore holding the trophy aloft and Stiles' toothless jigs of delight are etched on the mind of all those who witnessed them.

RESULTS

Group One
England 0 Uruguay 0; France 1 Mexico 1; Uruguay 2 France 1; England 2 Mexico 0; Mexico 0 Uruguay 0; England 2 France 0

Final table	P	W	D	L	F	A	Pts
England	3	2	1	0	4	0	5
Uruguay	3	1	2	0	2	1	4
Mexico	3	0	2	1	1	3	2
France	3	0	1	2	2	5	1

Group Two
West Germany 5 Switzerland 0; Argentina 2 Spain 1; Spain 2
Switzerland 1; Argentina 0 West Germany 0; Argentina 2
Switzerland 0; West Germany 2 Spain 1

Final table	P	W	D	L	F	A	Pts
West Germany	3	2	1	0	7	1	5
Argentina	3	2	1	0	4	1	5
Spain	3	1	0	2	4	5	2
Switzerland	3	0	0	3	1	9	0

Group Three
Brazil 2 Bulgaria 0; Portugal 3 Hungary 1; Hungary 3 Brazil 1;
Portugal 3 Bulgaria 0; Portugal 3 Brazil 1; Hungary 3 Bulgaria 1

Final table	P	W	D	L	F	A	Pts
Portugal	3	3	0	0	9	2	6
Hungary	3	2	0	1	7	5	4
Brazil	3	1	0	2	4	6	2
Bulgaria	3	0	0	3	1	8	0

Group Four
Soviet Union 3 North Korea 0; Italy 2 Chile 0; Chile 1 North Korea 1;
Soviet Union 1 Italy 0; North Korea 1 Italy 0; Soviet Union 2 Chile 1

Final table	P	W	D	L	F	A	Pts
Soviet Union	3	3	0	0	6	1	6
North Korea	3	1	1	1	2	4	3
Italy	3	1	0	2	2	2	2
Chile	3	0	1	2	2	5	1

Quarter-finals
England 1 Argentina 0; West Germany 4 Uruguay 0; Portugal 5
North Korea 3; Soviet Union 2 Hungary 1

Semi-finals
West Germany 2 Soviet Union 1; England 2 Portugal 1

Third-place play-off
Portugal 2 Soviet Union 1

Final

England (1) 4	West Germany (1) 2 (aet; 90 mins 2–2)
Hurst (3)	Haller
Peters	Weber

Top goalscorers: 9 Eusebio (Portugal); 5 Haller (West Germany);
4 Beckenbauer (West Germany), Bene (Hungary), Hurst (England),
Porkujan (Soviet Union).
Fastest goal: 1 minute, Pak Seung-zin (North Korea v Portugal).
Most goals scored: 17 (Portugal).
Total goals scored: 89 (average 2.78 per game).
Total attendance: 1,614,677 (average 50,458 per game).
Final attendance: 96,000.

MEXICO 1970

The decision to award the 1970 World Cup to Mexico was taken by FIFA at their Congress in Tokyo at the 1964 Olympic Games. However, many people were unhappy with the choice of venue because of the potential problems caused by Mexico's high altitude and heat. Watching Olympic athletes struggle in the 1968 Games in Mexico City did nothing to dispel these fears and the decision to play some of the games at 12 noon, to fit in with peak viewing for European countries, only made matters worse.

As it turned out, the 1970 tournament was perhaps the best ever to be staged and it was one of the first to become deeply impregnated in our minds. The reason for this was simple – colour television. This was the first time most people had seen international football in colour and the images of the deep blue of the Italians and glorious canary yellow of Brazil played out on a vivid green pitch were unforgettable.

The competition was played in exactly the same format as 1966, with four groups of four leading straight to the quarter-finals, but, for the first time, substitutions were introduced.

England set out for Mexico with a strong squad that was considered fully capable of retaining the Cup they had won four years earlier. The 4–3–3 system they had used in 1966 had become the more defensive 4–4–2, Banks was still in goal, the attack was augmented by Lee and Mullery, and Moore was at the peak of his career. Moore, unaffected by an attempt to frame him for the theft of a bracelet in Bogota, Colombia, led England superbly and a final against Brazil was widely predicted.

Brazil for their part were now managed by Zagalo, one of the stars of their 1958 and 1962 teams. Pelé was now at his peak and with the exciting Tostao, Jairzinho and Carlos Alberto this was a team of great attacking flair.

Of the other qualifiers, West Germany were eager to go one better than four years previously with the graceful Beckenbauer and Overath in midfield and a new scoring sensation, Gerd Muller, in attack. Italy also possessed a striker of great goal-scoring talent named Luigi Riva. However, the Italian team were not considered strong enough to progress far and Italian hopes were pinned on

Riva having an exceptional tournament.

With Uruguay also qualifying for the finals, it was decided that should any of the three teams win the trophy for a third time, they should be allowed to retain it.

There was none of the violence which had undermined the game in the two previous tournaments. Not one player was even sent off, equalling the achievement of 1950.

The opening game of the tournament between Mexico and the Soviet Union ended goalless, like its 1966 counterpart. These two teams qualified from Group One but not until Mexico had benefited from a series of controversial refereeing decisions in their games against both El Salvador and Belgium. However, to the delight of the home support, they were through to the knockout phase.

Group Two produced a couple of dull, dreary games. The Italians scored only one goal in three matches, beating Sweden 1–0 and drawing against Israel and then Uruguay, who were lucky to qualify with them.

England opened their challenge against Romania, winning 1–0 thanks to a goal from the 1966 final hero, Hurst. Brazil faced Czechoslovakia with a talented line-up but as has happened so frequently, it was their opponents who opened the scoring. This was perhaps what the Brazilians needed and Rivelino equalised with a free-kick bent around the defensive wall.

Brazil eventually strolled to a 4–1 victory with two goals from Jairzinho and one from Pelé but it was a shot from Pelé which narrowly failed to score which is best remembered. He saw that Czech goalkeeper Viktor was well off his goal line and from just inside his own half he lofted the ball over the goalkeeper's head only to see it bounce inches wide of the goal.

The meeting between England and Brazil was eagerly anticipated and resulted in a classic game played in intense heat which would have been a fitting finale to the tournament.

Brazil had been genuinely concerned that England were in the same group. They were without the influential Gerson while England were missing Newton. For the England players there was the added disadvantage of suffering a disturbed night's sleep as a result of hundreds of Mexicans fans singing and honking their horns outside the England hotel.

Despite these problems, and the debilitating effects of heat and altitude, England outplayed Brazil for long periods of the game. Moore was cool and creative in defence and even Pelé was kept quiet although he had a fierce and well-directed header miraculously saved by England's goalkeeper, Banks – a save which is universally accepted as the best ever.

Both teams had chances to win the game but it was Tostao's splendid run and pass to Pelé, who in turn laid the ball beautifully into the path of Jairzinho to score which proved to be the match-winner. Further chances fell to England but despite losing 1–0 this was reckoned to be just a prelude to the final. Both countries won their final group games although neither were that impressive.

In Group Four, one of the fancied outsiders, Peru, were coached by Didi, the Brazilian star of 1958 and 1962. However, their opening game against Bulgaria was shrouded in tragedy. A minute's silence was observed in memory of the thousands of people who had lost their lives in the Peruvian earthquake only two days before.

Against this background, it was perhaps understandable that Peru went two goals down. But they staged a remarkable come-back and after two shrewd substitutions they hit back immediately with a goal from Gallardo. Five minutes later, Chumpitaz equalised from a free-kick and the impressive Cubillas completed the recovery with a brilliant solo effort.

The following day on the same ground, Morocco gave West Germany a fright. The North Africans fully deserved their lead after 21 minutes and it took the Germans until the 56th minute before they could equalise. A draw would have been a fair result but 12 minutes from time, Gerd Muller, ever dangerous, scored his first World Cup goal.

Muller immediately added to his tally with a hat-trick against Bulgaria and completed a second successive hat-trick in the 3–1 defeat of Peru. However, both teams had already qualified.

The quarter-finals threw up a repeat of the 1966 final, pitching England against West Germany. Undoubtedly the most significant factor in the game happened the day before when the utterly dependable Banks came down with a stomach upset. Peter Bonetti replaced him in the England goal, but his performance would dog him for the rest of his career.

The match began well for England, Mullery and Peters giving them a 2–0 lead after 50 minutes. Beckenbauer got a goal back for the Germans, a low shot which crept under Bonetti's body but Alf Ramsey, the England manager, felt confident enough to substitute his most creative player, Bobby Charlton, to save him for the semi-finals.

It has always been recognised as a crucial mistake. Meanwhile, the Germans also made a tactical substitution, bringing on Grabowski who, with his fresh legs, tormented Cooper in the English defence. Seeler equalised for West Germany with just nine minutes remaining. On this occasion, it was the Germans who made the most of extra-time with Muller volleying the winner from close range. Bonetti did not escape blame and never played for England again. It was also a sorry end to what was to be Bobby Charlton's last game for England.

After scoring only one goal in three matches, Italy quadrupled their tally against Mexico with Riva getting two. However, it was not until the second-half substitution which brought on the inspirational Rivera that Italy gained the advantage.

Brazil also scored four in their dazzling victory over Peru. Gerson and Rivelino returned for Brazil but it was Tostao who did the most damage, although errors by Felix, the Brazilian goalkeeper, gave Peru a brief glimmer of hope.

The semi-finals pitted those old foes Brazil and Uruguay, the Uruguayans having beaten the Soviet Union, and Italy against West Germany. Uruguay registered a complaint that Brazil were playing at Guadalajara once again and that the game should be moved. Their protest was to no avail.

Nonetheless, they took the lead – with Felix again responsible for not covering his angles properly in the Brazilian goal – and held it until late in the first half when Clodoaldo equalised. Brazil started the second half well and Felix atoned for his previous mistake with a stunning save from Cubilla. With 14 minutes to go, Jairzinho waltzed past defenders, exchanged passes with Pelé and Tostao and drove the ball home. With seconds remaining, Rivelino crashed home a third from Pelé's lovely pass and Brazil were finalists once again.

In Mexico City, a thrilling and fluctuating match took place between Italy and West Germany. This was by no means a classic encounter but there were goals galore – not that there was any hint of this as Italy grimly held onto Boninsegna's seventh-minute lead for the best part of the match only for Schnellinger to grab an equaliser three minutes into injury time.

Having once again pulled themselves away from the jaws of defeat the Germans were faced with another 30 testing minutes just three days after their thrilling extra-time victory over England. Events meant that Beckenbauer was forced to play for an hour with his dislocated shoulder strapped – he was unquestionably brave but his influence was inevitably reduced.

Despite heat, fatigue and the cagey nature of the previous 90 minutes, the game really came alive in extra time. Muller (who else) scored inside five minutes of the restart but goals by Burgnich and Riva restored Italy's lead. With ten minutes to go Muller equalised with his tenth goal of the competition but Rivera scored virtually from the restart and not even the resilient Germans could come back again. They had played two tiring games, both of which had gone into extra-time.

So it was Brazil versus Italy in the final and whoever won would be the permanent holders of the Jules Rimet Trophy.

Pelé opened the scoring with a spectacular jump and header from a cross by Rivelino. Eight minutes before the interval, Boninsegna pounced on a defensive lapse to equalise. If Italy could have pressed home their psychological advantage at this point then the game may have taken a different course. But they did not. Brazil regained control and Gerson pivoted to hit a fierce, low drive past Albertosi in the Italian goal. From this point, Brazil turned on a magical display. Gerson's cross, was headed down by Pelé for Jairzinho to create World Cup history by scoring in every round.

The fourth was also one to savour. The Brazilians languidly worked the ball out of defence to Jairzinho on the left. He in turn found Pelé, who laid the ball immaculately to his right for Carlos Alberto to drive the ball imperiously into the goal.

The celebrations were spectacular with fans parading alongside their victorious players. Brazil had made the game look enjoyable to play and won the World Cup in glorious style.

RESULTS

Group One

Mexico 0 Soviet Union 0; Belgium 3 El Salvador 0; Soviet Union 4
Belgium 1; Mexico 4 El Salvador 0; Soviet Union 2 El Salvador 0;
Mexico 1 Belgium 0

Final table	P	W	D	L	F	A	Pts
Soviet Union	3	2	1	0	6	1	5
Mexico	3	2	1	0	5	0	5
Belgium	3	1	0	2	4	5	2
El Salvador	3	0	0	3	0	9	0

Group Two

Uruguay 2 Israel 0; Italy 1 Sweden 0; Uruguay 0 Italy 0; Israel 1
Sweden 1; Sweden 1 Uruguay 0; Israel 0 Italy 0

Final table	P	W	D	L	F	A	Pts
Italy	3	1	2	0	1	0	4
Uruguay	3	1	1	1	2	1	3
Sweden	3	1	1	1	2	2	3
Israel	3	0	2	1	1	3	2

Group Three

England 1 Romania 0; Brazil 4 Czechoslovakia 1; Romania 2
Czechoslovakia 1; Brazil 1 England 0; Brazil 3 Romania 2;
England 1 Czechoslovakia 0

Final table	P	W	D	L	F	A	Pts
Brazil	3	3	0	0	8	3	6
England	3	2	0	1	2	1	4
Romania	3	1	0	2	4	5	2
Czechoslovakia	3	0	0	3	2	7	0

Group Four

Peru 3 Bulgaria 2; West Germany 2 Morocco 1; Peru 3 Morocco 0;
West Germany 5 Bulgaria 2; West Germany 3 Peru 1; Bulgaria 1
Morocco 1

Final table	P	W	D	L	F	A	Pts
West Germany	3	3	0	0	10	4	6
Peru	3	2	0	1	7	5	4
Bulgaria	3	0	1	2	5	9	1
Morocco	3	0	1	2	2	6	1

Quarter-finals

West Germany 3 England 2 (aet); Italy 4 Mexico 1; Brazil 4 Peru 2;
Uruguay 1 Soviet Union 0

Semi-finals

Italy 4 West Germany 3 (aet); Brazil 3 Uruguay 1

Third-place play-off

West Germany 1 Uruguay 0

Final

Brazil (1) 4   Italy (1) 1
Pelé   Boninsegna
Gerson
Jairzinho
Carlos Alberto

Leading goalscorers: 10 Muller (West Germany); 7 Jairzinho
(Brazil); 5 Cubillas (Peru); 4 Bishovets (Soviet Union), Pelé (Brazil).
Fastest goal: 3 minutes, Petras (Czechoslovakia v Romania).
Most goals: 19 (Brazil).
Total goals: 95 (average of 2.97 per game).
Total attendance: 1,673,975 (average of 52,312 per game).
Final attendance: 107,000.

GERMANY 1974

Germany were awarded the tenth World Cup tournament at FIFA's 1969 Congress, so, like Mexico, Germany had the honour of staging the Olympic Games and then the World Cup within a space of two years.

A few days before the opening ceremony, Joao Havelange succeeded Stanley Rous as president of FIFA. The tournament also had a new trophy, called simply the FIFA World Cup, to replace the original which had been won outright by Brazil in 1970.

Many famous names were absent from the finals. England, Hungary and Czechoslovakia – teams with a proud football heritage – all failed to qualify but the most controversial absentee was the Soviet Union. Forced to play off against Chile, they drew the first leg in Moscow 0–0. They then refused to play the return leg, to be staged in the National Stage of Santiago, on the grounds that the stadium had been the scene of the murder of political prisoners, many of them communists, during the coup. After protracted meetings, FIFA ruled that the match should go ahead. Chile took to the field without the Russians, scored a goal and qualified for the finals.

For the first time since 1950, the system of the groups was extended beyond the first-round games. As before, 16 nations competed, divided into four groups of four but instead of a second-round knock-out tournament, the top two teams went into further groups with the winners becoming the finalists and the runners-up meeting in the third-place match.

In 1972, West Germany had proved they were the best team in Europe. Now it was time to prove they were the best in the world. Few who had seen them demolish the Soviet Union 3–0 in the final of the European Championship doubted that they could take the ultimate prize. Alongside Holland and Poland, the Germans had embraced the concept of 'total football' and with players of the stature of Beckenbauer, Breitner, Overath and Muller they had the ability to achieve World Cup glory.

The hosts were drawn in Group One with Chile and newcomers East Germany and Australia. But being favourites on home soil can often be a handicap and after an unconvincing 1–0 win in their opening game against Chile the home crowd whistled and jeered their team off the pitch.

The crowd's obvious displeasure stung the Germans into action against the hapless Australians and Overath opened the scoring in the 13th minute with a scorching drive. Muller then hit the bar with a diving header as the Germans created a tidal flow of attacking football.

Cullman increased their lead after 35 minutes with a header and the pattern of the game continued into the second half. Australia had little to offer although they did hit the post in a rare attack before Muller wrapped up the game with the third. Despite the margin of victory the crowd weren't overly happy, even though their team was through to the second round.

The final game of the group caught the imagination of the world as it brought an historic first-ever meeting between the two Germanys. 2,000 East German fans were allowed into the Hamburg stadium and even though both had already qualified there was a special edge to the game. The first half failed to produce a goal although both sides came close – Muller hitting the post following a trademark spinning turn and shot while at the other end the East Germans missed an open goal.

Though West Germany dominated the second half it was a quick break at the other end which enabled Sparwasser to make a wonderful run into the area and drive the ball past Maier. With just ten minutes left West Germany continued to attack but couldn't find a way past their disciplined opponents.

The historic result meant that both teams qualified but, by finishing second, West Germany avoided Holland in the second phase. It was maybe not such a bad result after all but even so, the team came under strong criticism for their lacklustre performance.

Brazil were no longer the same exciting team that had enthralled everyone four years previously. There was no Pelé, Tostao or Gerson and their new defensive style was much lamented. However, they qualified with Yugoslavia for the second round at the expense of Scotland and Zaire. Scotland, despite remaining unbeaten, went out on goal difference and only one goal's difference at that. They had scored two to Brazil's three against Zaire – neither of which approached the nine goals Yugoslavia had put past the African team.

This tournament was the World Cup of 'total football', the theory of which was that any player could do anything: attackers became defenders, defenders became attackers. It was not a form of tactics, but a style where players would not be limited to certain positions on the pitch. The team would be composed of highly skilful and versatile players, and the teams who were to demonstrate this to the best effect were West Germany and, particularly, Holland, who with Cruyff, Neeskens, Rep and Krol qualified for the second phase alongside Sweden.

In the final group, Italy made hard work of beating Haiti. They went a goal down early in the second half but goals from the experienced Rivera, Benetti, and Anastasi dispelled thoughts of a repeat of the nightmare of North Korea's win in 1966. On the same day, Argentina, who had finally been awarded the 1978 finals, faced Poland – one of the best teams in the tournament. In a good, open match, Poland scored two early goals but had the young Mario Kempes scored in the opening minutes things might have been different. Kempes' day was to come four years later but for now his team qualified behind Poland.

The two second-phase groups were composed of Holland, Brazil, Argentina and East Germany, and West Germany, Poland, Yugoslavia and Sweden.

In the opening second-phase matches Brazil beat the East Germans thanks to one of Rivelino's free-kick specials – his teammate, Jairzinho, stood in the East German defensive wall and ducked out of the way of Rivelino's fiercely struck shot.

Holland were getting better and better as the tournament progressed. Argentina were the next team powerless to prevent their irresistible attacking football as Cruyff scored two of the four goals in a virtuoso performance. But the Dutch were more than a one-man team as they proved against East Germany. With Cruyff being closely marked by Weise, the Dutch still had enough firepower in the shape of Neeskens and Rensenbrink to score twice to set up a decisive match against Brazil, who had also won both their games.

In a physical match, Brazil resorted to some dangerous tackles but Holland returned the treatment with interest. However, the game was saved by two brilliant strikes by Neeskens and Cruyff to send Holland into their first final.

The other second-round group saw a similar 'decider' situation develop. Both Poland and West Germany had won their first two group games – however, the Germans knew they could rely on a draw in their final game.

West Germany were improving and starting to play like potential champions. They had dominated much of the match against Yugoslavia with Breitner scoring with a tremendous right-foot drive from 25 yards. Muller also got on the score sheet – steering the ball into the net whilst lying on the ground after his first effort had been blocked. Just as importantly, Beckenbauer was back to his most majestic form. Improvement continued against Sweden in an entertaining game with Muller playing a leading role without actually scoring in the 4–2 win.

Poland had been less impressive and were considered fortunate to beat Yugoslavia and Sweden but it was now showdown time. The decisive game was played on a rain-soaked pitch but, despite the atrocious conditions, it was an entertaining affair. Maier, the German goalkeeper, brought off an excellent save from Lato in the first half to keep the Germans in the game. Muller had been very quiet all game but, with only 12 minutes to go, he latched on to a half-chance to score the goal that saw the hosts through to the final.

The world had the final they had eagerly wished for – two highly skilful teams, each with, in Cruyff and Beckenbauer, a worthy successor to Pelé's title of the world's greatest footballer.

And what a dramatic start. Holland kicked off and before a German player had even touched the ball they were a goal up. A superb run by Cruyff ended up with him being fouled inside the penalty area by Hoeness. Neeskens scored from the penalty spot with barely a minute gone. For nearly half an hour, the Dutch played with the arrogance of a team who assumed they had won and one can only assume that if they had pressed home their advantage they would have done so.

After 25 minutes, however, Jack Taylor, the English referee, awarded the Germans a more controversial penalty. Breitner brought the scores level and some years later revealed: 'When we were awarded the penalty, I knew straight away that I should be the player to take it. Muller, Beckenbauer or Overath would normally have taken it but they all appeared unsure so I grabbed the ball and took the responsibility. The goalkeeper moved to the left so I placed it to the right'.

For West Germany, Holland scoring so early was the best thing to happen. After the goal, the Dutch relaxed and played as if they thought they would win easily while the Germans got stronger.

Rep missed a simple chance to restore Holland's lead before Muller, the master poacher, won the World Cup with a well-taken goal on the turn just before half-time. Cruyff was cautioned for arguing but the Dutch had only themselves to blame for underestimating the opposition's powers of recovery.

Try as they might in the second half, the Dutch could not score and for the second time the World Cup went to West Germany.

RESULTS

Group One
West Germany 1 Chile 0; East Germany 2 Australia 0; West Germany 3 Australia 0; Chile 1 East Germany 1; East Germany 1 West Germany 0; Australia 0 Chile 0

Final table	P	W	D	L	F	A	Pts
East Germany	3	2	1	0	4	1	5
West Germany	3	2	0	1	4	1	4
Chile	3	0	2	1	1	2	2
Australia	3	0	1	2	0	5	1

Group Two
Brazil 0 Yugoslavia 0; Scotland 2 Zaire 0; Brazil 0 Scotland 0; Yugoslavia 9 Zaire 0; Scotland 1 Yugoslavia 1; Brazil 3 Zaire 0

Final table	P	W	D	L	F	A	Pts
Yugoslavia	3	1	2	0	10	1	4
Brazil	3	1	2	0	3	0	4
Scotland	3	1	2	0	3	1	4
Zaire	3	0	0	3	0	14	0

Group Three

Holland 2 Uruguay 0; Bulgaria 0 Sweden 0; Holland 0 Sweden 0;
Bulgaria 1 Uruguay 1; Holland 4 Bulgaria 1; Sweden 3 Uruguay 0

Final table	P	W	D	L	F	A	Pts
Holland	3	2	1	0	6	1	5
Sweden	3	1	2	0	3	0	4
Bulgaria	3	0	2	1	2	5	2
Uruguay	3	0	1	2	1	6	1

Group Four

Italy 3 Haiti 1; Poland 3 Argentina 2; Argentina 1 Italy 1; Poland 7
Haiti 0; Argentina 4 Haiti 1; Poland 2 Italy 1

Final table	P	W	D	L	F	A	Pts
Poland	3	3	0	0	12	3	6
Argentina	3	1	1	1	7	5	3
Italy	3	1	1	1	5	4	3
Haiti	3	0	0	3	2	14	0

Group A

Brazil 1 East Germany 0; Holland 4 Argentina 0; Holland 2
East Germany 0; Brazil 2 Argentina 1; Holland 2 Brazil 0;
Argentina 1 East Germany 1

Final table	P	W	D	L	F	A	Pts
Holland	3	3	0	0	8	0	6
Brazil	3	2	0	1	3	3	4
East Germany	3	0	1	2	1	4	1
Argentina	3	0	1	2	2	7	1

Group B

Poland 1 Sweden 0; West Germany 2 Yugoslavia 0; Poland 2
Yugoslavia 1; West Germany 4 Sweden 2; Sweden 2 Yugoslavia 1;
West Germany 1 Poland 0

Final table	P	W	D	L	F	A	Pts
West Germany	3	3	0	0	7	2	6
Poland	3	2	0	1	3	2	4
Sweden	3	1	0	2	4	6	2
Yugoslavia	3	0	0	3	2	6	0

Third-place play-off
Poland 1 Brazil 0

Final
West Germany (2) 2   Holland (1) 1
Breitner (pen)   Neeskens (pen)
Muller

Leading goalscorers: 7 Lato (Poland); 5 Neeskens (Holland), Szarmach (Poland); 4 Edstrom (Sweden), Muller (West Germany), Rep (Holland).
Fastest goal: 80 seconds, Neeskens (Holland v West Germany).
Most goals: 16 (Poland).
Total goals: 97 (average of 2.55 per game).
Total attendance: 1,744,022 (average of 46,685 per game).
Final attendance: 77,833.

ARGENTINA 1978

There were grave doubts about whether the 1978 World Cup should go ahead in Argentina, a country ruled by a military junta headed by General Videla who had ousted Isabelita Peron in 1976. After the coup, fears increased when thousands of people were tortured or simply went missing. The junta set up a body, the *Ente Autarquico Mundial*, to ensure that all the preparations for the tournament were completed in time but this looked unlikely when its chief, General Actis, was assassinated. Yet despite a background of terrorism and an unstable economy the tournament actually passed without a major incident.

The chain-smoking Argentinian manager, Cesar Menotti, having seen many of his country's best players move to Europe, decided that the bulk of his team would be home-based. But he did recall Mario Kempes from Valencia in Spain – a decision that was ultimately to win the World Cup.

Argentina made a winning if not sensational start to their campaign with a 2–1 win over Hungary in what was a tough qualifying group. They beat France 2–1 in their next game but this was largely down to two outrageous decisions by the referee. The first came from an incident when the French defender Tresor tackled Kempes and fell on the ball. The referee 'gave' a penalty to Argentina but the reason was unclear. Surely it was not a deliberate foul and if Tresor had handled the ball it was accidental. Passarella converted the penalty and France did well to fight back and equalise through Platini. Luque put Argentina back in front with a tremendous long-range shot but France pushed forward and should have been awarded a penalty themselves when Six was brought down. But for this clear infringement the referee gave nothing.

Italy and Argentina were assured of qualification but their game was important as the winners of the group would stay in Buenos Aires. Argentina had their chances but Italy's tight marking and solid defence gave Kempes few opportunities. Rossi instigated the winning goal by playing a smart one-two with Bettega who scored.

The Group Two game between Poland and West Germany was the opening match of the tournament and for the fourth successive time failed to provide any goals. With Lato, Deyna and Boniek, Poland had an excellent team whereas the Germans desperately missed the likes of Muller and Beckenbauer. Both teams qualified as expected but were given a surprisingly tough time by Tunisia. The North Africans first beat Mexico 3–1, before losing narrowly to Poland, and then held the Germans to a goalless draw in which they created the better chances.

Brazil blundered their way through Group Three, showing little of the attacking flair which had endeared them to so many fans around the world. However, one incident did spark interest in their opening game against Sweden. With the scores level at 1–1 Zico turned home a corner, apparently winning the match. But as the ball was heading into the net Clive Thomas blew his whistle for full-time. The Brazilians were outraged that the goal was not allowed but the referee bravely stood by his extraordinary decision.

In the end Brazil qualified with Austria who had the impressive Krankl up front.

In Group Four, Peru shattered the illusions of Ally MacLeod's Scotland by beating them 3–1 with Cubillas, a rising star in 1970, scoring two. The overconfident Scots were guilty of treating Peru too lightly and despite taking the lead through Jordan by half-time Peru were level. Who knows what may have happened had Masson scored from the penalty spot but from the point the spot kick was saved, Peru moved up a gear and Cubillas administered the last rites.

If that was bad, Scotland's misery was compounded by a 1–1 draw with the little-fancied Iran. Indeed, if it had not been for an extraordinary own goal Iran may have won the game.

Going into the final deciding game Scotland still had a mathematical chance of progressing to the second phase but needed to beat the Dutch by three clear goals. Considering their previous performances it sounded a ludicrous suggestion but on the day the Scots raised their game and after Archie Gemmill had jinked his way through the Dutch defence to make it 3–1 they were within sight of that margin. Their hopes were short-lived as three minutes later Johnny Rep scored from 25 yards and Scotland went out for a second successive time on goal difference. One Scot, Willie Johnston, arrived home earlier than his team-mates, having failed a dope test after the Peru game.

Following the same system as four years previously the second round was contested by two groups. Unfortunately, the first-round results had generated groups which split the continents. Group A consisted of Italy, West Germany, Holland and Austria whilst Group B contained Argentina, Peru, Brazil and Poland.

The opening game of Group A pitted Italy, winners of all their games, against West Germany. Italy had their chances but the game finished goalless. On the same day, Holland tore into the Austrian defence with Rep scoring twice, and Brandts, Rensenbrink and Willy van der Kerkhof completing an impressive 5–1 win. Goal difference would be used to determine the group winners in the case of a tie which rendered this score of huge importance.

As a result, West Germany had to forsake their defensive system against Holland and although they went an early goal up, Haan demonstrated his formidable shooting power from 30 yards to bring the scores level. Even the experienced Maier in the German goal could do nothing to stop the thunderbolt. West Germany re-established their lead but Rene van der Kerkhof (Willy's twin) threaded his way through the German defence to equalise.

After Italy had beaten Austria 1–0 they knew they had to beat the Dutch to have a chance of reaching the final. Going into their last game, West Germany also held a slim mathematical chance of reaching the final. They relied on Italy drawing with Holland and scoring a hatful of goals against neighbours Austria themselves.

Rummenigge gave the Germans the right start in the 19th minute, a lead they held until the normally dependable Vogts put the ball past his own keeper. Krankl then removed any hope the Germans might have had with two goals either side of Holzenbein's strike for Germany and the Austrians ran out 3–2 winners.

The Italy–Holland tie was effectively a semi-final, and committing themselves to attack, the Italians took a first half lead when Brandts put through his own goal whilst trying to clear the ball from danger. As well as giving away an own goal he caught the right knee of his goalkeeper, Jongbloed, who had to be substituted. The match was ill-tempered but the best football was played by the Dutch with Brandts atoning for his previous error by equalising from 20 yards. This paved the way for Haan to score another thunderous long-range effort from over 30 yards and Holland were through to their second successive final.

In Group B, Brazil finally started to play the sort of football the fans expected in beating Peru 3–0. That evening, Kempes scored twice against Poland as Argentina were spurred on by a fanatical crowd. This set up the crucial game between the South American favourites and emotions were certainly running high as both teams were desperate to remain unbeaten. The match remained goalless but four players were booked and four went off injured in a game where no prisoners were taken.

The goalless scoreline left the group wide open and Brazil were rightly furious that their game against Poland was to be played before Argentina's final game. With the group likely to be decided on goal difference, the hosts would know exactly how many goals they needed to win by.

Brazil put up their best performance to beat Poland 3–1, leaving Argentina needing to win by at least four goals. Grave doubts persist about the validity of their 6–0 rout of Peru as it seemed that they overran the opposition rather too easily – even though Peru hit a post early on. Luque scored two as did Kempes, taking his tally to four.

The crowds greeted Argentina for the final at the River Plate stadium with the now customary ticker-tape reception. However, the game was delayed first by the hosts' late arrival on the pitch and then by Argentine complaints about the strapping worn by Rene van der Kerkhof on an injured forearm. The Dutch, angered by what they saw as blatant gamesmanship, began overphysically and it took the skill of Ardiles and the finishing power of Kempes to bring the match distinction.

Kempes opened the scoring in the 38th minute, a lead they held until Nanninga headed the equaliser with less than ten minutes to go. The Dutch pushed forward with renewed vigour and Rensenbrink hit a post in the last minute. A shade the other way and the Dutch would have been champions. By such close margins are games decided. But it was not to be. Kempes scored his sixth goal of the tournament in the first period of extra-time, forcing his way past three defenders to make the score 2–1. And with five minutes left, and Holland committed to attack, Kempes played a neat one-two with Bertoni who scored an easy third.

The stadium erupted in celebration and the streets of Buenos Aries were packed with ecstatic crowds. Holland had again lost to the host nation but had contributed some exciting football in what turned out to be a successful tournament.

RESULTS

Group One

Italy 2 France 1; Argentina 2 Hungary 1; Italy 3 Hungary 1; Argentina 2 France 1; Italy 1 Argentina 0; France 3 Hungary 1

Final table	P	W	D	L	F	A	Pts
Italy	3	3	0	0	6	2	6
Argentina	3	2	0	1	4	3	4
France	3	1	0	2	5	5	2
Hungary	3	0	0	3	3	8	0

Group Two

Poland 0 West Germany 0; Tunisia 3 Mexico 1; Poland 1 Tunisia 0; West Germany 6 Mexico 0; Tunisia 0 West Germany 0; Poland 3 Mexico 1

Final table	P	W	D	L	F	A	Pts
Poland	3	2	1	0	4	1	5
West Germany	3	1	2	0	6	0	4
Tunisia	3	1	1	1	3	2	3
Mexico	3	0	0	3	2	12	0

Group Three

Brazil 1 Sweden 1; Austria 2 Spain 1; Austria 1 Sweden 0; Brazil 0 Spain 0; Brazil 1 Austria 0; Spain 1 Sweden 0

Final table	P	W	D	L	F	A	Pts
Austria	3	2	0	1	3	2	4
Brazil	3	1	2	0	2	1	4
Spain	3	1	1	1	2	2	3
Sweden	3	0	1	2	1	3	1

Group Four
Holland 3 Iran 0; Peru 3 Scotland 1; Holland 0 Peru 0; Iran 1
Scotland 1; Scotland 3 Holland 2; Peru 4 Iran 1

Final table	P	W	D	L	F	A	Pts
Peru	3	2	1	0	7	2	5
Holland	3	1	1	1	5	3	3
Scotland	3	1	1	1	5	6	3
Iran	3	0	1	2	2	8	1

Group A
Italy 0 West Germany 0; Holland 5 Austria 1; Holland 2
West Germany 2; Italy 1 Austria 0; Holland 2 Italy 1; Austria 3
West Germany 2

Final table	P	W	D	L	F	A	Pts
Holland	3	2	1	0	9	4	5
Italy	3	1	1	1	2	2	3
West Germany	3	0	2	1	4	5	2
Austria	3	1	0	2	4	8	2

Group B
Brazil 3 Peru 0; Argentina 2 Poland 0; Poland 1 Peru 0; Argentina 0
Brazil 0; Brazil 3 Poland 1; Argentina 6 Peru 0

Final table	P	W	D	L	F	A	Pts
Argentina	3	2	1	0	8	0	5
Brazil	3	2	1	0	6	1	5
Poland	3	1	0	2	2	5	2
Peru	3	0	0	3	0	10	0

Third-place play-off
Brazil 2 Italy 1

Final
Argentina (1) 3   Holland (1) 1 (aet)
Kempes (2)   Nanninga
Bertoni

Leading goalscorers: 6 Kempes (Argentina); 5 Cubillas (Peru),
Rensenbrink (Holland); 4 Krankl (Austria), Luque (Argentina).
Fastest goal: 31 secs, Lacombe (France v Italy).
Most goals: 15 (Argentina and Holland).
Total goals: 102 (average of 2.68).
Total attendance: 1,610,215 (average of 42,374 per game).
Final attendance: 77,260.

SPAIN 1982

The sweltering Spanish summer of 1982 saw the arrival of a young Argentine star, Diego Maradona. But his turn was to come, this tournament belonged to Paolo Rossi.

For the first time the number of finalists was enlarged from 16 to 24 to provide a more universal representation of nations. Due to the increased number of entrants another format was devised with the 24 teams divided into six groups of four. The top two teams then went into four further groups of three with the group winners progressing to a semi-final knockout stage. This meant, in effect, that the teams had to qualify all over again and there were concerns that this format might produce defensive, turgid games.

However, the tournament kicked off with a spectacular ceremony and for the first time in 20 years the opening game, between Argentina and Belgium, produced a goal. The South Americans were showcasing a new superstar of world soccer, Maradona, but he was brought down to earth by Belgium's uncompromising tactics. Despite frequently having all 11 men in defence, it was Belgium who scored with a rapid counter-attack.

These two teams eventually qualified at the expense of Hungary and El Salvador. In their encounter, Hungary had beaten El Salvador 10–1, a score which fuelled the arguments of critics who were opposed to expanding the number of finalists. However, El Salvador tightened up their act against Belgium and were in fairness the only so-called 'weaker' football nation not to do themselves justice.

Africa were now represented by two teams – Cameroon and Algeria. Cameroon were drawn with Italy, Poland and Peru in Group One but were by no means overawed by their illustrious opponents. In a group which saw five drawn games and only one win (Poland beating Peru), Cameroon were unfortunate not to qualify – only losing out by virtue of Italy having earned two 1–1 draws as opposed to Cameroon's one. But they left having played with discipline and flair and had been one of the most charismatic teams in the tournament.

Algeria gave further proof that the emerging teams were not to be underestimated with an upset comparable to the USA's 1950 victory over England and North Korea's humiliation of Italy in 1966. In their opening game in Gijon, they beat the mighty West Germany 2–1. In their second game the Algerians again took the initiative from the start but lost 2–0 to Austria who had effectively qualified having already beaten Chile. West Germany's victory over Chile gave them the same points total as Algeria so it all came down to the final matches. The lessons from the previous tournament had evidently not been learnt as Algeria's game against Chile was played a day before West Germany were due to meet Austria.

The Algerians once again gave a scintillating display and raced into an early 3–0 lead but they tired as the match progressed and conceded two second half goals. The next day witnessed one of the most disgraceful matches ever seen. A 1–0 win to West Germany would see them and Austria through and after the Germans had scored the game lost any meaning. Nonetheless, the Algerians' appeal to FIFA was rejected.

In Group Four, England got off to a scintillating start against France when Bryan Robson scored after only 27 seconds to record the fastest-ever World Cup goal. This was the first time England had reached the finals since 1970 and they celebrated the fact by qualifying with a 100 per cent record thanks to victories over Czechoslovakia and Kuwait.

With the host nation having won the past two tournaments, Spain were considered one of the likely favourites. Although their World Cup record was not particularly good, Spain boasted one of the best leagues in the world and a team of highly talented individuals. Sadly, only a dubious penalty saved them from defeat at the hands of Honduras, and they struggled to beat Yugoslavia with the help of another penalty. In their final group game, Spain faced Northern Ireland who needed a win to qualify. Spain could afford a defeat but by no more than one goal and once Armstrong had scored early in the second half there was every chance that the hosts would face an early exit. They survived but went into a tough second round group with West Germany and England.

In Group Six Brazil were back to their exhilarating style of old with fluent attacking football coupled with great individual skill. They fell a goal behind to the Soviet Union but never appeared to be troubled as first Socrates and then Eder scored tremendous goals. Scotland also took the lead against the South Americans,

Narey scoring a goal any one of his opponents would have been delighted with. But Zico, Oscar, Eder – with an audacious chip – and Falcao restored order and put the game beyond Scotland's reach.

Scotland had to beat the Soviet Union to qualify alongside Brazil and an early goal by Jordan gave them hope. Chivadze equalised on the hour and Scottish hopes were dashed when a defensive mix up allowed Shengelia to score. A goal from Souness three minutes from time guaranteed a tense end to the game but the Scots bowed out, again on goal difference.

The four groups for the second round contained some interesting ties. Group C was particularly strong with Brazil, Argentina and Italy competing for a semi-final place. In the first game, Italy gave their experienced defender Gentile the job of marking Maradona and he suffered from some rough tackles. However, after containing Argentina in the first half, Italy attacked in the second and scored twice before Passarella pulled one back for Argentina.

Worse was to come for the defending champions when they faced Brazil who turned on a truly wonderful performance to totally outplay their South American rivals. Eder, who had already scored two great goals produced another sensational free-kick which swerved and dipped before crashing against the bar. Zico reacted quickest to tap in a simple chance.

Brazil were so in control of the game that it was surprising that it was as late as the 67th minute before they extended their lead further, but shortly after Junior rounded off an excellent move to make it 3–0.

Near the end, Maradona's frustration finally got the better of him and he kicked out at Batista. The referee had no hesitation in sending him off. Diaz scored a goal late on for Argentina but everyone who saw the emphatic victory believed that this Brazilian side could emulate the style and performance of the 1970 vintage.

It was not to be Maradona's year but the star of the tournament was about to make his mark. Paolo Rossi had only returned from suspension in April 1982 having been banned for three years – reduced to two – for allegedly accepting a bribe and fixing a game in the Italian league. Rossi had always protested his innocence and now on the world stage he was to become the hero of Italy.

The decider between Brazil and Italy turned out to be a classic. It was a game Italy needed to win and within five minutes Paolo Rossi had put them ahead. But Brazil were not worried – they had fallen behind before and still run out easy winners. In the 12th minute Socrates duly equalised with a brilliant solo goal. Watching his mesmeric runs it was hard to believe that he smoked 40 cigarettes a day.

But Rossi, a natural predatory goalscorer, restored Italy's lead after 25 minutes following a defensive error. Still there was plenty of time and Falcao pulled the scores level with 22 minutes remaining. Brazil only needed to draw the game and had they played more defensively they would surely have gone through. But they continued to push forward looking for the winner and 15 minutes from time Rossi completed a memorable hat-trick.

Brazil had been the most outstanding team of the tournament but what they lacked, crucially, was a reliable goalscorer. Someone like Rossi.

Group B was also very tight. After a drab goalless draw against West Germany, England needed to beat Spain by two clear goals to win the group following West Germany's 2–1 win over the hosts. But this was to be a night of near misses and stout defending by the Spanish and even the introduction of Keegan and Brooking could not bring the vital goals England so desperately needed. So having conceded only one goal and remained unbeaten throughout, Ron Greenwood's England made a disappointing exit.

France had displayed some indifferent form at the beginning of the tournament but they now began to play to the best of their ability. With Platini, Giresse and Tigana in midfield they outplayed Austria and Northern Ireland to set up a semi-final against West Germany.

The first semi-final saw Italy meet Poland. The Poles had qualified by virtue of scoring more goals against Belgium than the Soviet Union managed. Italy were without Gentile but Poland were also without Boniek and it showed. Once again, Rossi was the inspiration, scoring both goals.

The game between France and West Germany was one of the all-time greats but was tainted by a disgusting incident. Littbarski scored for the Germans in the 18th minute but nine minutes later France equalised from the penalty spot after Rocheteau had been brought down in the area. The score did not change for the remainder of normal time although both teams had their chances. However, a crucial incident took place which was ultimately to turn the game. Eight minutes after coming on as a substitute, Battiston, the French defender, was put through by a superb pass from Platini and, with only the goalkeeper to beat, slipped the ball past him before being brought crashing to the ground by Schumacher. It was obvious that the Frenchman was badly injured as he lay on the ground unconscious. Remarkably, the referee took no action and Schumacher remained on the pitch.

Only two minutes into extra time, Tresor gave France the lead and when Giresse made it 3–1 they were seemingly on their way to their first final. Had Battiston still been on the field he might have strengthened a weakening defence but the Germans took a gamble and brought on Rummenigge who instigated Germany's revival with a goal still in the first period of extra-time. Fischer pulled the score back to 3–3 and the Germans had once again shown remarkable spirit to rescue a lost cause.

For the first time ever in the World Cup, penalties were used to decide a game. France seemed again to have the game won when Stielike missed but Six also missed for France and with the score at 4–4, Schumacher saved from Bossis and Hrubesch put West Germany into the final.

Two of the most entertaining and skilful teams were out and West Germany had reached the finals as one of the most unpopular sides ever.

Italy were a much improved side from the one that had started the tournament with three draws. They were without Antognoni and after eight minutes were also minus Graziani who damaged his shoulder. The first half was dominated by fouls and Cabrini's name was added to the record books when he had the unfortunate honour of being the first man to miss a penalty in a World Cup final.

It was almost pre-ordained that Rossi should break the dead-lock. Twelve minutes into the second half, he rose to meet a cross from Gentile and Italy were one up. After 68 minutes, Tardelli made it two with a scorching shot and Altobelli made sure of victory nine minutes from time.

Breitner scored a consolation goal but this was one occasion when the Germans' famed resolve deserted them and Italy deserved their third final win. However, it is worth remembering that both finalists had made less than auspicious starts against comparative minnows – Italy had failed to beat Cameroon and West Germany had lost to Algeria.

RESULTS

Group One
Italy 0 Poland 0; Cameroon 0 Peru 0; Italy 1 Peru 1; Cameroon 0 Poland 0; Poland 5 Peru 1; Cameroon 1 Italy 1

Final table	P	W	D	L	F	A	Pts
Poland	3	1	2	0	5	1	4
Italy	3	0	3	0	2	2	3
Cameroon	3	0	3	0	1	1	3
Peru	3	0	2	1	2	6	2

Group Two
Algeria 2 West Germany 1; Austria 1 Chile 0; West Germany 4 Chile 1; Austria 2 Algeria 0; Algeria 3 Chile 2; West Germany 1 Austria 0

Final table	P	W	D	L	F	A	Pts
West Germany	3	2	0	1	6	3	4
Austria	3	2	0	1	3	1	4
Algeria	3	2	0	1	5	5	4
Chile	3	0	0	3	3	8	0

Group Three
Belgium 1 Argentina 0; Hungary 10 El Salvador 1; Argentina 4 Hungary 1; Belgium 1 El Salvador 0; Belgium 1 Hungary 1; Argentina 2 El Salvador 0

Final table	P	W	D	L	F	A	Pts
Belgium	3	2	1	0	3	1	5
Argentina	3	2	0	1	6	2	4
Hungary	3	1	1	1	12	6	3
El Salvador	3	0	0	3	1	13	0

Group Four

England 3 France 1; Czechoslovakia 1 Kuwait 1; England 2
Czechoslovakia 0; France 4 Kuwait 1; Czechoslovakia 1 France 1;
England 1 Kuwait 0

Final table	P	W	D	L	F	A	Pts
England	3	3	0	0	6	1	6
France	3	1	1	1	6	5	3
Czechoslovakia	3	0	2	1	2	4	2
Kuwait	3	0	1	2	2	6	1

Group Five

Honduras 1 Spain 1; Northern Ireland 0 Yugoslavia 0; Spain 2
Yugoslavia 1; Honduras 1 Northern Ireland 1; Yugoslavia 1
Honduras 0; Northern Ireland 1 Spain 0

Final table	P	W	D	L	F	A	Pts
Northern Ireland	3	1	2	0	2	1	4
Spain	3	1	1	1	3	3	3
Yugoslavia	3	1	1	1	2	2	3
Honduras	3	0	2	1	2	3	2

Group Six

Brazil 2 Soviet Union 1; Scotland 5 New Zealand 2; Brazil 4
Scotland 1; Soviet Union 3 New Zealand 0; Scotland 2 Soviet Union 2;
Brazil 4 New Zealand 0

Final table	P	W	D	L	F	A	Pts
Brazil	3	3	0	0	10	2	6
Soviet Union	3	1	1	1	6	4	3
Scotland	3	1	1	1	8	8	3
New Zealand	3	0	0	3	2	12	0

Group A
Poland 3 Belgium 0; Soviet Union 1 Belgium 0; Poland 0 Soviet Union 0

Final table	P	W	D	L	F	A	Pts
Poland	2	1	1	0	3	0	3
Soviet Union	2	1	1	0	1	0	3
Belgium	2	0	0	2	0	4	0

Group B
England 0 West Germany 0; West Germany 2 Spain 1; England 0 Spain 0

Final table	P	W	D	L	F	A	Pts
West Germany	2	1	1	0	2	1	3
England	2	0	2	0	0	0	2
Spain	2	0	1	1	1	2	1

Group C
Italy 2 Argentina 1; Brazil 3 Argentina 1; Italy 3 Brazil 2

Final table	P	W	D	L	F	A	Pts
Italy	2	2	0	0	5	3	4
Brazil	2	1	0	1	5	4	2
Argentina	2	0	0	2	2	5	0

Group D
France 1 Austria 0; Austria 2 Northern Ireland 2; France 4 Northern Ireland 1

Final table	P	W	D	L	F	A	Pts
France	2	2	0	0	5	1	4
Austria	2	0	1	1	2	3	1
Northern Ireland	2	0	1	1	3	6	1

Semi-finals
Italy 2 Poland 0; West Germany 3 France 3 (5–4 on penalties)

Third-place play-off
Poland 3 France 2

Final
Italy (0) 3   West Germany (0)1
Rossi   Breitner
Tardelli
Altobelli

Leading goalscorers: 6 Rossi (Italy); 5 Rummenigge (West Germany); 4 Boniek (Poland), Zico (Brazil).
Fastest goal: 27 secs, Robson (England v France).
Most goals: 16 (France).
Total goals: 146 (average of 2.81 per game).
Total attendance: 1,766,277 (average of 33,967 per game).
Final attendance: 90,000.

MEXICO 1986

Colombia were chosen as the original hosts for the 13th World Cup but were forced to withdraw in 1982 as their facilities were not considered sufficient to stage a 24-team event.

Brazil, Mexico and the United States all applied for the right to host the tournament and surprisingly the vote went to Mexico. A terrible earthquake a year before the finals devastated Mexico City and nearly caused a second relocation but the tournament went ahead as planned. The problems of heat and altitude were again a major consideration but, despite these problems, the World Cup was a huge success.

There was yet another change to the format as the second phase reverted to a knock-out tournament. The top two in each group would qualify with the four best third-placed teams also going through.

The European challenge was led by the European champions, France, along with Denmark, West Germany and Poland. Algeria qualified for the second successive time and to avoid a repeat of the farce which saw them lose out four years previously, it was decided that all the final matches in the groups would be played simultaneously. Brazil and Argentina were fancied from South America and the home nations were well-represented as England, Scotland and Northern Ireland all qualified, as they had done in 1982.

The opening game of the tournament saw holders Italy create the better chances against Bulgaria but fail to add to Altobelli's first half strike. Six minutes from time Sirakov glanced a header past Galli to make the Italians rue their squandered opportunities.

The first opportunity to see Maradona came against the South Koreans and as the tackles came in thick and fast he responded by taking them apart to create openings for Argentina to run out comfortable 3–1 winners. From the start, he proved that he was going to be the most influential player of the tournament.

Maradona got on the scoresheet himself in the next game, equalising Altobelli's controversial penalty, and with a 2–0 win over Bulgaria, Argentina duly won Group A. Italy also qualified, as did Bulgaria although they were still to win a game in the World Cup finals.

Group B also saw three teams qualify. Mexico, inspired by their striker Sanchez, topped the group to the delight of the home crowd with Paraguay finishing second and Belgium squeezing through in third.

Group C started with Canada making their World Cup debut against France. With the game remaining goalless and the European champions becoming increasingly agitated at the Canadians' resolute defence a shock result was on the cards. But with a little over ten minutes to play Papin saved French blushes.

The next game saw the Soviet Union put six past Hungary in a warm-up for their toughest test against France. It obviously served its purpose as Rats opened the scoring against France with a stunning 30-yard drive. But the lead was short-lived as Fernandez equalised eight minutes later.

Subsequent victories meant that both teams finished with five points, but the Soviet Union had a superior goal difference. Debutants Canada lost all three of their games but were not disgraced.

Having impressed so many people in 1982, Algeria and Northern Ireland were hoping to build on their World Cup success. However, both were outclassed by Brazil and Spain in a group where third-placed teams failed to qualify. Northern Ireland's game against Brazil marked Pat Jennings' 41st birthday and 119th and last international cap. As if in tribute, the Brazilians gave their best performance and put three fabulous goals past the veteran keeper – before presenting him with a signed match ball after the game out of respect for a marvellous career.

With West Germany, Denmark, Scotland and Uruguay drawn together, Group E justified its nickname of 'the group of death'. This tournament marked Denmark's rise in world terms and they were in awesome form, winning all three games – including a 6–1 annihilation of Uruguay in which the powerful Elkjaer scored a hat-trick. Denmark and West Germany qualified, leaving Uruguay and Scotland to play for third place.

Scotland needed to win whereas Uruguay only required a draw to keep their slim hopes of qualifying alive. The Uruguayans hardly improved their chances when Batista was sent off in the first minute, but Scotland failed to capitalise on their numerical advantage and a bad-tempered match ended in a 0–0 draw. The point proved to be enough for Uruguay.

The teams in Group F had to contend with intense heat and humidity. After a poor start – losing to Portugal and managing only a draw against Morocco – England made several important changes which suddenly transformed them into a team of confidence and enthusiasm. From being on the brink of an early exit, Lineker scored three goals to beat Poland and take them through to the second phase. Morocco finished top of the group with a stunning 3–1 victory over Portugal and became the first African team ever to qualify for the second round.

The second round got underway in front of more than 100,000 Mexican fans as the hosts took on Bulgaria. The Bulgarians never looked like achieving their first-ever World Cup win as first Negrete, with a spectacular overhead kick, and then Servin completed the Mexican victory.

On the same day, Belgium, who had struggled to qualify, faced the Soviet Union in Leon. In a thrilling end-to-end game, Russia took a first-half lead through Belanov's long-range strike. With Ceulemans in inspirational form the Belgians struck back in the 54th minute through Scifo but 15 minutes later Belanov got his second. Ceulemans himself squared the game in the 75th minute and the game went into extra-time. Belgium took a 4–2 lead – the last another cracking volley from Claesen – but Belanov closed the margin to one from the penalty spot. In the dying minutes Pfaff tipped over a clever chip from Yevtushenko to give his team victory in one of the most entertaining World Cup games ever.

The South American favourites advanced further. Poland gave Brazil a few early scares but once they got into their rhythm there was no stopping the irresistible skills of Zico, Socrates and the exciting Careca in attack and they paced themselves to a 4–0 win.

Argentina expected a tough game against their close rivals Uruguay. Maradona created plenty of opportunities but none were converted and he also had a 30-yard free-kick rebound off the crossbar. Pasculli scored for Argentina just before half-time and although there were no further goals, Argentina were dominant and good for their win.

Italy were no longer the force they had been and they met a French side approaching their peak. Platini was the creative force behind the team and he had able support from Giresse and Tigana in midfield. Platini scored the first and Stopyra the second as Italy, without Rossi, were unable to offer much threat in attack.

West Germany continued to struggle and it was left to a last-minute free-kick from Matthaus to break the Morroccans. England, on the other hand, were visibly growing in confidence and Lineker notched two more goals in England's 3–0 win over Paraguay but only after Shilton had made two world-class saves early on.

The real surprise of the round was Denmark's defeat by the Spanish. Denmark had been the revelation of the tournament and everything seemed to be going well when they took the lead in the 33rd minute. Then a terrible error by Olsen allowed Butragueno to equalise for Spain just before half-time. The second-half was all Spain and in particular Butragueno who scored three more as Spain waltzed past the bewildered Danes 5–1.

In the first of the quarter-finals, France met Brazil in Guadalajara in an open attacking game. Careca opened the scoring for Brazil and Muller came close to making it two – his shot hitting the post. It was a stern test for France but in Platini, Giresse, Tigana and Fernandez they possessed arguably one of the greatest midfield line-ups of all time.

Shortly before half-time Platini converted a simple chance to square the game. With no further goals Brazil brought on the great Zico who had been used sparingly thus far. The Brazilian fans were ecstatic that their hero was on the field and almost immediately he had the chance to score from a penalty. However, his kick was saved by Bats and with no further goals in extra-time, the game went to a penalty shoot-out. Amazingly both Socrates and Platini missed their spot kicks but after Cesar had also failed it was left for Fernandez to put France joyfully into the semi-finals.

In the worst of the quarter-finals, West Germany and Mexico battled out a goalless draw and another penalty shoot-out was required. Mexico managed to score only one as Germany went through to join France.

The third quarter-final had a special significance as it was the first meeting between England and Argentina since the end of the Falklands War.

Argentina's disciplined defence controlled Lineker in the early stages and it was the South Americans and Maradona in particular who looked the most dangerous, but the game remained dead-locked until the 50th minute. Then came probably the most infamous goal in World Cup history. Maradona had initiated a move which resulted in the ball being sliced back into the England area by Hodge. Maradona followed in and as he rose to meet the high ball with his head he clearly fisted the ball past Shilton and into the net. Despite protests from the English players the Tunisian referee awarded the goal.

Four minutes later, England were two down and this time there was no denying the brilliance of Maradona. Collecting the ball in his own half he waltzed past the English defenders and slid the ball past Shilton to score one of the greatest goals in World Cup history.

Robson brought on Barnes and England belatedly started to attack. In the 80th minute a perfect cross from Barnes was headed in by Lineker for his sixth of the tournament and the same combination just failed to level the scores three minutes from time.

The last quarter-final saw Belgium take a first-half lead against Spain thanks to the hugely impressive Cuelemans. In a wide-open game, Spain committed to attack and their perseverance was rewarded when Senor volleyed the equaliser with five minutes remaining. Extra-time failed to end the stalemate and for the third quarter-final a penalty shoot-out was needed. It took only one miss by Spain but it was enough to put Belgium through 5–4.

The first semi-final, between France and West Germany was a repeat of that of 1982. Thankfully, there was no repeat of the dreadful tackle which had injured Battiston but neither was it as good as the 1982 vintage. France were curiously restrained and never really recovered from an eighth minute free-kick by Brehme which the otherwise excellent Bats let slip under his body. France were committed to pushing forward and although they had several good chances they left themselves increasingly open at the back and in the final minute Voller sealed the German victory.

In the other semi-final, there was just no stopping Maradona as he turned on a magnificent solo performance to take Argentina past Belgium and into the final. Early in the second half he beat two defenders to score his first goal and then later left three defenders for dead before slotting the ball past Pfaff for his second.

France were left to contest the third-place play-off for the second successive time and overcame Belgium 4–2.

With Maradona in such awesome form Argentina were the clear favourites. This probably suited the West Germans who had yet again quietly reached the final. They also boasted some fine players such as Rummenigge, Matthaus and Brehme and possessed the ultimate coach in Beckenbauer.

But this was Maradona's tournament and his influence, coupled with the midfield strength of Batista, Burruchaga and Valdano up front, combined to produce a tough but skilful team.

In a packed Azteca Stadium Argentina started the better and Brown opened the scoring with a header from a free-kick in the 22nd minute. Ten minutes into the second half Maradona found Enrique who in turn found Valdano who coolly side-footed Argentina 2–0 ahead.

The South Americans were coasting, the Germans looked in disarray but as ever they rose to the occasion and with 17 minutes left Rummenigge pulled a goal back from a corner. Eight minutes later, from an almost identical situation, Voller brought the scores level. But Maradona was not to be denied his hour of glory. A sweetly timed pass beat the German offside trap and Burruchaga raced away to score the winner.

Argentina had demonstrated that they were more than a one-man team but there was no denying that Maradona was worthy of the title world's best player.

RESULTS

Group A

Bulgaria 1 Italy 1; Argentina 3 South Korea 1; Argentina 1 Italy 1; Bulgaria 1 South Korea 1; Argentina 2 Bulgaria 0; Italy 3 South Korea 2

Final table	P	W	D	L	F	A	Pts
Argentina	3	2	1	0	6	2	5
Italy	3	1	2	0	5	4	4
Bulgaria	3	0	2	1	2	4	2
South Korea	3	0	1	2	4	7	1

Group B

Mexico 2 Belgium 1; Paraguay 1 Iraq 0; Mexico 1 Paraguay 1; Belgium 2 Iraq 1; Belgium 2 Paraguay 2; Mexico 1 Iraq 0

Final table	P	W	D	L	F	A	Pts
Mexico	3	2	1	0	4	2	5
Paraguay	3	1	2	0	4	3	4
Belgium	3	1	1	1	5	5	3
Iraq	3	0	0	4	1	4	0

Group C

France 1 Canada 0; Soviet Union 6 Hungary 0; France 1 Soviet Union 0; Hungary 2 Canada 0; France 3 Hungary 0; Soviet Union 2 Canada 0

Final table	P	W	D	L	F	A	Pts
Soviet Union	3	2	1	0	9	1	5
France	3	2	1	0	5	1	5
Hungary	3	1	0	2	2	9	2
Canada	3	0	0	3	0	5	0

Group D

Brazil 1 Spain 0; Algeria 1 Northern Ireland 1; Brazil 1 Algeria 0; Spain 2 Northern Ireland 1; Brazil 3 Northern Ireland 0; Spain 3 Algeria 0

Final table	P	W	D	L	F	A	Pts
Brazil	3	3	0	0	5	0	6
Spain	3	2	0	1	5	2	4
Northern Ireland	3	0	1	2	2	6	1
Algeria	3	0	1	2	1	5	1

Group E

West Germany 1 Uruguay 1; Denmark 1 Scotland 0; West Germany 2 Scotland 1; Denmark 6 Uruguay 1; Denmark 2 West Germany 0; Scotland 0 Uruguay 0

Final table	P	W	D	L	F	A	Pts
Denmark	3	3	0	0	9	1	6
West Germany	3	1	1	1	3	4	3
Uruguay	3	0	2	1	2	7	2
Scotland	3	0	1	2	1	3	1

Group F

Morocco 0 Poland 0; Portugal 1 England 0; England 0 Morocco 0;
Poland 1 Portugal 0; England 3 Poland 0; Morocco 3 Portugal 1

Final table	P	W	D	L	F	A	Pts
Morocco	3	1	2	0	3	1	4
England	3	1	1	1	3	1	3
Poland	3	1	1	1	1	3	3
Portugal	3	1	0	2	2	4	2

Second round

Mexico 2 Bulgaria 0; Belgium 4 Soviet Union 3 (aet); Brazil 4 Poland 0;
Argentina 1 Uruguay 0; France 2 Italy 0; West Germany 1 Morocco 0;
England 3 Paraguay 0; Spain 5 Denmark 1

Quarter-finals

France 1 Brazil 1 (4–3 on penalties); West Germany 0 Mexico 0
(4–1 on penalties); Argentina 2 England 1; Belgium 1 Spain 1
(5–4 on penalties)

Semi-finals

West Germany 2 France 0; Argentina 2 Belgium 0

Third-place play-off

France 4 Belgium 2

Final

Argentina (1) 3   West Germany (0) 2
Brown   Rummenigge
Valdano   Voller
Burruchaga

Leading goalscorers: 6 Lineker (England); 5 Butragueno (Spain), Careca (Brazil), Maradona (Argentina).
Fastest goal: 63 sec, Butragueno (Spain v Northern Ireland).
Most goals: 14 (Argentina).
Total goals: 132 (average of 2.54 per game).
Total attendance: 2,391,000 (average of 45,980 per game).
Final attendance: 114,500.

ITALY 1990

Italy were awarded the 1990 World Cup at the FIFA congress in 1984, becoming, with Mexico, only the second country to host two tournaments. There was considerable concern over the ambitious programme for rebuilding stadiums and new rail and road communications but, with huge investment, the magnificent stadiums were finished on time – just.

The format for the competition remained the same as in 1986 with the 24 nations divided into six groups of four. The top two in each group went through to the second round as well as the four best third-placed teams.

The host nation, along with West Germany, Holland, Brazil and Argentina, were considered the favourites to lift the trophy.

Other nations considered strong contenders, like France and Denmark, had failed to make it through the qualifying tournament. However, the Republic of Ireland qualified for the first time ever – eliminating Northern Ireland in the qualifying round. They joined England and Scotland from the home countries.

Argentina, Brazil, Colombia and Uruguay qualified from South America although it was in Brazil's group that one of the most outrageous attempts to qualify for the finals took place. Playing at home against Chile, Brazil were leading 1–0 when a flare, thrown from the crowd, appeared to hit Rojas, Chile's goalkeeper. He collapsed in distress and was carried from the field by officials. The Chilean players claimed they could not continue the match and refused to play on. However, television evidence clearly showed that the flare had not hit Rojas and the Chilean FA were fined by FIFA for their clumsy attempt at cheating and banned from the 1994 World Cup.

The enforced absence of Mexico, for fielding over-age players in a youth tournament, opened the door for Costa Rica and the United States to qualify from the CONCACAF group.

South Korea and the United Arab Emirates qualified from Asia whilst Africa was represented by Egypt and Cameroon, who, in their previous appearance in 1982, had remained undefeated.

In a tournament which failed to live up to its promise, Cameroon were to prove one of the revelations and announced their intent in the opening game of the finals. Before a crowd of 73,000 in the magnificent San Siro stadium in Milan, Cameroon took on the holders Argentina. This was to be no easy opener for the champions for whom Maradona was only a shadow of the player who had mesmerised opponents four year previously.

As the game wore on, and despite sometimes being over eager in the tackle, Cameroon started to create promising chances and an upset was on the cards. However, the Africans' hopes took a dive when Kana Biyik was red-carded for a challenge on Caniggia but five minutes later his brother Omam-Biyik rose to head the ball past Pumpido. Justice had been done, even though it was a soft goal that Pumpido should easily have saved. But Cameroon were ahead, and, roared on by the crowd, they kept it that way despite having Massing sent off for a crude challenge on Caniggia.

After this shock result, Cameroon set about qualifying for the second round with a 2–1 win against Romania. Their hero was Roger Milla who had come out of semi-retirement for the tournament and, at 38, became the oldest man to score in the World Cup. Despite losing their final game to the Soviet Union, they finished top of their group with Romania second and the defending champions, Argentina, only sneaking through as a best third-placed team.

In Group A, Italy were under tremendous pressure to succeed. The Italian league was the richest and best-supported in the world and all Italy now wanted victory for the national team. The last time Italy had won the World Cup, in 1982, they had started cautiously with three draws. This time they won all their opening games against Austria, the United States and Czechoslovakia, and discovered a player who was to hit a rich vein of scoring form – Salvatore 'Toto' Schillaci.

In their first game, Italy were by far the better attacking team but Austria proved stubborn opponents. Schillaci was brought on with only 15 minutes remaining and caused widespread celebration by heading the winning goal. Schillaci scored another against the Czechs, a game which saw him partnered in attack with Roberto Baggio, the young striker who had cost Juventus £7.5 million.

In Group C, Brazil also qualified with a 100 per cent record but this was not a team that could be favourably compared with the Brazil of 1970 or even 1982. The attacking flair had been replaced by a more European-style approach and although they created plenty of chances they struggled to convert them into goals.

The surprise of the group was Costa Rica. In their first game, against Scotland, they were expected to confirm their pre-tournament odds of rank outsiders. But with Scotland's now traditional ability to underperform against so-called minnows, the Central Americans held their own in the first half and then scored a well-worked winner shortly after the break.

After that embarrassment Scotland got back on track with a 2–1 win over Sweden but Costa Rica, having only lost narrowly to Brazil, came from behind to beat Sweden in their final game to qualify with the Brazilians. It was a timely reminder that the gap between the established soccer nations and the newcomers was diminishing.

The captain of the victorious West German team of 1974, Franz Beckenbauer, was now coach of the national side captained by the inspirational Matthaus. In their opening match against Yugoslavia, Matthaus scored two goals, the second a brilliant solo effort in which he ran with the ball from just inside his own half before driving a powerful shot from 25 yards.

The Germans ran out impressive 4–1 winners and then put on another fine display to crush the United Arab Emirates 5–1. In their final game they came up against Colombia who had made a welcome return after 28 years absence from the World Cup. The Colombians possessed one of the most creative players, in captain Valderrama, and one of the most eccentric in goalkeeper Higuita.

Having beaten the Emirates and lost to Yugoslavia the South Americans knew a draw would be sufficient to get through to the second phase and proceeded to spoil the flow of the game. This was nearly their undoing as Littbarski scored for West Germany just before full-time only for Rincon to grab an equaliser in injury-time.

In Group E, Spain and Belgium proved too strong for South Korea and Uruguay. The Uruguayans, despite having talented individuals like Sosa and Francescoli, were in decline as a force in world soccer. The game between the European teams proved to be one of the most entertaining with both goalkeepers making fine saves. Spain won the game 2–1 and headed the group. The encounter between South Korea and Uruguay was, on the other hand, a dire confrontation but victory for the South Americans kept them in the tournament.

The final group promised to be the closest of them all – and so it proved. England drew 1–1 with the Republic of Ireland in a tight game but it was somewhat surprising that Egypt, making their first appearance in 56 years, held Holland, the 1988 European champions, to the same score. In fact, the Dutch team seemed strangely below par, despite possessing the star players, Gullit, Van Basten and Rijkaard, and Egypt fully deserved their point after some enterprising play. If any proof was still needed, this confirmed that the African teams were threatening the soccer world order.

England and Holland then played out a goalless draw – as did Egypt and the Irish. With everything to play for going into the final games England finally broke the deadlock against Egypt when Wright rose to head home Gascoigne's free-kick. This decisive win took England to the top of the table as the other game finished as yet another draw although both Ireland and Holland qualified for the second round.

Egypt were out but Cameroon were still there to represent Africa and their fairy tale continued in the second round against Colombia. After a goalless 90 minutes, super-sub Milla came on to score twice in extra-time. His second was a personal disaster for the flamboyant Higuita who was dispossessed by Milla some 30 yards outside his area. Despite Redin's late strike, Cameroon held on to become the first African nation to reach the quarter-finals although more bookings meant that they would be without key players.

Next, Skuhravy scored three of Czechoslovakia's four against Costa Rica although the final score did not do full justice to the game. The Costa Ricans were trailing only 2–1 with 15 minutes to go when they were caught twice as they committed players to attack.

The much anticipated clash between Argentina and Brazil, countries with a great soccer tradition, turned out to be a disappointment. Brazil dominated the game but squandered numerous chances; they should have won easily but it was Maradona who made the most telling move. Having been virtually anonymous for most of the game, he played a delightful ball, despite being under pressure from Brazilian defenders, to Caniggia who then coolly took the ball around the goalkeeper, Taffarel. Brazil were out.

The same day, the two heavyweights of European football were battling it out in Milan. The game will be best remembered for an unsavoury incident in the first half. In the 20th minute, Holland's

Rijkaard was booked for a foul on the German striker Voller, who in turn was booked for complaining, with justification, that Rijkaard had spat at him. Shortly after, the two were involved in another dispute and they were both dismissed. As they left the field, Rijkaard again spat at Voller.

Despite this distasteful episode, the quality of football was very good with the Germans creating the better chances. In the second half, Klinsmann gave West Germany the lead and Brehme extended it with a shot which curled around the defence and into the net. With only minutes left Holland were awarded a dubious penalty but it had arrived too late. Koeman scored from the spot but West Germany won 2–1, the same score as the 1974 World Cup final.

The Republic of Ireland were enjoying their first ever finals immensely and, although they had yet to win a game, were through to the second phase to meet Romania who had the talented Hagi and Raducioiu in the line-up. Neither side scored in 120 minutes of play and in the dreaded penalty shoot-out Timofte missed his kick for Romania. The Irish had qualified for the last eight – still without winning a game in normal time.

Italy continued to make significant progress with their star striker, Schillaci, again breaking the deadlock, this time against Uruguay. Serena scored a second and the crowd erupted in delight. Italy had won every game, had not conceded a goal and were looking worthy favourites.

The final two matches of the second round saw Yugoslavia beat Spain thanks to some excellent finishing by Stojkovic in a tight match which went to extra-time.

Extra-time was also needed to separate England and Belgium. In a close match, the Belgians hit the post twice, one a tremendous strike from 25 yards by Scifo, and England striker Barnes scored with a volley – only for his effort to be controversially ruled offside. In the final minute of extra-time, with penalties beckoning, Gascoigne pushed forward only to be brought down. He floated the free-kick into the area where Platt timed his run to swivel and hit the ball on the volley past the Preud'homme. It was a great goal and came with only seconds left.

After such a shaky start, Argentina were now, amazingly, in the quarter-finals where they faced the classy Yugoslavians. Apart from his one touch of brilliance against Brazil, Maradona had been a shadow of his former self and his team-mates also compared poorly with their predecessors. Yugoslavia produced the more attacking football throughout and looked the more likely to score in a tedious game but after 120 minutes another penalty competition was required.

Although Maradona missed his penalty, Goycochea, who had come in as a replacement for Argentina's first-choice goalkeeper Pumpido, was the South American's hero as they won the penalty competition 3–2.

The Irish, yet to win a game, met Italy, who had won all their games. Although Schillaci scored the decisive goal for Italy, the Irish put up their best performance of the finals and played with the defiance and commitment that had endeared them to the watching millions.

West Germany rediscovered some of their earlier form and played some fine attacking football against Czechoslovakia. They took the lead when Klinsmann was fouled in the penalty area. Matthaus scored from the spot but further pressure was ably defended by the Czechs who despite having chances to equalise themselves were probably fortunate not to lose by more. The one blot on the game was the increase in play-acting by the Germans.

The fourth quarter-final was the best match of the tournament as Cameroon, without four players who had been booked in earlier games, came within ten minutes of reaching the last four. This prospect seemed miles away when England's new hero, Platt, headed them into the lead after 26 minutes. But Cameroon had already sent out warning signals and duly equalised on the hour from the penalty spot when Milla, who had only come on for the second half, was adjudged to have been fouled by Gascoigne.

Four minutes later and Milla was causing havoc again, playing a neat one-two with Ekeke who slotted the ball past Shilton. Cameroon were now in control and looking good value for a place in the semi-finals but England, to their credit, reorganised themselves and started to push forward again. Nine minutes from time a rash challenge on Lineker resulted in a penalty for England which Lineker himself converted.

England had come close to elimination but in the first half of extra-time they clinched their place when Lineker was again brought down in the penalty area and again converted his penalty kick.

Cameroon had brought a fresh and uninhibited approach to the finals and their progress had been a true reflection of their ability. They had made England struggle but the Europeans now had a date with their old foes West Germany.

The first semi-final, however, pitted the hosts against Argentina who, for the first time in the tournament, showed more enterprise. Italy started well and went into the lead after 17 minutes when Schillaci scored his fifth goal of the tournament. But with the weight of expectation, Italy began to show signs of nerves. Twenty years before, the Italians would have resolutely defended their lead but now they relinquished control of the game and in the 67th minute Caniggia scored a deserved equaliser. The game went into extra-time which produced some unsavoury arguing from the Argentinians when Giusti was sent off but another penalty shoot-out inexorably beckoned.

Both teams scored from their first three kicks but then Goycochea once again demonstrated his amazing ability against spot kicks, saving from Donadoni and Serena. The unthinkable had happened. To the bitter disappointment of the home crowd, Italy were out despite playing some of the most attractive and attacking football in the competition.

The Germans were strong pre-match favourites to join Argentina in the final but rather than adopt a cagey approach, England went on the attack from the kick-off and, playing some of their finest football for years, rocked the Germans. In a thrilling game, England dominated West Germany and were desperately unlucky when Brehme's free-kick took a wicked deflection off Parker and went past Shilton. But England rallied and with ten minutes remaining Lineker equalised with a great strike from a difficult angle with two defenders in close attendance. Both sides hit the post in extra-time but with no further goals the game went to penalties. Lineker, Beardsley and Platt scored for England, but it was to no avail as first Pearce and then Waddle missed. In a sporting gesture, Matthaus, the German captain, delayed his celebrations to sympathise with the English players.

Both semi-finals had been decided on penalties and they had proved a grossly unfair way to decide a match.

The third-place play-off, normally a rather muted occasion, this time produced a match of quality and excitement. Baggio put the

Italians ahead but Platt equalised with a great header nine minutes from time. However, it was appropriate that Schillaci should have the last word. With only five minutes to go he was brought down in the penalty area and converted the kick himself to become the leading scorer in the tournament.

West Germany were expected to win the final with ease. With Italy, they had been the best team in the tournament and Matthaus had proved to be the world's best player. But just when everyone wanted to see the Germans put on an exhibition their form deserted them and we witnessed the worst final in history.

The Germans committed themselves to attack but could not convert their chances. This set the standard for the whole game as Argentina seemed wholly prepared to wait and take their chances in a penalty competition and rely on their outstanding goalkeeper.

Both teams were guilty of play-acting. In the 68th minute, the German striker Klinsmann looked as though he had been hit by a train when tackled by Monzon – a ruse which succeeded in presenting the Argentinian with the unhappy distinction of becoming the first player to be sent off in a World Cup final.

With only five minutes to go, the referee awarded West Germany a penalty after Voller had been fouled in the area. The Argentinian players were furious as he had turned down a similar looking offence for them only minutes earlier. However, Brehme coolly slotted the ball home even though Goycochea made a valiant attempt and was only inches away from saving it.

The game deteriorated badly in the last few minutes. Kohler, the German defender, appeared to be wasting time and collapsed as if he had been pole-axed when Dezotti tried to retrieve the ball off him. Dezotti was also sent off by the referee as several Argentinian players jostled the official in a disgraceful show.

It was a shame that the Germans had not beaten Argentina in the style that they had shown earlier in the tournament. This final did nothing for the game and what is the ultimate match for any footballer or fan was tarnished by this episode.

RESULTS

Group A
Italy 1 Austria 0; Czechoslovakia 5 United States 1; Italy 1
United States 0; Czechoslovakia 1 Austria 0; Italy 2 Czechoslovakia 0;
Austria 2 United States 1

Final table	P	W	D	L	F	A	Pts
Italy	3	3	0	0	4	0	6
Czechoslovakia	3	2	0	1	6	3	4
Austria	3	1	0	2	2	3	2
United States	3	0	0	3	2	8	0

Group B
Cameroon 1 Argentina 0; Romania 2 Soviet Union 0; Argentina 2
Soviet Union 0; Cameroon 2 Romania 1; Soviet Union 4 Cameroon 0;
Argentina 1 Romania 1

Final table	P	W	D	L	F	A	Pts
Cameroon	3	2	0	1	3	5	4
Romania	3	1	1	1	4	3	3
Argentina	3	1	1	1	3	2	3
Soviet Union	3	1	0	2	4	4	2

Group C
Brazil 2 Sweden 1; Costa Rica 1 Scotland 0; Brazil 1 Costa Rica 0;
Scotland 2 Sweden 1; Costa Rica 2 Sweden 1; Brazil 1 Scotland 0

Final table	P	W	D	L	F	A	Pts
Brazil	3	3	0	0	4	1	6
Costa Rica	3	2	0	1	3	2	4
Scotland	3	1	0	2	2	3	2
Sweden	3	0	0	3	3	6	0

Group D

Colombia 2 UAE 0; West Germany 4 Yugoslavia 1; Yugoslavia 1
Colombia 0; West Germany 5 UAE 1; Colombia 1 West Germany 1;
Yugoslavia 4 UAE 1

Final table	P	W	D	L	F	A	Pts
West Germany	3	2	1	0	10	3	5
Yugoslavia	3	2	0	1	6	5	4
Colombia	3	1	1	1	3	2	3
UAE	3	0	0	3	2	11	0

Group E

Belgium 2 South Korea 0; Spain 0 Uruguay 0; Spain 3 South Korea 1;
Belgium 3 Uruguay 1; Spain 2 Belgium 1; Uruguay 1 South Korea 0

Final table	P	W	D	L	F	A	Pts
Spain	3	2	1	0	5	2	5
Belgium	3	2	0	1	6	3	4
Uruguay	3	1	1	1	2	3	3
South Korea	3	0	0	3	1	6	0

Group F

England 1 Republic of Ireland 1; Egypt 1 Holland 1; England 0
Holland 0; Egypt 0 Republic of Ireland 0; England 1 Egypt 0;
Holland 1 Republic of Ireland 1

Final table	P	W	D	L	F	A	Pts
England	3	1	2	0	2	1	4
Rep of Ireland	3	0	3	0	2	2	3
Holland	3	0	3	0	2	2	3
Egypt	3	0	2	1	1	2	2

Second round
Cameroon 2 Colombia 1 (aet); Czechoslovakia 4 Costa Rica 1;
Argentina 1 Brazil 0; West Germany 2 Holland 1; Republic of Ireland 0
Romania 0 (5–4 on penalties); Italy 2 Uruguay 0; Yugoslavia 2
Spain 1 (aet); England 1 Belgium 0 (aet)

Quarter-finals
Argentina 0 Yugoslavia 0 (3–2 on penalties); Italy 1
Republic of Ireland 0; West Germany 1 Czechoslovakia 0; England 3
Cameroon 2 (aet)

Semi-finals
Argentina 1 Italy 1 (4–3 on penalties); West Germany 1 England 1
(4–3 on penalties)

Third-place play-off
Italy 2 England 1

Final
West Germany 1   Argentina 0
Brehme (pen)

Leading goalscorers: 6 Schillaci (Italy); 5 Skuhravy
(Czechoslovakia); 4 Lineker (England), Matthaus (West Germany),
Michel (Spain), Milla (Cameroon).
Fastest goal: 4 minutes, Susic (Yugoslavia v United Arab Emirates).
Most goals: 15 (West Germany).
Total goals: 150 (average of 2.21 per game).
Total attendance: 2,515,000 (average of 48,365 per game).
Final attendance: 73,603.

USA 1994

Football fans the world over threw up their hands in surprise and despair when FIFA announced that the 15th World Cup finals would be held in the USA. No-one doubted the USA's pedigree as one of the greatest sporting nations with enthusiastic fans, but dissenting voices pointed to the lack of a professional football league and newspaper polls which ranked football some way below lacrosse in the average American's sporting interests. Yet, as is often the case, the finals proved to be one of the best tournaments.

In an attempt to improve the spectacle, FIFA also introduced three points for a win in the first-round group matches and relaxed the offside law so that a game was to be stopped only if a player was interfering with play – a measure which continues to raise controversy after every game. FIFA also aimed to crackdown on tackles from behind, violent behaviour and timewasting. There would be a total of 235 bookings and 15 send-offs in the finals. On the positive side there were 141 goals scored at an average of 2.7 per game – it was just a shame that the final proved so fruitless.

However, tragedy struck the World Cup during the qualifiers. In April 1993, a plane carrying 18 members of the Zambian national team and 12 other Zambian citizens crashed off the coast of Gabon on its way to a World Cup tie in Senegal. Despite this tragedy, the Zambian side, full of inexperienced players, went into their final qualifying game against Morocco needing only a draw to reach the finals. But they lost 1–0 and Morocco qualified for their third finals.

Morocco were joined by Cameroon, the heroes of Italia '90, but perhaps Africa's strongest representative was Nigeria, who made their much-belated finals debut. For some time Nigeria had been a powerful force in international junior competitions, as well as African tournaments, and if ever there was an African team to go all the way to the deciders, this was it.

With the United States qualifying automatically as hosts, CONCACAF was given only one automatic place in the finals. Mexico, who had been banned from the finals four years earlier for fielding over-age players in a youth tournament, claimed the spot easily, to the delight of their fans.

Argentina made heavy work of qualification when finishing second in South America's Group One. Colombia won the group easily inflicting a humiliating 5–0 home defeat on Argentina in the process. It was Argentina's worst-ever defeat and if Paraguay had beaten Peru in the same group, the two-time winners would not even have had the opportunity of scrambling through. As it was, they faced Oceania champions Australia in a play-off which they narrowly shaded with a 1–0 win in Buenos Aires.

There was little respect shown for the established names in South America's Group Two either. In the thin air of La Paz, Bolivia shook Brazil 2–0, the first time Brazil had been beaten in a World Cup qualifier and an achievement celebrated in Bolivia with as much passion as if they had won the World Cup itself. It was a different story in the return which Brazil won 6–0 but Bolivia, thanks to their home form, qualified alongside their more illustrious rivals.

In Asia, it looked, at one stage, as if North Korea and Iraq would qualify for the States – neither of whom had the best relations with the hosts. But in the end it was Saudi Arabia and South Korea who won through, much to the relief of the organisers.

With Africa having been awarded a third qualifying spot, European nations were now competing for just 12 places. This led to tough qualifying groups and some surprise casualties. In Group Two, England were fancied to qualify alongside Holland but Norway had other ideas. They beat San Marino 10–0 but ensured their place in the finals by taking three out of four points off both England and Holland. This left the two 'favourites' to battle out a decider in Rotterdam. Holland won 2–0 but it was a match loaded with controversy caused in part by Koeman's foul on Platt when it seemed the Englishman would score. Not only did Koeman avoid being sent off but he rubbed salt into England's wound by scoring from a free-kick shortly afterwards. Bergkamp put the game beyond reach six minutes later.

Scotland also failed to qualify so football fans in the British Isles all became honorary Irishmen to follow the progress of the Republic of Ireland in the States. Under the inspirational management of Jack Charlton, the Republic qualified for their second successive World Cup finals but only by the smallest margin – finishing joint second with Denmark on points and goal difference. However, they edged out the Danes on goals scored.

Denmark were the European champions at the time, but even their dramatic exit was overshadowed by that of France. Needing just one point from their final two games – both at home – the French looked home and dry. Against Israel, they lost 3–2, despite being 2–1 up with only seven minutes remaining. Then, against Bulgaria, they took a 1–0 lead only for Kostadinov to score twice – the winner coming in injury time.

Elsewhere, three-times winners Italy struggled before overcoming Portugal to qualify alongside Switzerland.

The break-up of the Soviet Union caused all sorts of problems and Russia was the only team to qualify for the finals. Qualification was made easier by the withdrawal of Yugoslavia from Group Five and the Russians' only defeat was at the hands of group winners Greece. However, as both teams were safely through by then, the result was academic.

Soldier Field in Chicago had the honour of hosting the opening ceremony and first match. Despite assurances that the Americans could 'certainly put on a show' the opening ceremony was strangely subdued – enlivened only by Diana Ross' embarrassing attempts at taking a penalty.

The opening game between champions Germany and Bolivia was not much better in terms of entertainment. Klinsmann scored the only goal of the game and Bolivia's star striker Etcheverry was sent off just moments after coming on as a substitute. Still, the Germans were at least the first title-holders to win their opening game as they, rather than the hosts, were handed the pleasure of getting the tournament under way.

In Group C, Spain overcame the dismissal of Nadal midway through the first half by grabbing a 2–0 lead against South Korea early in the second. A comfortable win seemed likely until first Hong then Seo scored in the last five minutes to earn warm congratulations from their football fan leader President Kim Young-sam.

Four days later, Germany virtually booked their place in the second round with a 1–1 draw against Spain. With Hierro filling in at the back for the suspended Nadal, Spain took a surprise but deserved lead when Goycochea floated in a far-post cross which Illgner allowed to creep inside his right-hand post. Just on half-time, Moller volleyed narrowly over but three minutes into the second half Germany were level. Hassler curled in a free-kick which Klinsmann headed firmly past Zubizaretta.

Although there were chances galore when Bolivia faced South Korea the game remained goalless thanks to some dreadful finishing from both sides. Bolivia continued their tradition of having a man sent off – this time, the left-back Cristaldo.

In the final games of the group, South Korea came within inches of a 3–3 draw with the World Cup holders, after Germany had set up a 3–0 first half lead. First Hwang and then Hong, from fully 30 yards, pulled two back and had it not been for Illgner's acrobatic saves, Korea would surely have got a deserved equaliser. Spain's 3–1 victory over Bolivia ensured that both European teams went through to the last 16 but two points were not enough for Korea to qualify in third place.

One German, however, would not play any further part in the finals. Midfielder Effenberg made rude gestures at fans during the win over Korea and was booted out of the squad by manager Vogts.

The Americans got their own World Cup campaign under way with a useful draw against the Swiss at the Pontiac Silverdome, the first World Cup game to be played indoors. They went behind to a curling free-kick from Bregy but equalised with an even better one from Wynalda five minutes later.

Also in Group A, Romania produced the first upset of the finals with victory over Colombia – one of the pre-tournament favourites. Colombia dominated possession but Romania made the most of their chances on the break. First, Raducioiu held off three defenders to open the scoring and then Hagi floated the ball over the keeper from near the touchline. It looked lucky but probably wasn't. Valencia pulled one back for the South Americans but Raducioiu snatched a third, again on the break, shortly before the final whistle.

In a group of contrasting fortunes, Switzerland then made a mockery of the over-cautious approach to their opening game by hammering Romania 4–1. Sutter, Chapuisat and the returning Knup (two) scored the goals which turned the group upside down. But this was small beer compared to what was happening elsewhere in the group.

Against Colombia, the United States astonished even their own fans with their best-ever performance. The US nearly scored after 28 minutes through Wynalda but five minutes later they were really in front when Colombian defender Escobar, who was trying to cut off Harkes' cross, only managed to stab it past his goalkeeper. Stewart put the US further ahead in the 50th minute and Valencia's last minute reply came too late to spoil the US party.

Colombia went on to beat Switzerland 2–0 but Romania's 1–0 win over the hosts meant that the South Americans finished bottom of the table and were out of the competition.

But there were far more tragic consequences for Escobar. After he returned home he was shot dead outside a restaurant in his home town of Medellin. The exact reason for his murder remains unknown although gambling losses involving drug barons is thought to be the cause. Messages of condolence flooded into Colombia after his murder.

Group B offered the clear favourites in Brazil, alongside Cameroon, Russia and Sweden. The Africans had arrived in the US short of money, practice and morale and a goal from Ljung as early as the seventh minute to put Sweden ahead could have exacerbated matters. But in the sunshine of the Rose Bowl stadium the indomitable Lions turned on the old magic and Embe capitalised on a defensive lapse to put Cameroon level after half an hour.

A second loss of concentration in defence by the Swedes just after the restart allowed Omam-Biyik to steal in between Andersson and goalkeeper Ravelli and prod the ball home. But Larsson, on as a sub, struck a 30-yard effort which Bell tipped onto the crossbar only for Dahlin to volley home the rebound. The result – a thoroughly entertaining draw.

Brazil opened their campaign by walking on to the pitch holding hands like an infant school class – enthusiastically supported by all but a handful of the 81,061 crowd. They soon took control against a dispirited Russian team – a number of whom had been upset at the appointment of coach Sadyrin. The only concern for Brazilian coach Perreira was that although Dunga and Mauro Silva controlled midfield they scored only once in the first half with Romario, unmarked at the far post, toe-poking in Bebeto's cross.

Eight minutes into the second half Brazil increased their lead when Romario's sharp turn in the box was halted by Ternavski. Rai sent Kharin the wrong way and after that it was just a question of how well Kharin could repel the Brazilian attack. If it hadn't been for several smart saves the score would have much worse.

Three days later, Brazil became the first team to secure a place in the second round place when they dismantled Cameroon. After a cagey start, the first break came in the 38th minute when Romario raced on to a Mauro Silva pass to slip the ball past Bell.

In the second half, Cameroon defender Song was sent off for a late tackle on Bebeto and, at 17, became the youngest player ever to be sent off in the World Cup finals. Cameroon were obviously intent on breaking records as they immediately brought Roger Milla on as a substitute for Embe – he was now the oldest player in World Cup history. Amid all the confusion Brazil capitalised when Marcio Santos headed in the subsequent free-kick.

Milla had little opportunity to make his mark although he did cause Brazil more problems than the Russians had done in the previous game. Bebeto wrapped up a comfortable win in the 72nd minute, rolling the ball in from a tight angle.

Sweden repelled a feeble revival attempt by Russia despite going behind to a Salenko penalty as early as the third minute. The Swedes equalised with a penalty of their own with Brolin beating Kharin after Dahlin had been brought down by Gorlukovich. The Russian had been booked earlier in the game and four minutes after half-time was sent off for another foul on Dahlin with whom he had had a game-long running battle. The Swedes took advantage of their extra man and Dahlin produced a spectacular diving header to put them into the lead in the 59th minute. The final half of the game was all Sweden and Dahlin headed his second nine minutes from the end.

A terrible challenge by Dahlin in that game earned the Swedish striker his second booking in two games and he faced suspension from Sweden's following match against Brazil. Of their previous five encounters, Brazil had won four with the other drawn and so they went into this game as favourites to make it five out of six. Instead Sweden took the game to Brazil and scored first through Andersson. The Brazilians looked rattled but after Romario had equalised two minutes into the second half both teams seemed content to play out the draw.

Having looked a hapless, dispirited bunch, Russia crushed Cameroon 6–1 in their final game. Salenko scored a first half hat-trick and went on to become the only player ever to score five in one match in the finals. Even a goal by Milla with his first touch after coming on as substitute was not enough to inspire his team-mates. However, he earned himself an entry in World Cup lore as the oldest player to score in the finals.

Group D was the most fascinating of the tournament, featuring Argentina, Bulgaria, Nigeria and Greece. Maradona had declared himself fit and ready to play in his fourth World Cup finals and coach Basile picked him for their opener against Greece.

Batistuta opened the scoring for Argentina in the first minute and they were never threatened by a Greek side that seemed over-awed by the occasion. Batistuta netted a hat-trick with Maradona himself scoring the third in Argentina's 4–0 win.

Nigeria fulfilled all their promise with a powerful destruction of the Bulgarians who were still looking for the first-ever win in the finals. Yekini, having swept in the first, roared in delight with his arms stretched through the goal netting. Meanwhile, Stoichkov had a magnificently struck goal from a free-kick disallowed because it was supposed to be indirect. Just before half-time, Amokachi put Nigeria two ahead after muscling past a defender and nine minutes after the restart Amunike completed the scoring with a diving header.

In good heart, Nigeria went on to face Argentina and in a wild end-to-end opening took the lead through Siasia after just seven minutes. Thoughts of their defeat against Cameroon in 1990 surfaced but this side were made of sterner stuff and two goals from Caniggia – his second the 1,500th goal in World Cup history – secured victory.

The Nigerian defenders resorted to some violent play and committed by far the majority of fouls. They had three players booked to Argentina's one – but Caniggia's booking could be considered somewhat unfortunate as he was shown the yellow card for getting off the stretcher, rather than going off and coming back on when he required treatment.

Maradona once again turned in an excellent performance and with Caniggia, Redondo, Simeone and Batistuta playing well, Argentina looked as if they could go a long way.

But all hopes fell apart when Maradona failed a drugs test after the match. He had used a cocktail of ephedrine-based drugs in his battle to get fit and was immediately withdrawn from the Argentine squad. Despite stating that he had not realised they were a banned substance, he was thrown out of the World Cup – another dramatic chapter in the turbulent life of Maradona.

All of a sudden, Argentina's strategy and spirit vanished and from being a leading fancy they now stumbled badly. It was not a good time to meet Bulgaria who, at their 18th attempt, had finally won their first World Cup game (admittedly against Greece, the worst team in the finals) and were eager to double their tally.

Following a tight first half it was Stoichkov who provided the inspiration on the hour, sliding the ball past Islas on the break. He even doubled up as a defender when Tsvetanov was sent off as Bulgaria time and again managed to find the telling block in defence.

The Bulgarian's reward arrived in the last minute when Sirakov headed home a corner – a vital goal which put them second and Argentina third. Nigeria topped the group following their 2–0 win over Greece.

Group E was the tightest of the finals with all four teams finishing on four points. In the end it was the defence-minded Norwegians who failed to qualify for the next round, although at one stage it seemed that Italy would make an embarrassing early exit.

In an eagerly anticipated game the Italians faced the Republic of Ireland at the Giants Stadium in New Jersey – a venue guaranteeing both teams huge support. Ireland, lobster pink after just ten minutes, went ahead in the 11th. A mistake by Baresi, of all people, allowed Houghton the time to run across the Italian defence to send a looping shot beyond Pagliuca and just under the bar.

Sheridan came close to extending Ireland's lead in the second half when his rasping drive came back off the bar but they were good for their win against a disappointing Italian side.

Italy next faced the impressive Norwegians who had scored late to beat Mexico in their opening game. Defeat here would ensure an early return home and the Italians set the early pace, forcing smart saves from Thorsvedt. Then in the 21st minute, disaster struck for Italy as Pagliuca was sent off for a foul on Leonhardsen. The Italian coach Sacchi sent on reserve keeper Marchegiani but obviously had to remove an outfield player. Astonishingly, the man he chose was Roberto Baggio, his one universally acknowledged match-winning player.

With the Norwegians happy to continue defensively, there was little action for the rest of the half. Shortly after the restart the influential Baresi limped off the field and things got worse in the 68th minute when Italy were forced to introduce their third permitted substitute when Casiraghi was replaced by Massaro.

Italy took the opportunity of a free-kick to make the change and no sooner had Massaro taken his place when Signori swung over a cross for Dino Baggio to head powerfully home.

The drama was still some way from being over. Maldini damaged his right ankle but continued the game hobbling around in midfield while Massaro took over at left back.

Norway had a goal disallowed but under the circumstances, no-one could have begrudged Italy their monumental battling success.

The following day, Ireland met Mexico in the heat of Orlando and set off at a furious pace in search of an early goal. Mexico held firm and, as half-time approached, took the lead with a nicely worked move which resulted in Garcia striking a fierce 20-yard drive past Bonner. This left the Irish chasing the game in sweltering heat and humidity.

In the 66th minute Garcia scored his second, shortly after which the action immediately switched to the touchline as Ireland manager Charlton had his infamous altercation with the FIFA officials who seemed intent on preventing Aldridge from taking the field even though Coyne had left it. Despite this problem, Ireland fought back well and seven minutes from time were rewarded with a consolation goal from Aldridge. It was to prove vital as goal difference was to become a decisive factor in the group.

After his touchline antics, Charlton was banned from the bench but while his team went for a win against Norway, the Norwegians still seemed transfixed by a defensive strategy. It was hard to believe that this was the same team which had rocked England and Holland in the qualifiers but they ended up paying the price for sitting back.

In the other game, Massaro opened the scoring for Italy early in the second half. At this stage Mexico were bottom of the group while Italy looked increasingly confident and led the group. Ten minutes later, Bernal's swerving shot past Marchegiani lifted Mexico to the top of the table and it was Italy's turn to hang on desperately to third place.

Over in Group F, the Dutch were without Gullit and Van Basten but were expected to qualify comfortably alongside Belgium. In their opening game, Belgium faced Morocco but despite the tremendous heat it was the Europeans who set the early tempo. Degryse shot narrowly wide after seven minutes but then headed Belgium in front just three minutes later. They could have scored more but in the end Morocco could have considered themselves unlucky after Chaouch hit the woodwork twice.

The next day, Holland got off to a nervy start and went behind in the 18th minute when Faud Amin headed in a free-kick. Saudi Arabia nearly extended their lead before Holland equalised five minutes into the second half through Jonk.

Dutch manager Advocaat later admitted that the Saudis had played better than Holland. The Dutch gained a fortunate win when in the closing minutes Saudi keeper Mohammed Al Deayea misjudged a lob and presented Dutch winger Taument with a barely deserved winner.

The next game brought together Belgium and Holland in the presumed showdown of the group. In an enthralling match, with play swinging from end to end, Belgian goalkeeper Preud'homme laid claim to being the best goalkeeper in the tournament with an outstanding display.

Both sides created chances with Preud'homme saving well from Koeman and Rijkaard, while Grun, Scifo and Degryse went close at the other end. The deadlock was broken in the 65th minute when a Degryse corner from the left sped across the face of the Dutch area and Albert drove the ball home. Albert should have scored a second but with Preud'homme equal to anything and everything, the Dutch would find Belgium held on for a memorable win.

In the first all-Arab game in the World Cup finals, Saudi Arabia, in only their second game, beat Morocco. They took an eighth minute lead from the penalty spot only for Morocco to come back strongly and equalise through Chaouch in the 27th.

On the stroke of half-time, Saudi midfielder Amin hit a long range effort which the Moroccan goalkeeper Azmi fumbled weakly into the net. Saudi keeper Al Deayea performed heroics in the second half to lift his team into second place above Holland.

In the closing game of the group, Holland faced Morocco – a tricky fixture for the talented but out-of-sorts Dutch. They needed to win to be certain of a place in the second round. Morocco had nothing to lose and their overphysical approach led to a flurry of bookings.

Chances were few but three minutes from the interval Bergkamp pounced on a half-chance to clip the ball in from close range.

Their lead was short-lived as Nader equalised right after the break and with news that Saudi Arabia were leading Belgium, the Dutch were staring elimination in the face. But in the 79th minute Roy put the Dutch back in the lead and there they sat, precariously guarding their position as group leaders.

In the other game, the Saudi striker Owairan scored one of the goals of the World Cup when he burst from his own half to carve through the Belgian defence with a spectacular run before cracking a rising drive past Preud'homme.

The first round had witnessed high tension and drama but at the end only eight teams from the 24 were eliminated. Argentina and Italy both qualified by narrow margins but the only surprise was the non-qualification of Colombia and this was overshadowed by the tragic death of Escobar.

In the first of the second round ties, reigning champions Germany faced Belgium on a cool afternoon in Chicago. German coach Vogts brought in Helmer to replace the disgraced Effenberg and this switch gave veteran striker Voller the chance to start the game. He didn't waste his opportunity to shine and his close range effort gave Germany a sixth minute lead. Obviously pleased with his start, Voller decided to help out in defence rather than leaving it to the professionals and missed a clearance to give Grun the chance to equalise in the eighth minute.

Four minutes later and what was anticipated as a low scoring tactical game was enlivened by another goal – this time with Voller laying on Klinsmann to rifle the ball past Preud'homme. Not to be outdone, Voller had a header tipped over by the excellent Preud'homme, but there was no denying the German forward from the resulting corner as he headed his second and Germany's third goal home.

Were it not for the brilliance of Preud'homme and, when he was beaten, a dramatic goal line clearance from De Wolf, Germany would have scored more. As it was, Belgium clawed themselves back into the game and could have felt justifiably aggrieved that the game didn't go into extra-time.

In the 76th minute, Weber was brought down in the German area in what was a clear penalty offence. Swiss referee

Rothlisberger however, did not see it that way and waved play on. With a minute to go, Albert skipped through the German defence to score past Illgner and set up a rousing finale which saw even Preud'homme in his opponent's area for a corner. In the end the Germans hung on and deserved the win.

Switzerland, under the guidance of English-born manager Hodgson, had surprised many people including themselves by reaching the finals. They had come through a tough first round but were now facing Spain without their influential attacking midfielder Sutter.

The Swiss started confidently with Chapuisat, usually the source of most good moves. Strangely, it was an attacking move by him which led to Spain scoring in the 15th minute. As the Swiss midfielder picked up the ball and started moving forward he was crunched by a tackle from Nadal who had returned after his two-match suspension. The ball fell to Hierro who exploited a gap to slide a 25-yard shot past Pascolo.

As the match progressed, Switzerland had little choice but to press forward for the equaliser and might have pulled it around but for Zubizarreta's extraordinary reflex save. However, the outcome was settled when Enrique raced on to Sergi's ball and beat Pascolo to make it 2–0. His style of celebration, of running around with his shirt pulled over his head, has been much copied since.

Beguiristain scored a third from the penalty spot but the 3–0 scoreline was a little harsh on the Swiss who had acquitted themselves well in the tournament.

After their excellent displays against Belgium and Holland, Saudi Arabia went into their game against Sweden with some confidence. However, the Swedes were a well-drilled team which had played together for some time and with Andersson and Dahlin up front with Brolin tucked in just behind, they possessed a formidable strike force.

This was proved within the first five minutes as Dahlin headed home Andersson's cross to put Sweden ahead. Despite creating the better chances, they failed to add to the score and were visibly tiring in the heat as half-time approached. Suitably refreshed, the Swedes added to their lead within five minutes of the start of the second half when Andersson shot inside Al Deayea's left-hand post.

Saudi Arabia had impressed many observers in the first round matching everyone in technical ability. Now they showed great courage and introduced two attacking substitutes Al Ghesheyan and Al Muwallid. After Al Muwallid had shot just over, Al Ghesheyan pulled a goal back in the 85th minute cutting in the area and rifling in a typically spectacular shot. Saudi piled men forward in search of the equaliser but were caught on the counter as Brolin and Dahlin conspired to give Andersson the chance to kill the game.

Over in Pasadena, Argentina were still reeling from Maradona's expulsion and matters were worsened by the loss of Caniggia. They needed to be at full strength to take on the Romanians who in their captain Hagi had the so-called Maradona of the Carpathians.

As ever, Romania allowed their opponents time and space in which to knock the ball about but were merciless on the counter-attack. Dumitrescu opened the scoring in the 11th minute with a curling free-kick which deceived Islas in the Argentinian goal. Although Batistuta pulled a goal back from the penalty spot five minutes later, Argentina were no match for the quick-thinking Romanians. Dumitrescu again cut through the midfield and fed Hagi on the right whose perfect, defence-splitting pass found Dumitrescu again who tucked the ball neatly past the keeper. It was simple yet elegant.

Hagi himself made it 3–1 in the 56th minute with a glorious right-footed drive following a sublime pass from Dumitrescu. Although Balbo scraped home a second for Argentina they had been out-thought and outplayed.

The Irish had already overcome the odds once by defeating the Italians but two blunders destroyed their hopes of success over Holland. After just ten minutes the speedy Dutch forward Overmars pounced on a misjudged headed backpass from Phelan and his squared ball was put away by Bergkamp.

Shortly before half-time, Jonk was allowed space in midfield to shoot from 30 yards. Bonner, normally so reliable in the Irish goal, suffered a lapse of concentration and instead of getting his body behind the ball, fumbled it into the net. It was too much for the Irish who toiled manfully but lacked the necessary firepower in attack to cause the Dutch any undue alarm.

The hosts had amazed everyone by reaching the second round but now faced the toughest test of all, Brazil. But if you're going to go then it's best to go with style.

Given that the game was being played on 4 July, Independence Day, the hopes of the 84,000 fans were high. When Brazil were reduced to ten men for the entire second half after Leonardo was sent off for elbowing Ramos, some might even have dreamt of an upset. However, despite being a man down, the South Americans still dominated play and Bebeto's 74th minute goal after good work from Romario was enough to end the American dream.

Italy had scraped through the first round and looked set to continue the high drama against Nigeria. The African nation had been impressive in their opening games and took the lead, against the run of play, from a corner in the 27th minute. Maldini's attempted clearance only bounced off his knees to Amunike who struck the rebound past Marchegiani.

Nigeria looked confident of holding the Italians and their chances had a massive boost when Zola was sent off for the mildest of challenges having only been on as a sub for 16 minutes. Five minutes later, and Nigeria should have been awarded a penalty when Maldini pulled back Yekini in the penalty area.

But the Italians rode their luck and with two minutes remaining Roberto Baggio found enough space in the area to squeeze the ball past Rufai. Having got back in the game when all looked lost, the Italians relaxed and started to play better football – an indication of their experience of high pressure games. In the first half of extra-time, Eguavoen climbed all over Benarrivo who willingly accepted the penalty. Baggio scored from the spot and Italy held on to their hard-earned win.

The final second round game between Mexico and Bulgaria witnessed some of the most bizarre refereeing decisions of the tournament. Bulgaria took an early lead when Stoichkov, who could have taught Grumpy a few lessons in the earlier games, hit a thunderous drive after a surging run.

The referee was handing out yellow cards like party invites and Mexico's equaliser was something of a gift – a dubious penalty that even the Mexicans seemed surprised at being awarded. The game was never bad-tempered and there were few serious fouls. Four minutes after half-time, Kremenliev was shown a second yellow card and, as if not to be accused of bias, the referee then sent off Garcia for an equally innocuous offence. With no further goals the game went to penalties and, as if in retribution, Mexico missed their penalties with some style and Bulgaria went through to join six European teams as well as Brazil in the quarter-finals.

Having ridden their luck so far in the competition, Italy started brightly against Spain in the first quarter-final. After Roberto Baggio had seen his goal-bound shot deflected in the 13th minute, his namesake (no relation) Dino Baggio struck a tremendous 25-yard drive past Zubizarreta.

Having been guilty of some late tackles in the opening encounters, Spain started to develop their own attacks with Caminero going close twice in the first 30 minutes. Caminero made it third time lucky in the 59th minute when his shot took a deflection past the reinstated Pagliuca. Now Spain were on the up and they might have won the game, had their substitute, Salinas, not squandered a straightforward chance. As it was, Pagliuca's save from Salinas was a crucial point and the reprieve must have lifted the Italians as five minutes later Roberto Baggio ran clear, rounded Zubizarreta, and put Italy ahead once again.

In the last minute Spain should have been awarded a penalty when Tassotti elbowed Enrique in the face but neither official saw the offence and Italy escaped. The Italian later received a lengthy ban from FIFA but Italy were in the semi-finals.

Brazil and Holland contested the second quarter-final at the Cotton Bowl in Dallas and after a cautious first half, the game burst into life. First, Romario reacted quickly to Bebeto's cross to put Brazil ahead in the 51st minute. Just after the hour, it was Bebeto's turn to score although Dutch defenders were furious that the linesman had kept his flag down when Romario walked back from an offside position just as the through ball for Bebeto was played.

Holland were forced forward and within two minutes Bergkamp pierced the Brazilian defence to pull a goal back. Bergkamp was again influential in Holland's next goal as his determination won a corner from which Winter rose to head past the badly positioned Taffarel.

This was Brazil's sternest test so far but as the game went into the final 15 minutes they found a winner from an oft-used source. The Brazilians have always been the masters of extravagant free-kicks and Branco treated his fans to a long-distance special to win the game and put Brazil into the semi-finals for the first time since 1970.

After struggling for so long to win a World Cup game, Bulgaria had now won three games on the trot. Few saw them having much chance against the world champions, Germany, but it turned out to be one of the most exciting games in World Cup history.

In a tight first half, both teams went close with Balakov hitting the post and then Klinsmann seeing his diving header instinctively saved by Mikhailov. The do-or-die spirit of Ivanov led to him receiving several minutes' treatment after he had thrown himself in front of a full-blooded drive by Moller.

Within minutes of the restart Klinsmann clattered into the penalty area and Matthaus predictably scored from the spot. The status quo had been established and it looked as if Germany, who had been given a scare, would hold out for the win. In the 73rd minute Moller struck a fine shot against the post and although Voller netted the rebound, he was offside.

Two minutes later Buchwald brought down Stoichkov who curled a brilliant free-kick over the wall and beyond a statue-like Illgner. Three minutes later, as the buzz was still dying down, Lechkov's header put Bulgaria into the semi-finals. The unbelievable had happened.

The last quarter-final was the second game to be decided by penalties and saw Sweden reach the semi-finals for the first time since 1958. Sweden might have scored in the opening minutes but Dahlin headed against the post and the remainder of the first half passed in stalemate.

The pace of the game picked up in the second half and at 75 minutes the Swedes thought they had taken the lead through Ingesson but the forward was penalised. However, three minutes later, Sweden worked a clever free-kick in which Mild slid the ball beyond the outside of the wall for Brolin, running at an angle, to smack the ball past Prunea.

With just two minutes on the clock however, Raducioiu levelled the score from close range to force the tie into extra-time. Ten minutes in, Hagi and Dumitrescu worked an opening but the ball took a fortunate deflection off Patrik Andersson for Raducioiu to score his second. Swedish dreams of a semi-final place seemed over when Schwarz was sent off for a second bookable offence. But Kennet Andersson's rise to head the ball past Prunea sent the tie to the dreaded penalty shoot-out.

Sweden got off to a disastrous start when Mild blazed over and it wasn't until Ravelli saved Petrescu's kick that they got back on level terms. With the score at 4–4, Larsson scored Sweden's first sudden death penalty and Ravelli saved from Belodedici to set up the prize draw against Brazil.

In the semi-final, Bulgaria were unlucky to meet an Italian side which having scraped through thus far, chose this game to perform in the style which had been so eagerly anticipated of them. In a dazzling first half spell Roberto Baggio scored two corkers as Italy threatened to run riot with Donadoni and Maldini also going close.

Just before half-time, Stoichkov pulled one back from yet another penalty, but the second half proved something of an anti-climax. Despite claims for handball and a foul on Lechkov, Bulgaria's tendency to play for free-kicks worked against them in the end. A silly challenge by Costacurta brought him a yellow card which, added to an early one, meant that he would miss the final.

In Pasadena, the heat, travelling and number of games had taken their toll on the weary Swedes who hung on as best they could against the dominance of Brazil. Despite nice touches, deft flicks and a hatful of chances for Brazil, the game remained goal-less at half-time thanks mainly to some loose finishing and a series of good stops from Ravelli who was celebrating his 116th inter-national.

The same pattern continued into the second half and again Ravelli pulled out some tremendous saves despite his mad, wild-eyed grimaces to camera. Brazil had all the possession and in the 63rd minute they also had numerical advantage when Thern was sent off for kicking out at Dunga.

With ten minutes to go, Romario finally rose to head home a cross and send Brazil into the final.

If the Swedes had appeared lacklustre and tired in their semi-final, the same and more could be said for the Bulgarians when the two teams met in the dreaded third-place play-off. First half goals from Brolin, Mild, Larsson and Kennet Andersson effectively killed the game and the final 4–0 scoreline was perhaps an unfair reflec-tion on the Bulgarians who had made such progress in these finals. Bulgaria's biggest regret was that Stoichkov could not add to his six-goal tally and so remained the tournament's equal top-scorer with Salenko.

And so to the final in Pasadena in front of 94,194 expectant fans. Italy's coach Sacchi surprised many people by playing Roberto Baggio, despite a hamstring strain, and recalling veteran sweeper Baresi just three weeks after a cartilage operation. Brazil's coach Parreira named a virtually unchanged side.

The first half was a cagey affair with Brazil testing the disciplined Italian defence. In the 12th minute Dunga fired in a cross but Romario, unmarked, only managed to head the ball into Pagliuca's grateful arms. Five minutes later and Baresi, of all people, played a wonderful defence-splitting pass only for Taffarel to save Massaro's shot.

It was Brazil that created the better chances and it was Pagliuca who was by far the busier keeper, twice parrying fierce free-kicks from Branco and also dropping low to save well from Romario.

The second half followed much the same pattern although the tension was lifted by a bizarre incident. In the 75th minute, Mauro Silva, the driving force for Brazil in midfield, shot from 20 yards and watched Pagliuca spill the ball only for it to rebound off the post and back into his arms. The goalkeeper kissed the post in thanks.

With the score still 0–0 after 90 minutes the game entered extra-time with Brazil again having the clearer chances. Cafu and Maldini had been having a fascinating duel since the Brazilian came on as a sub in the first half and he had twice created scoring chances. His first cross evaded Pagliuca but Bebeto, at the far post, was also strong footed and could only prod the ball back to Pagliuca.

Another cross from Cafu to the far post found Romario who amazingly put the ball wide when it seemed easier to score.

Throughout the final Baresi was an absolute colossus in defence and made numerous saving tackles. Baggio, on the other hand, was having a quiet game. No doubt suffering from the hamstring injury, he was never as sharp as in the games leading up to the final and his one clear effort in extra-time was indicative of his performance – shooting weakly when in the clear. No-one wanted to hear the final whistle, indicating as it would, the penalty shoot-out.

Italy made the worst possible start when Baresi blasted over the bar but Pagliuca kept Italy level by saving from Marcio Santos. Albertini then scored for Italy, Romario squared for Brazil. Evani put Italy ahead and Branco levelled for Brazil. Taffarel saved from the unfortunate Massaro and with Dunga scoring for Brazil it was up to Baggio, the hero of so many games, to score and keep Italy's hopes alive. His shot sailed over the bar and Brazil became champions for the fourth time.

Brazil were undoubtedly the best team in the finals but this was a sad way to end it all. After a thoroughly enjoyable tournament the abiding memory was of a final which was one game too far. The players had run out of attacking flair in what should have been the showpiece event. It was a desperately unsatisfactory way to decide the world champions but USA '94 still ranks as one of the best-ever staged.

RESULTS

Group A
USA 1 Switzerland 1; Romania 3 Colombia 1; USA 2 Colombia 1; Switzerland 4 Romania 1; Romania 1 USA 0; Colombia 2 Switzerland 0

Final table	P	W	D	L	F	A	Pts
Romania	3	2	0	1	5	5	6
Switzerland	3	1	1	1	5	4	4
USA	3	1	1	1	3	3	4
Colombia	3	1	0	2	4	5	3

Group B
Cameroon 2 Sweden 2; Brazil 2 Russia 0; Brazil 3 Cameroon 0; Sweden 3 Russia 1; Russia 6 Cameroon 1; Brazil 1 Sweden 1

Final table	P	W	D	L	F	A	Pts
Brazil	3	2	1	0	6	1	7
Sweden	3	1	2	0	6	4	5
Russia	3	1	0	2	7	6	3
Cameroon	3	0	1	2	3	11	1

Group C

Germany 1 Bolivia 0; Spain 2 South Korea 2; Germany 1 Spain 1;
South Korea 0 Bolivia 0; Spain 3 Bolivia 1; Germany 3 South Korea 2

Final table	P	W	D	L	F	A	Pts
Germany	3	2	1	0	5	3	7
Spain	3	1	2	0	6	4	5
South Korea	3	0	2	1	4	5	2
Bolivia	3	0	1	2	1	4	1

Group D

Argentina 4 Greece 0; Nigeria 3 Bulgaria 0; Argentina 2 Nigeria 1;
Bulgaria 4 Greece 0; Nigeria 2 Greece 0; Bulgaria 2 Argentina 0

Final table	P	W	D	L	F	A	Pts
Nigeria	3	2	0	1	6	2	6
Bulgaria	3	2	0	1	6	3	6
Argentina	3	2	0	1	6	3	6
Greece	3	0	0	3	0	10	0

Group E

Rep of Ireland 1 Italy 0; Norway 1 Mexico 0; Italy 1 Norway 0;
Mexico 2 Rep of Ireland 1; Italy 1 Mexico 1; Rep of Ireland 0 Norway 0

Final table	P	W	D	L	F	A	Pts
Mexico	3	1	1	1	3	3	4
Rep of Ireland	3	1	1	1	2	2	4
Italy	3	1	1	1	2	2	4
Norway	3	1	1	1	1	1	4

Group F

Belgium 1 Morocco 0; Holland 2 Saudi Arabia 1; Saudi Arabia 2
Morocco 1; Belgium 1 Holland 0; Holland 2 Morocco 1;
Saudi Arabia 1 Belgium 0

Final table	P	W	D	L	F	A	Pts
Holland	3	2	0	1	4	3	6
Saudi Arabia	3	2	0	1	4	3	6
Belgium	3	2	0	1	2	1	6
Morocco	3	0	0	3	2	5	0

Second round
Brazil 1 USA 0; Holland 2 Rep of Ireland 0; Romania 3 Argentina 2;
Sweden 3 Saudi Arabia 1; Bulgaria 1 Mexico 1 (3–1 on penalties);
Germany 3 Belgium 2; Spain 3 Switzerland 0; Italy 2 Nigeria 1 (aet)

Quarter-finals
Brazil 3 Holland 2; Sweden 2 Romania 2 (5–4 on penalties);
Bulgaria 2 Germany 1; Italy 2 Spain 1

Semi-finals
Brazil 1 Sweden 0; Italy 2 Bulgaria 1

Third-place play-off
Sweden 4 Bulgaria 0

Final
Brazil 0 Italy 0 (3–2 on penalties)

Leading goalscorers: 6 Stoichkov (Bulgaria); Salenko (Russia)
Fastest goal: 1 minute. Batistuta (Argentina v Greece)
Most goals: 15 (Sweden)
Total goals: 141 (average of 2.7 per game)
Total attendance: 3,567,415 (average of 68,604 per game)
Final attendance: 94,194

TEN ALL-TIME
WORLD CUP GREATS

FRANZ BECKENBAUER

Franz Beckenbauer was an outstanding captain and a supreme attacking sweeper. Born in Munich in 1945 he was playing for Bayern Munich before he was 18 and had established himself as a regular member of the national side by the age of 20. He was known as 'Der Kaiser' because of his supposed arrogance, but, in fact, he is a shy and pleasant man.

In the 1966 World Cup Beckenbauer scored twice against Switzerland in his first World Cup game and also found the net against Uruguay and the Soviet Union. In the final, Beckenbauer man-marked Bobby Charlton and although he kept the England man quiet, West Germany lacked the creative touches in midfield which Beckenbauer normally provided.

In the 1970 World Cup, the two teams met again in the quarter-finals. Beckenbauer had now developed his role as an attacking sweeper and his ability to read the game was crucial to West Germany's success. Although England took a 2–0 lead, Beckenbauer orchestrated the Germans' recovery and subsequent victory.

In 1972 Beckenbauer led a great West German team to the European Championship and was named European Footballer of the Year, a title he was awarded again in 1976. But his greatest triumph came in 1974 when he captained West Germany to a 2–1 victory over Holland in the World Cup final.

He retired from international football in 1977 after winning 103 caps for his country but soon joined the New York Cosmos where he won two North American Soccer League (NASL) championships. He was appointed national coach in 1984 and took West Germany to the 1986 and 1990 World Cup finals; becoming only the second man (after Mario Zagalo of Brazil) to win the World Cup as a player and manager when West Germany beat Argentina in the 1990 final.

PELÉ

He was born Edson Arantes do Nascimento but to football fans all over the world he is known as Pelé. Born in 1940 in Tres Coracoes, Brazil, he went on to become the greatest player of all time.

Amazingly, Pelé played for just two clubs throughout his career. A natural athlete, he excelled at football and made his senior debut for his beloved Santos when he was only 15. He made his international debut at the age of 16 in 1957 – coming on as a substitute to score against Argentina.

Pelé missed the first two games of the 1958 World Cup before making his World Cup debut against Russia. He hit his first World Cup goal against Wales, before scoring a hat-trick against France in the semi-final. He completed his first World Cup with two more in Brazil's 5–2 win over Sweden in the final.

Injury in the second game of the 1962 World Cup prevented Pelé from taking any further part in the competition and ruthless tackling in the game against Portugal four years later led to him threatening never to play in the World Cup again.

But before the 1970 triumph came the little matter of scoring his 1,000th goal in November 1969 against Vasco de Gama at the Maracana Stadium in Rio. Despite Pelé's incredible scoring record he was also quick to create opportunities for others. In the 1970 World Cup final he headed Brazil into the lead before setting up Jairzinho and then Carlos Alberto with wonderful passes. Throughout the competition Pelé demonstrated a wonderful range of skills, the most outrageous example probably being a lob from his own half against Czechoslovakia which missed the target by inches.

Pelé played his final game for Santos in 1974 but came out of retirement to join his second club, the New York Cosmos. He played his farewell game for the Cosmos in front of a 75,000 crowd in 1977.

The mark that Pelé has left on world football is immeasurable. He became the mark by which greatness is measured. His goalscoring achievements were staggering and his great enthusiasm for the game should be a lesson to all. He is still an ambassador for the game.

JOHAN CRUYFF

Cruyff was born in a poor district of Amsterdam in 1947. His mother worked as a cleaner at Ajax, the club with which he was to gain so much success. Cruyff became one of the outstanding players of the 1970s and one of the greatest all-round players the world has seen. Tall yet slightly built, Cruyff had stunning acceleration and the ability to change direction instantly. His speed was deceptive but his excellent control was there for all to see. Perhaps his only failing was his demonstrative temperament.

In 1947, football in Holland was played largely on an amateur or semi-professional basis but by 1970, Holland had grown to be one of the most successful footballing countries in Europe. At the age of ten, the young Cruyff was playing in the Ajax youth scheme (which has also seen the development of stars like Van Basten and Bergkamp). He made his debut for the first team at the age of 17 and helped Ajax win the championship in only his second season. Then followed the league and Cup double as Cruyff became the top goalscorer in the Dutch league. Cruyff won his first international cap at the age of 19 against Hungary and steered Ajax to three consecutive European Cup victories between 1971 and 1973.

Following this phenomenal success, many European teams were keen to sign the Dutch star and in 1973 Cruyff joined Barcelona for a then record fee of £922,000. Later that year, he was voted European Footballer of the Year for the second time.

Holland qualified for the 1974 World Cup in Germany and Cruyff more than anyone orchestrated their progress to the final where they lost to the hosts. However, their fluid style of play, known as 'total football', impressed the world.

Cruyff helped Holland reach the 1978 World Cup finals but refused to go to Argentina for the finals. He was only 31 and could perhaps have swung the balance for Holland.

He subsequently came out of retirement and spent three years in the North American Soccer League before returning to Spain in 1981 to play for Levante. The following year he returned to Ajax, winning another league title with them and then another with Feyenoord who he joined in 1984.

Cruyff's success continued when he went into management. He led Ajax to a European Cup Winners' Cup success and Barcelona to two Spanish Cup wins, a European Cup Winners' Cup success, four league titles (1991–1994) and the European Cup in 1992.

He scored 33 goals in 48 internationals for Holland and was named European Footballer of the Year three times.

DIEGO MARADONA

The boy wonder, Diego Armand Maradona, was born in Buenos Aires on 30 October 1960 to a poor family. He showed exceptional ability at an early age and made his senior debut for Argentinos Juniors ten days before his 16th birthday. In his second season he became Argentina's youngest-ever international when he was selected to play against Hungary at the age of 16.

Such was his talent that the national team's coach, Luis Cesar Menotti, was worried that the youngster would suffer as a result of the pressure of media attention, particularly in the build-up to the 1978 World Cup, which was being held in Argentina. Menotti made the brave and unpopular decision to leave him out of the squad for the finals. Luckily for Menotti, Argentina won the World Cup.

Maradona was in outstanding goalscoring form for his club when he was signed by Boca Juniors in 1980. He then joined Barcelona for a then world-record fee of nearly £5 million in 1982.

His reputation in world football had reached such a height that when he appeared for his country in the 1982 World Cup finals in Spain he was a marked man. He made his World Cup debut on his new home ground, the Nou Camp stadium in Barcelona, but was subjected to some rough tactics. However, he scored twice against Hungary as Argentina got through to the second round. Against Italy he faced the experienced defender, Gentile, who followed Maradona all over the pitch, chopping him down time and again. Maradona took his frustration out on Brazil in the next game and was sent off for kicking out at Batista. His and Argentina's tournament was over.

Maradona brought success to Barcelona but in the summer of 1984 he joined Napoli for another record fee of £6.9 million. He spent his early years there collecting championships with a team which had historically given way to the dominance of the northern clubs in Serie A.

But it is perhaps the summer of 1986 that best summarises the genius of Maradona as a player. This time the World Cup was held in Mexico and the Argentinian was now at his peak.

In the opening game he was involved in all three goals against South Korea and this set the scene for the rest of the tournament. Although a marked man, he was stronger, quicker and more mature – he took the knocks but most of the time defenders found themselves chasing his shadow. He made a good Argentinian team into an excellent one and against England and Belgium scored two of the most memorable goals in the history of the World Cup.

Maradona helped Napoli to the league and Cup double in 1987 and the league in 1990. In the World Cup of that year, Maradona was no longer the force he had been although he led Argentina to the final.

Since then Maradona's career has been plagued by injury, drug scandals and constant media attention. He was banned from the 1994 World Cup finals when he failed a drugs test after the first-round match against Nigeria. He had used a cocktail of ephedrine-based drugs in his battle to get fit and was immediately withdrawn from the Argentine squad.

He has made several unsuccessful comebacks and in January 1998 suggested that he might return to Napoli although it was unclear in what capacity.

GERD MULLER

Gerd Muller was a striker with an instinctive feel for scoring goals. Nicknamed 'Der Bomber', he may not have scored spectacular goals from distance but once inside the penalty area he always seemed to be quickest to the ball, and was lethal from this range.

Born in November 1945 in Bavaria, Muller began playing for his local club, Nordlingen, before joining Bayern Munich who also signed another talented youngster, Franz Beckenbauer, around the same time. With the great Sepp Maier in goal, Bayern Munich then started out on the most successful phase of their history. They won the German Cup in 1966 and 1967, the European Cup Winners' Cup in 1967 and the Bundesliga in the 1968/69 season. Throughout this time, Muller was scoring at a prolific rate.

Muller made his national team debut in 1966 in West Germany's first game after their World Cup final defeat. By 1970 he was averaging a goal a game and helped West Germany reach the World Cup finals where they were one of the favourites to win. He scored in their 2–1 victory over Morocco and announced his presence in true style with successive hat-tricks against Bulgaria and Peru. These victories set up a repeat encounter against England, winners of the 1966 final.

England took a 2–0 lead but the Germans levelled the score before Muller volleyed the winner. In the semi-final against Italy, Muller scored two more to take his total for the tournament to ten but it was not enough to stop the Italians going through 4–3. Recognition of his performances followed when he was voted European Footballer of the Year.

Bayern Munich continued to dominate the Bundesliga with Muller, the league's leading scorer for three successive years. In 1974, West Germany reached the World Cup final where they faced Holland. With the score at 1–1 Muller received the ball in the area and scored with a brilliant goal on the turn that left Krol, the Dutch defender, struggling to keep his balance. It was only a half-chance but the goal demonstrated the striker's instinct and characterised his style. He would spend hours practising darting runs and quick turns, confident that he could turn more quickly than big defenders.

This World Cup-winning goal took Muller's total to a record aggregate of 14 in World Cup finals and marked his last match in international football. He had scored 68 goals in 62 internationals. His tally of goals in the Budesliga was 365 and he also scored 36 goals in the European Cup – Europe's toughest club competition.

JUAN ALBERTO SCHIAFFINO

Juan Alberto Schiaffino masterminded the Uruguayan team in two World Cups and confounded the critics who had claimed that with his slight physique he would be no match for the toughest defenders. He became one of the best attacking players of his generation.

Born in Montevideo in 1925, Schiaffino joined the Penarol youth team at 17 and quickly earned his place in the first team. The slender young man was a fine passer of the ball and demonstrated great vision. He was quick, had excellent control and was a superb finisher.

Schiaffino was selected for the national team and in the 1950 World Cup finals in Brazil he scored four in a runaway 8–0 success over Bolivia which put them into the final pool with Brazil, Sweden and Spain.

After a desperate 2–2 draw against Spain and coming from behind twice to beat Sweden 3–2, Uruguay faced the overwhelming favourites, Brazil, in the final, held at the Maracana stadium. It seemed a formality for the hosts and they piled continuous pressure on Uruguay, eventually scoring two minutes into the second half. But Uruguay were a spirited side and determined not to let Brazil settle. Schiaffino worked tirelessly throughout and his efforts were rewarded with an equaliser in the 66th minute. He then instigated another move for Ghiggia to score. Unbelievably, Uruguay had won and the team received a hero's welcome when they returned to Montevideo.

Four years later, Schiaffino was part of a talented Uruguayan team which beat Scotland 7–0 and England 4–2 on the way to the semi-finals. Here, they met the mighty Hungarians but, despite going 2–0 down, Uruguay again showed great resilience to equalise and force the game into extra-time. Both Uruguayan goals came from Hohberg but it was Schiaffino who had created both chances. In extra-time, Schiaffino was injured and this allowed Hungary to regain their advantage.

Schiaffino was now at the height of his career and shortly after the 1954 World Cup finals, AC Milan paid a world record fee of £72,000 for him. He enjoyed a long career in Italy before retiring in 1962.

In 1976, Schiaffino took charge of his old club Penarol and even had a brief spell as the national team manager.

GORDON BANKS

Gordon Banks rivals Russia's Lev Yashin as the greatest goalkeeper to play in the World Cup. And if he is remembered for just one incident, it must surely be the one-handed save he made from Pelé in the 1970 World Cup. Pelé met Jairzinho's cross with a powerful downward header which seemed certain to be a goal. But Banks flung himself to his right and managed to scrape the ball off the line and send it upwards over the crossbar. It is still considered the finest reaction save ever made.

Born in Sheffield in 1937, Banks signed first for Chesterfield and, after finishing his National Service, for Leicester City. He made his international debut against the old enemy Scotland in 1963 who, ironically, were to be the opposition in his last international match nine years and 73 caps later.

Banks was an agile and brave goalkeeper who quickly established himself as first choice for England. He had great positional sense and natural elasticity. At his peak, Banks was regarded as the greatest goalkeeper in the world, yet he never played for a fashionable club.

In the 1966 World Cup, he remained unbeaten in England's first four games and it was not until the semi-final that Eusebio managed to put the ball past him – and that was only from the penalty spot. For sheer drama the final was one of history's finest but Banks, and England, achieved their dream.

England arrived in Mexico for the 1970 World Cup finals with a stronger squad than that which had won the cup four years previously. Banks was still keeping all at bay but England looked shaky in their opening game against Romania, despite winning 1–0. Then followed the game that would have proved a fitting final. Brazil, with Pelé, Jairzinho, Rivelino and Tostao, were a formidable side but England matched them in every department. Banks could do nothing to stop Jairzinho's drive but his save from Pelé's header kept England in the match.

Despite this loss, victory over Czechoslovakia set up a quarter-final clash against West Germany. Two days before the game, Banks learned that we was to be awarded the OBE but on the morning of the game he was taken ill with a stomach ailment and was unfit to play. England should still have won as they took a 2–0 lead but errors from the replacement goalkeeper, Peter Bonetti, and a tactical mistake – bringing off Bobby Charlton rather than the tiring Terry Cooper – allowed the Germans to win the game 3–2.

At the beginning of the 1972/3 season, Banks was involved in a car crash where he suffered serious damage to his right eye. This effectively finished his career although he had two seasons with Fort Lauderdale in America.

EUSEBIO

Eusebio was a vital ingredient in the success of Portuguese football at both club and international level throughout the 1960s.

Born in Mozambique in 1942, Eusebio da Silva Ferreira was a supreme artist with the ball and a superb athlete. At the age of 19, he moved from his local club to join Benfica of Lisbon. He quickly established himself as a lethal striker, scoring twice in Benfica's 5–3 defeat of the mighty Real Madrid in the 1962 European Cup final.

Eusebio won the first of his international caps for Portugal in 1961 and was voted European Footballer of the Year the same year, an honour he was to receive again in 1965.

His brilliant performances and stunning goals in the 1966 World Cup made him the tournament's top scorer with nine goals – four coming in the amazing fightback against North Korea. Although no one man is greater than the team, Eusebio proved himelf the exception in this extraordinary game. The North Koreans had already sent Italy to an ignominious defeat and within 25 minutes of their quarter-final against Portugal, one of the cup favourites, they were 3–0 up. Eusebio refused to accept defeat and almost single-handedly dragged his team back into contention with two goals before half-time. After an hour he equalised and then scored a fourth before Augusto completed Portugal's 5–3 victory.

It was to be a different story in the semi-final as England's well-organised team denied Eusebio the opportunity of making his usual impression. Perhaps the most abiding memory is of a distraught Eusebio being comforted by team-mates after their 2–1 defeat by the eventual champions.

Eusebio will be best remembered for his tremendous speed and one of the most ferocious right-foot shots ever seen. He was the leading scorer in the Portuguese league every year from 1964 to 1973 and helped Benfica to considerable domestic and European success.

A knee injury in the 1970s effectively finished his first-class career although he reappeared in Mexico and the United States and in 1976 helped Toronto Metros-Croatia win the Football Bowl.

BOBBY CHARLTON

Bobby Charlton possessed a sublime talent on the pitch throughout his playing career and continues to be a significant roving ambassador for the game to this day.

Born in 1937, Charlton signed for Manchester United in 1954 as one of United's 'Busby Babes', the nickname given to the group of exciting young players signed by manager Matt Busby. Charlton remained faithful to Manchester United for his entire career.

The 'Busby Babes' seemed destined to become one of the finest club teams ever seen but tragically the heart of the team was killed in an aircrash at Munich airport on the team's return to England after a European Cup match in February 1958. Eight players, three officials and eight journalists died in the disaster.

Bobby Charlton was the link between that great team and the next great Manchester United side. He made his first appearance for England in 1958 and played a crucial role in England's re-emergence as a world football power in the 1960s, playing alongside players like Banks, Moore and Greaves.

Charlton had started out as an attacker but he soon developed a deeper-lying role from where he could make devastating runs or deliver long, accurate passes. This role was very demanding but Charlton's athleticism and will to win were equal to it. And all these qualities were evident in England's finest achievement – the 1966 World Cup win.

In their opening game England had been held to a goalless draw by the defensive tactics of Uruguay. In England's second match,

Mexico adopted similar tactics, challenging the hosts to take the initiative. The crowd was getting restless when Charlton collected the ball in his own half, beat two defenders, and unleashed a fierce right-footed shot that gave Calderon, the Mexican goalkeeper, no chance. Charlton also had a hand in England's second goal with a great defence-splitting pass to Greaves whose shot rebounded for Hunt to score. Those two incidents restored the nation's faith in their team.

In the semi-final, England met Portugal and once again Charlton gave an exhibition of the art of goalscoring. His first was side-footed from 20 yards and his second was hit on the run with such power and accuracy that even the Portuguese players applauded the Manchester United star. Charlton's role in the final was somewhat cancelled out by Franz Beckenbauer but, by the same token, he did not allow the young German to have such an influential role either. To cap a memorable year, Charlton was named European Footballer of the Year.

Manchester United had won the league title in 1965 and repeated the feat in 1967. The following year, Charlton captained them to European Cup glory, scoring twice in the historic victory over Benfica as United became the first English club to win the trophy. The combination of Charlton, George Best and Denis Law still evokes wonderful memories for all those who saw United play in their heyday.

In the 1970 World Cup finals England had struggled through their opening group and faced West Germany in the quarter-final. Charlton was playing his 106th time for his country and all seemed to be going well when they went 2–0 ahead. But Beckenbauer reduced the deficit and, shortly after, Alf Ramsey took off Charlton. Although he was tiring, many thought that this was a tactical mistake – such was Charlton's influence over his team and opponents that it could only have given the Germans fresh heart. No doubt the point will be debated forever but West Germany went on to win the match. This marked Charlton's final game for his country – a disappointing end for England's then most-capped player and still their record goal-scorer.

Charlton bowed out at Old Trafford in April 1973 after scoring 247 goals in 754 games. In 1984 he joined the United board, combining his work with football schools for youngsters.

His finishing apart, Bobby Charlton will always be remembered for his powerful running and sudden bursts of acceleration which enabled him to swerve away from opponents at speed before switching the direction of attack with an accurate long pass.

MICHEL PLATINI

The French national team of the 1980s was one of the most artistic and talented sides to have ever graced the World Cup finals. And they were also one of the unluckiest. In Spain in 1982 and again four years later in Mexico, they deserved a place in the final but were beaten by West Germany on both occasions.

Although the team included such talented players as Jean Tigana, Alain Giresse, Dominique Rocheteau and Marius Tresor, the player who was the lynchpin and exemplified the true artistry and flair of French football was Michel Platini.

Born in 1955, Platini began his career in 1972 at Nantes, his home-town club, where his father was the coach. In 175 appearances Platini scored 98 league goals, including one against Nice which won the French Cup. Seven years later he was bought by Saint Etienne who sold him to Italian giants Juventus in 1982 for £1.2 million.

Platini made his international debut in 1976 and represented his country in the 1978 World Cup finals. France did not get past the first round then but they made significant progress in 1982 when they reached a semi-final against West Germany. The Germans took the lead but, with Platini in sparkling form, an equaliser was always likely. When France were eventually awarded a penalty Platini kissed the ball before placing it on the spot and then fired home.

The game went into extra-time when the French scored twice, and they seemed to be on their way to the final. Perhaps the French should have consolidated their lead or perhaps they lacked the resilience of the Germans who scored twice to level the game. In the penalty shoot-out which followed Bossis fired his shot at the German goalkeeper and the French were out.

Two years later, France demonstrated in the European Championship that they were the best team in Europe, if not the world. For Platini the tournament was a great personal triumph that elevated his reputation to the level of players such as Pelé, Cruyff and Beckenbauer. He scored nine goals in the five games, including one of his special curling free-kicks in the final against Spain. Platini's free-kicks were deadly; a skill gained by years of practice in swerving shots around a wall of wooden dummies.

In the same year, Platini won the second of three successive European Footballer of the Year awards and the first of two World Footballer of the Year titles. He enjoyed great success with Juventus in Italy and in European club competitions – all of which guaranteed him recognition as a world-class player.

By the time of the 1986 World Cup finals, the French team was reaching its peak. Platini had confirmed his status as one of the best players in the world and it was his goal which defeated reigning champions Italy. In the next round the French faced Brazil in what turned out to be one of the most entertaining games in World Cup history. Brazil took the lead but again Platini was on hand to slot the ball home coolly for the equaliser. The game went to extra-time and penalties and, although Platini missed, the French won through to the semi-finals.

Drained by their efforts and the 100-degree heat they had endured in the classic quarter-final France could not lift their game against West Germany and once again failed to reach the final, losing 2–0.

Platini retired the following year after winning 72 caps for France and scoring a record 41 goals. He was appointed manager of the French national team but resigned after a disappointing European Championship finals in 1992.

He has since been one of the chief organisers behind France 98 and if the championship has anything like the style and flair Platini showed on the pitch it will be a tremendous spectacle.

WORLD CUP RECORDS

The first World Cup goal was scored by Lucien Laurent for France after 19 minutes against Mexico in 1930.

Frenchman Juste Fontaine scored a record 13 goals in six matches in the 1958 finals.

Gerd Muller scored ten goals for West Germany in 1970 and four goals in 1974 for the highest aggregate of 14 goals.

Jairzinho (Brazil) scored seven goals in six games in 1970. The only other player to score in every match in a finals is Alcide Ghiggia of Uruguay with four goals in four games in 1950.

Oleg Salenko became the only player ever to score five goals in one match in the finals in Russia's 6–1 win over Cameroon in 1994.

Ramon Gonzales of Paraguay earned the dubious distinction of scoring the first own goal in the game against the United States in 1930.

Guillermo Stabile scored the first World Cup finals hat-trick, for Argentina against Mexico in 1930. Geoff Hurst is the only player to score a hat-trick in a World Cup final in England's 4–2 win against West Germany in 1966.

The highest number of goals scored in a World Cup tournament is 141 in 1994. However, that was in 52 games and the average was 2.7 per game. For a true goal-fest, 1954 was the winner when 140 goals came at an average of 5.38 per game. Austria's 7–5 victory over Switzerland certainly helped towards the total.

The highest number of goals scored by one team is 27 by Hungary in 1954. It was little consolation for losing to Germany in the final though.

England scored just 27 seconds into their opening match against France in 1982. Bryan Robson's goal beat the previous record by three seconds.

The record margin of victory in a World Cup final tournament is nine goals: Hungary 10 El Salvador 1 (1982); Hungary 9 South Korea 0 (1954); Yugoslavia 9 Zaire 0 (1954). The highest aggregate is 12: Austria 7 Switzerland 5 (1954).

Brazil were unbeaten in 13 consecutive World Cup matches between 1958 and 1966, winning 11 and drawing two. They were finally beaten 3–1 by Hungary. Italy hold the record for most successive wins, seven between 1934 and 1938.

At the age of 17 years and 41 days, Norman Whiteside of Northern Ireland became the youngest-ever player in the finals when he played against Yugoslavia in the 1982 finals.

Dino Zoff became the oldest player, at 40, to win a World Cup winners' medal when he captained Italy to their 1982 success.

Cameroon's Roger Milla had the distinction of being the oldest player in World Cup history when he appeared, aged 42, as a substitute in the 6–1 defeat by Russia in 1994. He became the oldest player to score when he claimed Cameroon's consolation goal in that match.

Peru's captain, Mario de las Casas, earned the unwelcome distinction of being the first player to be sent off, in the game against Romania in 1930.

Cameroon defender Song was sent off in the 1994 tournament against Brazil to become, at 17, the youngest player ever sent off in the World Cup finals.

Gianluca Pagliuca became the first goalkeeper to be sent off, in Italy's first-round game against Norway in 1994.

Peru were the first winners of FIFA's Fair Play award with no cautions in the 1970 finals.

The 1994 final between Brazil and Italy was the first to be decided by penalties. Brazil had become the first country to win the World Cup final three times when they earned the right to keep the Jules Rimet Trophy in 1970. They now stand alone on four wins, ahead of Italy and Germany on three each.

Nearly 200,000 people packed into the Maracana stadium in Rio for the 1950 final between Brazil and Uruguay though only 150,000 tickets had been sold.

The total attendance (3,567,415) and average attendance (68,604) of the 1994 finals were both record figures.

FIXTURE GUIDE

There's no getting away from it, you'll be spending the next month in front of the television. So that you don't miss any vital game and to help you make the best of any 'free' time, here's a useful day-by-day fixture guide to the finals.

For the first time, teams will play all their games in different stadiums. The top two teams in each of the eight groups go through to the knockout stages. Three points are scored for a win and one for a draw. If teams are level on points, the positions are determined by goal difference, then goals scored, then the result against the competing team. If matches are level after 90 minutes in the knockout games, a 'golden goal' will decide the outcome in 30 minutes' extra time. If there is no goal, the match will be decided by a penalty shoot-out.

The usual carve-up between BBC and ITV has been agreed. The BBC will show the opening ceremony followed by Scotland v Brazil on 10 June and England's match against Tunisia five days later. ITV will show the Brazil match live in their Scottish regions and then screen the two home nations' second group matches – Scotland v Norway and England v Romania. The final group games will be on the BBC who will have first pick of the quarter-finals. ITV will have first choice of the second round games.

FIRST ROUND

Wednesday 10 June
    Group A: **Brazil v Scotland**; Stade de France, 15.30, BBC
    Group A: **Morocco v Norway**; Montpellier, 19.00, ITV

Thursday 11 June
    Group B: **Italy v Chile**; Bordeaux, 15.30, BBC
    Group B: **Cameroon v Austria**; Toulouse, 19.00, ITV

Friday 12 June
    Group C: **Saudi Arabia v Denmark**; Lens, 15.30, BBC
    Group C: **France v South Africa**; Marseilles, 19.00, ITV
    Group D: **Paraguay v Bulgaria**; Montpellier, 12.30, ITV

Saturday 13 June
    Group E: **Holland v Belgium**; Stade de France, 19.00, BBC
    Group E: **South Korea v Mexico**; Lyon, 15.30, ITV
    Group D: **Spain v Nigeria**; Nantes, 12.30, BBC

Sunday June 14
    Group F: **Yugoslavia v Iran**; Saint Etienne, 15.30, BBC
    Group H: **Jamaica v Croatia**; Lens, 19.00, ITV
    Group H: **Argentina v Japan**; Toulouse, 12.30, ITV

Monday 15 June
    Group F: **Germany v USA**; Parc des Princes, 19.00, BBC
    Group G: **Romania v Colombia**; Lyon, 15.30, ITV
    Group G: **England v Tunisia**; Marseille, 12.30, BBC

Tuesday 16 June
    Group A: **Scotland v Norway**; Bordeaux, 15.30, ITV
    Group A: **Brazil v Morocco**; Nantes, 19.00, ITV

Wednesday 17 June
    Group B: **Chile v Austria**; Saint Etienne, 15.30, ITV
    Group B: **Italy v Cameroon**; Montpellier, 19.00, ITV

Thursday 18 June
    Group C: **France v Saudi Arabia**; Stade de France, 19.00, BBC
    Group C: **South Africa v Denmark**; Toulouse, 15.30, ITV

Friday 19 June
    Group D: **Nigeria v Bulgaria**; Parc des Princes, 15.30, ITV
    Group D: **Spain v Paraguay**; Saint Etienne, 19.00, BBC

Saturday 20 June
    Group E: **Holland v South Korea**; Marseille, 19.00, ITV
    Group E: **Belgium v Mexico**; Bordeaux, 15.30, BBC
    Group H: **Japan v Croatia**; Nantes, 12.30, ITV

Sunday 21 June
    Group H: **Argentina v Jamaica**; Parc des Princes, 15.30, ITV
    Group F: **Germany v Yugoslavia**; Lens, 12.30, BBC
    Group F: **USA v Iran**; Lyon, 19.00, BBC

Monday 22 June
    Group G: **Colombia v Tunisia**; Montpellier, 15.30, BBC
    Group G: **Romania v England**; Toulouse, 19.00, ITV

Tuesday 23 June
    Group A: **Scotland v Morocco**; Saint Etienne, 19.00, BBC
    Group A: **Brazil v Norway**; Marseille, 19.00, BBC
    Group B: **Italy v Austria**; Stade de France, 14.00, BBC
    Group B: **Chile v Cameroon**; Nantes, 14.00, BBC

Wednesday 24 June
    Group C: **France v Denmark**; Lyon, 14.00, BBC
    Group C: **South Africa v Saudi Arabia**; Bordeaux, 14.00, BBC
    Group D: **Spain v Bulgaria**; Lens, 19.00, ITV
    Group D: **Nigeria v Paraguay**; Toulouse, 19.00, ITV

Thursday 25 June
    Group E: **Belgium v South Korea**; Parc des Princes, 14.00, BBC
    Group E: **Holland v Mexico**; Saint Etienne, 14.00, BBC
    Group F: **Germany v Iran**; Montpellier, 19.00, ITV
    Group F: **USA v Yugoslavia**; Nantes, 19.00, ITV

Friday 26 June
    Group G: **Romania v Tunisia**; Stade de France, 19.00, BBC
    Group G: **Colombia v England**; Lens, 19.00, BBC
    Group H: **Japan v Jamaica**; Lyon, 14.00, ITV
    Group H: **Argentina v Croatia**; Bordeaux, 14.00, ITV

SECOND ROUND (KNOCK-OUT)

Saturday 27 June
    Winner Group A v Runner-up Group B
    Parc des Princes, 19.00. Winner: 1
    Winner Group B v Runner-up Group A
    Marseille, 14.30. Winner: 2

Sunday 28 June
    Winner Group C v Runner-up Group D
    Lens, 14.30. Winner: 3
    Winner Group D v Runner-up Group C
    Stade de France, 19.00. Winner: 4

Monday 29 June
    Winner Group E v Runner-up Group F
    Toulouse, 19.00. Winner: 5
    Winner Group F v Runner-up Group E
    Montpellier, 14.30. Winner: 6

Monday 30 June
    Winner Group G v Runner-up Group H
    Bordeaux, 14.30. Winner: 7
    Winner Group H v Runner-up Group G
    Saint Etienne, 19.00. Winner: 8

Wednesday 1 and Thursday 2 July: Rest days

QUARTER-FINALS

Friday 3 July
Winner 2 v Winner 3
Stade de France, 14.30. Winner: B
Winner 1 v Winner 4
Nantes, 19.00. Winner: A

Saturday 4 July
Winner 6 v Winner 7
Lyon, 19.00. Winner: D
Winner 5 v Winner 8
Marseille, 14.30. Winner: C

Sunday 5 and Monday 6 July: Rest days

SEMI-FINALS

Tuesday 7 July
Winner A v Winner C
Marseille, 19.00
Wednesday 8 July
Winner B v Winner D
Stade de France, 19.00

Thursday 9 and Friday 10 July: Yet more rest days

THIRD-PLACE PLAY-OFF

Saturday 11 July
Stade de France, 19.00

FINAL

Sunday 12 July
Stade de France, 19.00

DAY-BY-DAY:
YOUR WORLD CUP
TOURNAMENT GRID

GROUP A
Brazil • Scotland • Morocco • Norway

Brazil v Scotland; Stade de France, 10 June 15.30
Morocco v Norway; Montpellier, 10 June 19.00
Scotland v Norway; Bordeaux, 16 June 15.30
Brazil v Morocco; Nantes, 16 June 19.00
Scotland v Morocco; Saint Etienne, 23 June 19.00
Brazil v Norway; Marseille, 23 June 19.00

Group A final table	P	W	D	L	F	A	G/D	Pts
A1								
A2								
A3								
A4								

GROUP B
Italy • Chile • Cameroon • Austria

Italy v Chile; Bordeaux, 11 June 15.30
Cameroon v Austria; Toulouse, 11 June 19.00
Chile v Austria; Saint Etienne, 17 June 15.30
Italy v Cameroon; Montpellier, 17 June 19.00
Italy v Austria; Stade de France, 23 June 14.00
Chile v Cameroon; Nantes, 23 June 14.00

Group B final table	P	W	D	L	F	A	G/D	Pts
B1								
B2								
B3								
B4								

GROUP C
France • South Africa • Saudi Arabia • Denmark

France v South Africa; Marseilles, 12 June 19.00
Saudi Arabia v Denmark; Lens, 12 June 15.30
France v Saudi Arabia; Stade de France, 18 June 19.00
South Africa v Denmark; Toulouse, 18 June 15.30
France v Denmark; Lyon, 24 June 14.00
South Africa v Saudi Arabia; Bordeaux, 24 June 14.00

Group C final table	P	W	D	L	F	A	G/D	Pts
C1								
C2								
C3								
C4								

GROUP D
Spain • Nigeria • Paraguay • Bulgaria

Paraguay v Bulgaria; Montpellier, 12 June 12.30
Spain v Nigeria; Nantes, 13 June 12.30
Nigeria v Bulgaria; Parc des Princes, 19 June 15.30
Spain v Paraguay; Saint Etienne, 19 June 19.00
Spain v Bulgaria; Lens, 24 June 19.00
Nigeria v Paraguay; Toulouse, 24 June 19.00

Group D final table	P	W	D	L	F	A	G/D	Pts
D1								
D2								
D3								
D4								

GROUP E
Holland • Belgium • South Korea • Mexico

Holland v Belgium; Stade de France, 13 June 19.00
South Korea v Mexico; Lyon, 13 June 15.30
Holland v South Korea; Marseille, 20 June 19.00
Belgium v Mexico; Bordeaux, 20 June 15.30
Belgium v South Korea; Parc des Princes, 25 June 14.00
Holland v Mexico; Saint Etienne, 25 June 14.00

Group E final table	P	W	D	L	F	A	G/D	Pts
E1								
E2								
E3								
E4								

GROUP F
Germany • USA • Yugoslavia • Iran

Yugoslavia v Iran; Saint Etienne, 14 June 15.30
Germany v USA; Parc des Princes, 15 June 19.00
Germany v Yugoslavia; Lens, 21 June 12.30
USA v Iran; Lyon, 21 June 19.00
Germany v Iran; Montpellier, 25 June 19.00
USA v Yugoslavia; Nantes, 25 June 19.00

Group F final table	P	W	D	L	F	A	G/D	Pts
F1								
F2								
F3								
F4								

GROUP G
Romania • Colombia • England • Tunisia

Romania v Colombia; Lyon, 15 June 15.30
England v Tunisia; Marseille, 15 June 12.30
Colombia v Tunisia; Montpellier, 22 June 15.30
Romania v England; Toulouse, 22 June 19.00
Romania v Tunisia; Stade de France, 26 June 19.00
Colombia v England; Lens, 26 June 19.00

Group G final table	P	W	D	L	F	A	G/D	Pts
G1								
G2								
G3								
G4								

GROUP H
Argentina • Japan • Jamaica • Croatia

Argentina v Japan; Toulouse, June 14 12.30
Jamaica v Croatia; Lens, June 14 19.00
Japan v Croatia; Nantes, 20 June 12.30
Argentina v Jamaica; Parc des Princes, 21 June 15.30
Japan v Jamaica; Lyon, 26 June 14.00
Argentina v Croatia; Bordeaux, 26 June 14.00

Group H final table	P	W	D	L	F	A	G/D	Pts
1								
2								
3								
4								

SECOND ROUND (KNOCK-OUT)

Saturday 27 June
Winner Group A v Runner-up Group B

....
Parc des Princes, 19.00. Winner: 1

Winner Group B v Runner-up Group A

....
Marseille, 14.30. Winner: 2

Sunday 28 June
Winner Group C v Runner-up Group D

....
Lens, 14.30. Winner: 3

Winner Group D v Runner-up Group C

....
Stade de France, 19.00. Winner: 4

Monday 29 June
Winner Group E v Runner-up Group F

....
Toulouse, 19.00. Winner: 5

Winner Group F v Runner-up Group E

....
Montpellier, 14.30. Winner: 6

Monday 30 June
Winner Group G v Runner-up Group H

....
Bordeaux, 14.30. Winner: 7

Winner Group H v Runner-up Group G

....
Saint Etienne, 19.00. Winner: 8

Wednesday 1 and Thursday 2 July: Rest days

QUARTER-FINALS

Friday 3 July
Winner 2 v Winner 3

....
Stade de France, 14.30. Winner: B

Winner 1 v Winner 4

....
Nantes, 19.00. Winner: A

Saturday 4 July
Winner 6 v Winner 7

....
Lyon, 19.00. Winner: D

Winner 5 v Winner 8
....
Marseille, 14.30. Winner: C

Sunday 5 and Monday 5 July: Rest days

SEMI-FINALS
Tuesday 7 July
Winner A v Winner C

....
Marseille, 19.00

Wednesday 8 July
Winner B v Winner D

....
Stade de France, 19.00

Thursday 9 and Friday 10 July
Yet more rest days

THIRD-PLACE PLAY-OFF

Saturday 11 July
Stade de France 19.00

FINAL

Sunday 12 July
Stade de France 19.00

Champions: ....

Verdict of the final: ....

Verdict of the championship:....................................

Match of the tournament: ....

Player of the tournament:..

Top goalscorer: ....

Best moment:...

Worst moment:...